The Road to Mi

'A wise, humane and delightful study. Mead has discovered an original and highly personal way to make herself an inhabitant both of the book and of George Eliot's imaginary city' Harold Bloom

'Admirable, endearing [and] evocative . . . A poignant testimony to the power of fiction' Joyce Carol Oates

'A beguiling mix of memoir, literary criticism and biography' *Sunday Times*

'Always lucid and sometimes soaringly beautiful . . . Her reading of *Middlemarch* is close, generous and intelligent' *Observer*

'A thoughtful and perceptive account of Eliot's masterpiece . . . This is a valuable and most readable homage' *Herald*

'A fresh and vibrant portrait of Eliot, an entrancing memoir and a passionate homage to the riches of rereading' *Newsday*

'Pays tribute not only to Eliot, but also to all book lovers who see novels as good friends worthy of frequent revisits' *New York Post* 'Must Reads'

'I wish more critical books were this literary and this readable' *Evening Standard*

'A lively literary memoir' *The Times*

'Companionable' *Spectator*

'It would be difficult to find a novel more likely to reward multiple rereadings than Eliot's – or a richer, more complete or more moving demonstration of its lasting power than [this book]' *Salon*

The Road to Middlemarch

My Life with George Eliot

Rebecca Mead

GRANTA

Granta Publications, 12 Addison Avenue, London W11 4QR

First published in Great Britain in hardback by Granta Books, 2014
Paperback edition published by Granta Books, 2014

First published in the United States in 2014 as *My Life in Middlemarch*
by Crown Publishers, a division of Random House LLC, New York,
a Penguin Random House Company.

A CIP catalogue record for this book is available from the
British Library.

1 3 5 7 9 10 8 6 4 2

ISBN 978 1 84708 516 0

Book design by Elizabeth Rendfleisch
Offset by Avon DataSet Ltd, Bidford on Avon, Warwickshire
Printed and bound by CPI Group (UK) Ltd, Croydon, CR0 4YY

www.grantabooks.com

For my mother, and in memory of my father

Contents

Prelude

*"Here was something beyond the shallows of
ladies' school literature."*

—*MIDDLEMARCH*, CHAPTER 3

When I was seventeen years old and still living in the seaside
town where I spent my childhood, I would go for a few hours
every Sunday morning to the home of a retired teacher of English
literature to talk about books. She was the wife of an admiral in
the Royal Navy and had been enlisted by my school to tutor me,
along with a couple of my classmates, for our university entrance
examinations.

My town is in the southwest of England, in a mostly rural
county that is cut through by narrow roads and hedgerowed lanes
that discreetly delineate the ancestral holdings of landed families.
The admiral and his wife lived in a village just outside town, and
their living room overlooked chalky hills. Here we sat, week after
week, reading narrowly but closely: analysing Metaphysical poets
and dissecting tragic themes in Shakespeare. The biggest book
we read was *Middlemarch*, by the Victorian novelist George Eliot,

who was born Mary Ann Evans near Nuneaton, not far from Coventry, in 1819.

I had the Penguin English Library edition, a brick of a paperback nine hundred pages long. On the front cover was a detail from a painting of a young woman in a full white skirt and a long black tunic, climbing some stone steps to scale a fence and reach a wooded thicket that abuts a golden hillside. The painting dates from 1839, but the scene looks exactly like a stretch of countryside that lay within five minutes' walk of my parents' house.

I was aching to get away from this landscape. Oxford was the immediate goal, but anywhere would do. My town had no colleges, no theatres, no museums. It seemed to me to offer no opportunity to live a cultured, intellectual life, which was what I avidly aspired to do, even if I had only a very imprecise notion of what that might consist of. I noted the subtitle of *Middlemarch*— "A Study of Provincial Life"—and as I looked out of my teacher's window over hills that were frequently sodden with rain, grazed by forlorn sheep, my home seemed to me barely less provincial than the Midlands of the 1830s the book described.

The novel, which charts the intersecting lives of a number of residents of an English town, was riveting, from the very first sentence of its first chapter. "Miss Brooke had that kind of beauty which seems to be thrown into relief by poor dress," it reads, and you know immediately that you are in the company of an unconventional heroine. On that first encounter, I identified completely with Miss Dorothea Brooke, an ardent young gentlewoman who yearns for a more significant existence. This identification was in spite of the difference between our social stations. Dorothea lives at Tipton Grange, a large estate equipped with household staff.

My family lived in a modest house with a small garden, built in the 1950s, and I only had to go back a few generations to find ancestors who had belonged to the household staff of properties like the Brookes'.

Dorothea, who at the novel's outset is nineteen, disdains the attentions of her neighbour and suitor, Sir James Chettam, an altogether too amiable baronet, "who said 'Exactly' to her remarks even when she expressed uncertainty." Instead, she makes a spectacularly unwise marriage to the Reverend Edward Casaubon, a pedantic, middle-aged scholar labouring on his notes for an endlessly deferred masterwork with the deadly title *The Key to All Mythologies*, whom she initially mistakes for a sage in parson's clothing.

Parallel with the story of Dorothea, we have that of Dr. Tertius Lydgate, an idealistic young physician newly arrived in town. He aims to establish a practice along modern principles and to make great discoveries, but his ambitions are fatally curtailed by marriage to Rosamond Vincy, the wilful, empty-headed town beauty. We meet Will Ladislaw, a youth of tempestuous passions, full of high-flown aspirations to be an artist or a poet; a cousin of Mr. Casaubon, Ladislaw is drawn—in the most honourable of fashions—to his cousin's new young wife, who comes also to depend upon him. We meet Rosamond's brother, Fred Vincy, the feckless but well-intentioned son of the town's mayor; and we meet the young woman Fred has set his hopes on, clever, practical, sardonic Mary Garth, the daughter of a financially squeezed land agent. We come to know Nicholas Bulstrode, the sanctimonious, overbearing banker, who insists that others conform to religious principles that—it is no surprise ultimately to discover—he has not always observed himself. And we learn about the Reverend Camden Farebrother, the humane, generous clergyman who understands the frailties of his flock because, being an occasional gambler and a habitual smoker, he is well aware of his own.

This book, which had been published serially in eight volumes almost a hundred years before I was born, wasn't distant or dusty, but arresting in the acuteness of its psychological penetration and the snap of its sentences. Through it, George Eliot spoke with an authority and a generosity that was wise and essential and profound. I couldn't believe how good it was.

And I couldn't believe how relevant and urgent it felt. At seventeen I was old enough to have fallen in love, and I had intellectual and professional ambitions, just like Eliot's characters. I was, after all, working hard to get into one of England's ancient universities, something no one in my family had ever done before. The questions with which George Eliot showed her characters wrestling would all be mine eventually. How is wisdom to be attained? What are the satisfactions of personal ambition, and how might they be weighed against ties and duties to others? What does a good marriage consist of, and what makes a bad one? What do the young owe to the old, and vice versa? What is the proper foundation of morality? I marked passages with a fluorescent pen: from chapter 37, as Dorothea realizes Casaubon's intellectual inadequacies: "Now when she looked steadily at her husband's failure, still more at his possible consciousness of failure, she seemed to be looking along the one track where duty became tenderness"; from chapter 64, where Lydgate and Rosamond's marital relations are at their most strained: "In marriage, the certainty, 'She will never love me much', is easier to bear than the fear, 'I shall love her no more.'" These seemed like things worth holding on to. The book was reading me, as I was reading it.

My copy's back cover cited what I later came to realize was the most celebrated characterization of the novel: Virginia Woolf's observation that *Middlemarch* is "one of the few English novels written for grown-up people." I was ready for adult literature. I was eager to become well read. I had not grown up in a house full of books, though I was encouraged to be a reader. My family made weekly trips to the library, and my father belonged to a book-of-the-month club from which he ordered me big, presentation volumes: a compendium of fairy tales, a collection of canonical poetry in which I read the most familiar works of John Keats and Rupert Brooke and Philip Larkin. Because I loved words, the Christmas after I turned eleven my parents gave me a hardback edition of *Roget's Thesaurus*. My father inscribed it to me, formally, with a fountain pen, while my mother covered the dust jacket with sticky-backed plastic to protect it from tearing.

A few months after receiving that gift I passed the examination to get into the local grammar school, and in my teenage years, literature, no less than pop music or fashion, became a common cultural currency. My friend Sarah, who had swinging blonde hair and long tanned legs, came in one day having discovered F. Scott Fitzgerald. Because of her I read and loved *Tender Is the Night,* and now when I come to Fitzgerald's description of Nicole Diver, with her brown legs and her "thick, dark, gold hair like a chow's," it's Sarah I see. A quiet, intense girl called Kate whose brown hair fell in a heavy braid down her back, and who seemed weighted with mystery and sadness, urged Virginia Woolf upon me. I read *To the Lighthouse* and *The Waves* and admired them while being sure I was missing more than I was understanding, which was exactly how I felt about Kate. Someone else came across D. H. Lawrence, and then we all read *The Rainbow* and *Sons and Lovers*, and, of course, *Lady Chatterley's Lover*, which was stimulating and perplexing at the same time.

Books gave us a way to shape ourselves—to form our thoughts and to signal to each other who we were and who we wanted to be. They were part of our self-fashioning, no less than our clothes. In my case, these were draping layers of black, antiquated lace and silk acquired at thrift shops, fastened with paste jewellery given to me by my grandmother. I was pale and thin, and ringed my eyes with thick black eyeliner so beyond my budget that I slept in it to conserve my supply, touching it up in the mornings. I inwardly hoped that my dress threw my intelligence into relief.

Though I would not have been able to say so at the time, I sought to identify myself with the kind of intelligence I found in *Middlemarch*—with its range, its wit, its seriousness, its erudition, its deep feeling. I admired the little I knew of George Eliot's life: her daunting, self-willed transformation from provincial girlhood to metropolitan pre-eminence, a good story to hear if one is an anxiously ambitious girl from a backwater town. I was intrigued by her adoption of a masculine pseudonym, by which she continued to be known throughout her life as a novelist, even after her identity was revealed early in her fiction-writing career. I knew that some important critics considered *Middlemarch* to be the greatest novel in the English language, and I wanted to be among those who understood why. I loved *Middlemarch*, and I loved being the kind of person who loved it. It gratified my aspirations to maturity and learnedness. To have read it, and to have appreciated it, seemed a step on the road to being one of the grown-ups for whom it was written.

NEARLY thirty years later, I found myself in a marble corridor at the New York Public Library, pressing a buzzer to get into the rare books collection. I moved to New York when I was twenty-one, just after graduating from college, where I had spent countless hours in libraries. As a student I had installed myself for long days of study at an oak desk piled high with books of poetry, novels, and critical texts, my pages of handwritten notes illuminated by a window set with stained glass. The library had been a place for studying, but it had also been a place for everything else: seeing friends, watching strangers, flirting and falling in love. Life happened in the library.

I didn't go to libraries so much any more. I'd become a journalist, so rather than immersing myself in books I tended to consult them fleetingly, then shelve them. I read much less for pleasure than I liked, and my grasp on literature—the field in which I'd sought to distinguish myself at seventeen—grew a little shakier every year, like a foreign language I didn't have sufficient opportunity to speak.

And in all my years in New York, I'd never had reason to go to the rare books collection, a cooled, darkened room lined with glass-fronted cabinets that now a librarian was buzzing me into. I'd requested to see a volume from its holdings, a notebook that had belonged to George Eliot. She started using it in 1868 and made notes there for a few years, precisely the period in which she wrote what would turn out to be her greatest work. "I have set myself many tasks for the year—I wonder how many will be accomplished?" she wrote in her journal on 1 January 1869. Among those projected tasks: "A Novel called Middlemarch."

Scholars have catalogued the notebook's contents, but my reasons for going to spend time with it were not so much scholarly as they were personal, almost mystical. I wanted to know what was in the notebook—but more than that, I wanted a tactile encounter with something that had been Eliot's, as if the ink and paper itself might reveal something I didn't already know about her, and about *Middlemarch*.

Middlemarch was one book I had never stopped reading, despite all the distractions of a busy working life. I went back to it as a student: "Discuss George Eliot's treatment of 'oppressive narrowness' and its effect on her characters" was the essay title I selected to answer in my first-year exams at college, where the hard chair and the grand hall amounted to my own escape from oppressive narrowness. I read it again in my twenties, when I was working my way up from an entry-level job, preoccupied by ill-fated romantic entanglements but captivated by city life. In my thirties, trying to establish myself as a writer to be taken seriously, I was struck with new, poignant force by the story of Lydgate— the ambitious would-be reformer who becomes, instead, a society doctor known for a treatise on gout, "a disease which has a good deal of wealth on its side," in Eliot's pointed observation.

The novel opened up to me further every time I went back to it; and by my early forties it had come to have yet another resonance. In a far from singular crisis, I had recently become consumed by a sense of doors closing behind me, alternative lives unlived: work I might have done, places I might have moved to, men I might have married, children I might have borne. In this light, a book that had once seemed to be all about the hopes and desires of youth now seemed to offer a melancholy dissection of the resignations that attend middle age, the paths untrodden and the choices unmade.

So why was I back in the library? It was, I suppose, in a bid to become a little less melancholy, a little less resigned. For the past two decades I'd thrived professionally by delving for a few weeks or months at a time into a wide variety of different subjects, many of which it might never have occurred to me on my own to have an interest in. But I was growing restless, and I felt ready to turn my deep attention to something that mattered to me. I wanted to recover the sense of intellectual and emotional immersion in books that I had known as a younger reader, before my attention was fractured by the exigencies of being a journalist. I wanted to go back to being a reader.

Still, being a journalist for all these years had taught me a few things: how to ask questions, how to use my eyes, how to investigate a subject, how to look at something familiar from an unfamiliar angle. What would I find, I wondered now, if I used this experience to read *Middlemarch* differently from the ways I'd read it before? What if I tried to discern the ways in which George Eliot's life shaped her fiction, and how her fiction shaped her? I wasn't so naive as to think that novels could be biographically decoded, but novels are places in which authors explore their own subjectivity, and I wanted to think about what George Eliot might have sought, and what she might have discovered, in writing *Middlemarch*.

And cloaked in this quasi-objective spirit of enquiry was an-other set of questions, these ones more personal, and pressing, and secret. What would happen if I stopped to consider how *Middle-march* has shaped my understanding of my own life? Why did the novel still feel so urgent, after all these years? And what could it give me now, as I paused here in the middle of things, and sur-veyed where I had come from, and thought about where I was, and wondered where I might go next?

So here I was, a student of sorts, back in an imposing library after a quarter of a century's absence. I took my seat at a carrel opposite a young man who was bending over a work by E. M. Forster, and after a few minutes the librarian returned with a leather-bound volume the size of a slender paperback, which she settled into a book rest.

I opened to the first page, and as I did so I became vaguely aware of a slight scent in the air that was at once out of place and oddly familiar: the smell of a spent hearth. For a moment, I won-dered if there could be a fireplace in the adjoining room—a silly thought, quickly dismissed. But then it dawned on me that the smell was coming from the notebook itself.

Glancing at the young man reading his Forster, I inclined towards the notebook and surreptitiously inhaled. There was something there beyond the usual mustiness of an old, infre-quently opened book, I was sure—something that smelled like the lingering trace of a fire burning in a long-cooled grate. Perhaps, I quickly said to myself, one of the notebook's previous owners had shelved it near a fireplace. Since George Eliot's death it had passed through many hands. First were those of Charles Lewes, her stepson, and his wife, Gertrude; their daughter, Elinor Carrington Ouvry, had sold it at auction in 1923, where it had been purchased by Walter T. Spencer, a London bookseller who later sold it to Owen D. Young, the diplomat and founder of the Radio Corporation of America, whose collection was acquired by the New York Public Library in 1941. The notebook might have sat on a shelf in an ill-ventilated room on either side of the Atlantic. And maybe the smell wasn't smoke at all. Perhaps it was just the aging pages decaying, surrendering infinitesimal fragments to the atmosphere every time they were opened.

Still, there the smell was. And maybe—just *maybe*—the book had absorbed molecules of smoke from a fireplace at the Priory, the house in St. John's Wood, London, that George Eliot bought in 1863 and in which she lived with George Henry Lewes, the exuberant critic and writer whom she spoke of as her husband despite the fact that he remained legally married to someone else. Perhaps the notebook—inscribed by George Eliot's hand and containing a record of her thought and mind—had also been imbued with a trace of her material world, and could lead me back there.

The Priory was a substantial house a few steps from Regent's Park and close to Regent's Canal, on a street called Northbank. Eliot lived and worked there until Lewes's death, in 1878. On Sunday afternoons they opened the house to friends and to some lucky admirers, whom they received in a drawing room decorated with Persian rugs, casts of antique statues, paintings and engravings, and books. She might have kept the volume in her study upstairs, on the first floor, where her desk stood before a tall window overlooking the garden. The room was boldly decorated with green wallpaper, a dado of dull red, and yellow skirting boards and doors. "Herein were the many wonderful books written," said Elizabeth M. Bruce, an American writer who visited the house when it was put up for sale after George Eliot's death, in 1880. "We felt within it as pilgrims at a shrine may feel. We were moved by an impulse to enter with unsandalled feet."

Or perhaps the notebook had been used in the library downstairs—"a cheerful room like the others, lined with well filled bookshelves," observed Charles Eliot Norton, an American professor of art at Harvard, who visited the Priory in January 1869. (He noted, irritably, that the house was "surrounded with one of those high brick walls of which one grows so impatient in England.") Over the fireplace was a portrait of George Eliot by Sir Frederic Burton. The portrait was made in 1865, when George Eliot was in her mid forties. Her face is framed by abundant, shiny, light-brown hair, and there is a soft expression in her grey, heavy-lidded eyes.

Norton considered the portrait "odious" and "vulgarizing," and it is certainly sentimental. Eliot looks wise and beneficent, like the headmistress at a good girls' boarding school. The portrait seems too respectable—which is how William Hale White, a writer who had known Eliot in her thirties, characterized the first, overly reverent biography of her, *George Eliot's Life, as Related in Her Letters and Journals.* That book was published in 1885 and written by John Walter Cross—who was George Eliot's widower, a man twenty years her junior whom she had married a year and a half after George Henry Lewes's death and only seven months before her own. White remembered Eliot quite differently, and he gave a suggestive characterization of her. "She was really one of the most sceptical, unusual creatures I ever knew, and it was this side of her character which to me was the most attractive," he said. White hoped that in some future literary portrait, "the salt and spice will be restored to the records of George Eliot's entirely unconventional life."

The Burton portrait, executed in pastel-coloured chalk, is lacking in salt or spice, but many who knew her thought it a good likeness. Her mouth is closed and she has a sober expression, although the faintest trace of a smile line can be seen on her cheek. She smiled rarely—"like a fitful gleam of pale sunshine," wrote Sophia Lucy Clifford, another guest at the weekly gatherings at the Priory, who later became a novelist herself. The thrill of witnessing that smile and hearing George Eliot's low, measured voice—a voice that many remarked was very beautiful—"was beyond all description, and had the effect of making you feel that there was nothing in this world you would not do for her; and that to be with her, even on one of those rather terrible Sunday afternoons, for a single hour, was a great achievement in your life."

I paged through the notebook carefully, looking at the hand-numbered pages, their contents carefully indexed at the back. (Why had I never thought to index a notebook? My own organization of research tends to be haphazard and disorderly, like that of Mr. Brooke, Dorothea's scatterbrained uncle and guardian, who demands of Casaubon to know his method of arranging documents. "In pigeon-holes, partly," replies a startled Casaubon. "Ah, pigeon-holes will not do," says Mr. Brooke. "I have tried pigeon-holes, but everything gets mixed in pigeon-holes: I never know whether a paper is in A or Z.") Eliot had listed the episodes of *The Canterbury Tales*, made notes on Hindu literature, named the colleges of Oxford University. She had transcribed lines from Wordsworth, Blake, and Spenser, and made notes in Italian on Machiavelli. There were quotations from sacred Jewish literature, the Hebrew letters carefully if inexpertly copied, and I remembered a line from the first chapter of *Middlemarch*, about Dorothea's unusual hopes for marital life even before she has met Casaubon: "The really delightful marriage must be that where your husband was a sort of father, and could teach you even Hebrew, if you wished it." This wonderful sentence shows Eliot's dexterity with comedy and with pathos: Dorothea is so wrong, and so earnest, and so completely recognizable in her well-intentioned misprision.

After a while I closed the notebook, but before I left I took one more look around the reading room. In a corner stood a small desk that had once belonged to Charles Dickens, Eliot's near contemporary. I thought about his wildly popular American tours—draining but profitable excursions into celebrity that were the sort of thing Eliot avoided completely. She never travelled to America, as a literary celebrity or otherwise, though in 1872, when she was in the midst of *Middlemarch*, an acquaintance from New England urged her to visit. She declined, writing, "Boston I always imagine to be a delightful place to go straight to and come straight back from. But the Atlantic is too wide for that."

I've crossed the wide Atlantic many times, and it never gets any easier. In my early twenties, I went home to visit my parents once a year or so, and they would come to see me; in my thirties I would stop off for a day or two in England en route to or from an assignment somewhere more extraordinary—Paris, Mumbai, Tokyo—feeling jet-lagged and glamorous. And then, as my parents became elderly and their lives constricted, I went back more often, for walks with my mother that would be filled with accounts of doctors' visits, and dinners at which my father would pour Rioja with an increasingly shaky hand. Five days here, a week or two there: I did not want to stop and count the meager total. When I first left England as a young woman, I didn't consider that there would be a finite, and unknowable, number of times I would return. Eventually, though, each goodbye came to be freighted with the possibility that it might be the last.

Upon Dickens's desk was a flower in a vase and a calendar set to the date of his death: 9 June 1870. In the years Eliot lived with Lewes she came to know Dickens socially, and he had been to lunch at the Priory not long before his death. "I thought him looking dreadfully shattered then," she wrote in a letter afterwards. Dickens was a famous writer before she even became a novelist, and he had been an early admirer of the mysterious new author who went by the pseudonym of George Eliot. When *Scenes of Clerical Life*, her first work of fiction, was published in 1858, Dickens astutely wrote to the author via the book's publisher, John Blackwood, with the sly observation, "If they originated with no woman, I believe that no man ever before had the art of making himself, mentally, so like a woman, since the world began." Eliot's identity was revealed after the publication of her first novel, *Adam Bede*, in 1859. This time, Dickens wrote to her in person and offered praise in terms that would thrill any writer: " 'Adam Bede' has taken its place among the actual experiences and endurances of my life."

I left Dickens's desk, walked through the library's marble corridors, and emerged on Forty-Second Street. I turned into

Bryant Park and claimed a chair on a gravel path under one of the towering London plane trees, a species named for the city of my birth growing in the city I had chosen. I thought about Eliot's notebook, and of what it suggested about the germination and the growth of *Middlemarch*. I considered, too, how aptly Dickens had identified the strange potency of a great book—the way a book can insert itself into a reader's own history, into a reader's own life story, until it's hard to know what one would be without it.

Reading is sometimes thought of as a form of escapism, and it's a common turn of phrase to speak of getting lost in a book. But a book can also be where one finds oneself; and when a reader is grasped and held by a book, reading does not feel like an escape from life so much as it feels like an urgent, crucial dimension of life itself. There are books that seem to comprehend us just as much as we understand them, or even more. There are books that grow with the reader as the reader grows, like a graft to a tree.

This kind of book becomes part of our own experience, and part of our own endurance. It might lead us back to the library in mid life, looking for something that eluded us before.

Chapter 1

Miss Brooke

"Something she yearned for by which her life
might be filled with action at once rational
and ardent."

—*MIDDLEMARCH*, CHAPTER 10

On 2 December 1870, not long after her fifty-first birthday, George Eliot made an entry in her journal. "I am experimenting in a story, which I began without any very serious intention of carrying it out lengthily," she wrote. "It is a subject which has been recorded among my possible themes ever since I began to write fiction."

She had been working on this story in the mornings for the previous month and so far she'd written forty-four pages—four chapters. Most days, Eliot retreated upstairs immediately after finishing breakfast, at 8 a.m., and worked steadily for five hours. Affairs were arranged so that she was as free from domestic concerns as possible. Two servants—sisters named Grace and Amelia—kept the household running along well-established lines. "She never knew what was to be for dinner until she came down to it," one of her servants later told a visitor.

She and Lewes, her partner of the last decade and a half, often lunched alone, but on that day a friend joined them. Maria Congreve was a bright young woman almost twenty years Eliot's junior: "one of those women of whom there are few—rich in intelligence without pretension, and quivering with sensibility, yet calm and quiet in her manners," Eliot once reported with approval to another friend. Over lunch, Eliot mentioned that she was feeling more cheerful than she had been of late, and that the sense of anxiety by which she often felt crippled had abated.

Later that evening, by the fire in the study, Eliot read aloud to Lewes an article about the ongoing Franco-Prussian War: Paris was enduring its second month under siege. The article made her cry, and she was troubled that she had spoken at lunch of her own relative contentment when there was so much suffering elsewhere. Before she retired to bed she wrote a note to Mrs. Congreve. "It rang in my ears that I had spoken of my greater cheerfulness as due to a reduced anxiety about myself and my doings, and had not seemed to recognize that the deficit or evil in other lives could be a cause of depression," she wrote. "I was not really so ludicrously selfish while dressing myself up in the costume of unselfishness. But my strong egoism has caused me so much melancholy, which is traceable simply to a fastidious yet hungry ambition, that I am relieved by the comparative quietude of personal cravings which age is bringing."

The manuscript upstairs was also concerned with egoism, melancholy, and ambition—and with the question of what an individual might do to alleviate the suffering of others. The story she had begun "without any very serious intention of carrying it out lengthily" would become "Miss Brooke," Book One of *Middlemarch*.

In describing the subject of the story as being among the possible themes she had long been considering for fictional treatment, Eliot was probably referring to her ingenious revision of the marriage plot. What might happen if, instead of ending with a wedding, a novel were to begin with one—that of a young woman and a much older man to whom she is eminently ill-suited? The marriage plot was a well-established form in nineteenth-century literature, exquisitely mastered by Jane Austen, whose novels George Eliot had reread immediately before she made her own first effort at fiction. And the first four chapters of "Miss Brooke" present a decidedly Austenian scenario. There are two well-born sisters, both unmarried, one filled with sense and the other—like Mrs. Congreve—quivering with sensibility. (Dorothea "was usually spoken of as being remarkably clever, but with the addition that her sister Celia had more common-sense.") The clever older sister is under a wilful romantic misapprehension. Failing to recognize that her amiable, titled neighbour is courting her, she instead imagines that he is enchanted by her younger sister.

The older sister has entirely other ideals. She hopes to find a husband of exalted intellectual and moral stature. She imagines she would have been happily wed to "John Milton when his blindness had come on; or any of the other great men whose odd habits it would have been glorious piety to endure." Before too long, she meets a clergyman and scholar who appears to her—if to no one else around her—to be endowed with greatness, "a modern Augustine who united the glories of doctor and saint." Naturally, she constructs mentally a future in which she unites the glories of wife and helpmeet in her relation to this paragon of learning. "There would be nothing trivial about our lives," she thinks. "Everyday-things with us would mean the greatest things."

It's fun to speculate about what Jane Austen might have done with this premise: would Casaubon have dwindled into Mr. Collins-like irrelevance, Will Ladislaw turned out to be a Wickham-like scoundrel, and Lydgate emerged as a Darcy-like black horse? One thing is beyond doubt: if this were Jane Austen's story, the courtship of the blossoming Dorothea by the dry-as-dust Casaubon would have been a comedy. And, in fact, when John Blackwood, George Eliot's publisher, read Casaubon's excruciatingly stilted letter of proposal to Dorothea he wondered whether it was too comical to be plausible. (The letter reads, in part: "I have discerned in you an elevation of thought and a capability of devotedness, which I had hitherto not conceived to be compatible either with the early bloom of youth or with those graces of sex that may be said at once to win and to confer distinction when combined, as they notably are in you, with the mental qualities above indicated.") Blackwood queried the tone. "It is exceedingly funny," he wrote. "But I mean is it not too transparently so not to strike even a girl so devoted to wisdom as poor dear Dodo."

There is an Austenian irony in Eliot's presentation of Dorothea's ardent nature. Celia, the small, steady voice of sense, recognizes her sister's fondness for self-denial—"she likes giving up," Celia tells Sir James. The author knowingly editorializes upon Dorothea's misplaced infatuation. "Dorothea's inferences may seem large," Eliot writes. "But really life could never have gone on at any period but for this liberal allowance of conclusion, which has facilitated marriage under the difficulties of civilization." The reader is invited to recognize the absurdity of Dorothea's instant devotion to Casaubon, and also to recognize the absurdity of social proprieties—the "difficulties of civilization," in a marvellously restrained phrase—that require a man and a woman to marry before they have more than a passing acquaintance with each other.

But as George Eliot presents it, Dorothea's inward predicament could not be more serious. When the reader meets her she is troubled, restless, discontented. "For a long while she had been oppressed by the indefiniteness which hung in her mind, like a thick summer haze, over all her desire to make her life greatly effective," Eliot writes. "What could she do, what ought she to do?" The pages vibrate with Dorothea's yearning for a meaningful life. Her soul is too large for the comedy of manners into which she at first appears to have been dropped. She is bigger—her longings are grander—than the conventional story that others would write around her.

This theme—a young woman's desire for a substantial, rewarding, meaningful life—was certainly one with which Eliot had long been preoccupied. It was a theme that she had been turning over in her mind when she wrote that late-night letter to Mrs. Congreve, confessing the alarmingly unbounded extent of her own ambition and ardour. And it's a theme that has made many young women, myself included, feel that *Middlemarch* is speaking directly to us. How on earth might one contain one's intolerable, overpowering, private yearnings? Where is a woman to put her energies? How is she to express her longings? What can she do to exercise her potential and affect the lives of others? What, in the end, is a young woman to do with herself?

These questions had been among George Eliot's most pressing ones since long before she became George Eliot—back when she was Mary Ann Evans, an anxious, moody, brilliant Warwickshire girl with ambitions almost too large to bear.

ALTHOUGH a school friend later remarked to an early biographer that it was impossible to imagine George Eliot as a baby, and "that it seemed as if she must have come into the world fully developed, like a second Minerva," the evidence suggests that she was, at one point, a squalling infant much like any other. "Mary Ann Evans was born at Arbury Farm at five o'clock this morning," her father, Robert Evans, noted in his diary for 22 November 1819.

She was his fifth child, the third by his second wife, Christiana, and Robert Evans was already in his mid forties when she was born. Evans, like his father before him, had started out as a carpenter and builder, but by the time Mary Ann arrived he had become the trusted estate manager of Francis Newdigate, the local landowner, who lived at a grand house named Arbury Hall. Evans was not a large man, at least on the evidence of a handsome purple-and-green plaid velvet waistcoat that survives in a local museum. But he was known for his physical strength and for his strong moral rectitude. A terrifying anecdote, approvingly recounted in John Walter Cross's *George Eliot's Life, as Related in Her Letters and Journals*, tells of an occasion when Evans was riding on top of a coach in Kent. The woman next to him complained that the hulking sailor on her other side was being offensive. "Mr. Evans changed places with the woman, and taking the sailor by the collar, forced him down under the seat, and held him there with an iron hand for the remainder of the stage," Cross reports.

Mary Ann adored her father, and in her fiction the noble-hearted, practical-handed artisan is a recurring type, one whom her critics have sometimes found too good to be true. One such is Adam Bede, the eponymous hero of her first novel, whom Henry James described as lacking "that supreme quality without which a man can never be interesting to men,—the capacity to be tempted." In *Middlemarch*, there is Caleb Garth, like Robert Evans an estate manager, whose chief fault is that he is too willing to think the best of people. (This is a virtue disguised as a failing, as when an interview subject tells a prospective boss that his worst flaw is being too concerned with detail.) When, in her early thirties, a few years after her father's death, Eliot spoke in an essay of "virtue or religion as it really exists—in the emotions of a man dressed in an ordinary coat, and seated by his fireside of an evening, with his hand resting on the head of his little daughter," it seems an idealized picture from her own childhood. After her father died she saved his wire-rimmed spectacles in their tortoise-shell case and kept them for the rest of her life—an intimate souvenir, as if his perceptive eyes might still watch over her.

Less information survives about Eliot's mother, Mrs. Robert Evans, the former Christiana Pearson. In his *Life*, Cross portrays her as the fulcrum of the family, always busy with her knitting, delivering herself of epigrammatic opinions like Mrs. Poyser in *Adam Bede*. But she seems to have been ill for much of Mary Ann's childhood, her condition doubtless exacerbated by repeated childbearing as well as by grief. George Eliot referred to herself as the youngest child in her family, but that wasn't the whole story. Twin brothers, William and Thomas, were born in March 1821, when Mary Ann was barely a toddler; they both died when they were just ten days old. The lost boys are buried in the family tomb at their parish church, in Chilvers Coton, which is where Christiana was also laid after she died, probably of breast cancer, when Mary Ann was sixteen.

Mary Ann was a bright little girl, already reading the romances of Sir Walter Scott when she was seven years old. Scott was her father's favourite, too, and he encouraged his clever daughter to read, though books were not exactly plentiful in the Evans household. Once a neighbour loaned a copy of Scott's *Waverley* to Mary Ann's sister Chrissey, five years her senior; it was returned before Mary Ann could finish reading it, and so she started writing the story out herself from scratch. Like lots of imaginative children, she told herself stories peopled by characters from the fictions she consumed. "I could not be satisfied with the things around me; I was constantly living in a world of my own creation, and was quite contented to have no companions that I might be left to my own musings and imagine scenes in which I was chief actress," she later wrote. She preferred the company of adults to children and was regarded as something of an odd duck—"a queer, three-cornered, awkward girl," said a neighbour. Once, when given the assignment of writing an essay about God, she sat down and drew a picture of a large, watchful eye.

At Miss Wallington's, the school in Nuneaton she attended between the ages of nine and thirteen, and later at the Miss Franklins' school in Coventry, instructors and students recognized that she had an unusually powerful intellect. Not that a powerful intellect was strictly necessary, or even preferable, when it came to a girl's education: her studies included French and English but also dancing and needlework. In *Middlemarch*, she acidly illuminates the deficiencies of what was considered a desirable education for a young lady by characterizing the ignorant and trivial Rosamond Vincy as "the flower of Mrs. Lemon's school," where "the teaching included all that was demanded in the accomplished female—even to extras, such as the getting in and out of a carriage." The Herbert Art Gallery & Museum in Coventry has among its holdings an example of work supposedly executed by Mary Ann Evans and some of her classmates at the Miss Franklins' school: a little white cloak with a ruffled edge perhaps intended for a doll, though it would also be fit for a baby's christening, or its funeral.

Mary Ann was good at things other than needlework. Her essays in English were "reserved for the private perusal and enjoyment of the teacher, who rarely found anything to correct," a classmate said. She was the best pianist in the school, came at the top of all her classes, and cried when school closed for the holidays—"to the astonishment and perhaps disgust of her schoolfellows," one of them reported. Another former classmate said that Mary Ann always seemed a different order of creature, and added, "Her schoolfellows loved her as much as they could venture to love one whom they felt to be so immeasurably superior to themselves"— an observation with enough of a sting in the tail to be worthy of George Eliot herself.

After leaving school she continued to write to a favourite teacher, Maria Lewis, who was only a few years her senior. From these letters and others to an aunt and uncle, scholars and biographers have gleaned much of what has been established about Eliot's early life, and many critics have found this correspondence extremely unpalatable. By her teens, Mary Ann had become enthusiastically evangelical, and priggishly judgemental. She liked giving up. She disapproved of singing, other than hymns; she dismissed novels as dangerous and frivolous. "I am ready to sit down and weep at the impossibility of my understanding or barely knowing even a fraction of the sum of objects that present themselves for our contemplation in books and in life," she wrote. "Have I then any time to spend on things that never existed?" It would be satisfying to discover that the young George Eliot resembled Elizabeth Bennet, the clever if initially misguided heroine of *Pride and Prejudice*. Instead, she brings to mind Lizzy's prim younger sister, Mary, who, charged with playing the piano at a dance, wants to supply concertos instead of reels.

She was equally quick to deliver her opinions about the choices of others, however unearned her authority to judge. "When I hear of the marrying and giving in marriage that is constantly being transacted I can only sigh for those who are multiplying earthly ties which though powerful enough to detach their heart and thoughts from heaven, are so brittle as to be liable to be snapped asunder at every breeze," she wrote, at the wise old age of seventeen. She seems determined to be joyless. After a sightseeing trip to London with her brother Isaac, who was three years older—the first time she has been to the capital—she declares herself "not at all delighted with 'the stir of the great Babel.'" (The highlight of her week was seeing the Greenwich Hospital, Christopher Wren's masterpiece on the Thames, which housed veteran sailors.)

Gordon S. Haight, a professor of English at Yale who in 1968 published the first scholarly biography of George Eliot, noted with considerable understatement in his nine-volume edition of her collected correspondence, "It must be conceded that the letters before 1842 are generally lacking in charm."

And yet to me what is most excruciating about these letters is not exactly their dedicated priggishness, or their unsympathetic religiosity, or their writer's perverse insistence on remaining unimpressed by one of the world's great cities. Rather what I find almost too painful to bear is their nakedness and their earnestness—their embarrassing pretentiousness, their mannered affect of maturity. ("You will think I need nothing but a tub for my habitation to make me a perfect female Diogenes, and I plead guilty to occasional misanthropic thoughts," she writes in one.) Lacking in charm they may be, but they were not written to charm, and certainly they were not written to charm professors of English literature at Yale. They were written out of passion and exuberance and boredom and ostentation, and her desire to discover what she was thinking by putting it on the page—which is to say they are letters written by a young woman who is trying to work out who she is, and where she is going.

That raw season in which I sat on my narrow childhood bed, propped up on pillows and reading *Middlemarch* for the first time, I also spent many hours writing letters to a cousin of more or less my own age. And if my teenage correspondence was much less learned than George Eliot's, the letters I wrote were no less painfully self-exposing, filled with the enthusiasm and obliviousness and unearned world-weariness of youth. There were rudimentary discussions of leftist politics that I understood in a cursory way and believed in with the fervour of ignorance; a nascent feminism into which I channelled my confusions about the dawning of sexual maturity; fascinated but affectedly blasé accounts of the discovery of sex itself, and its attendant complications; long catalogues of the pop music I was listening to; even longer lists of the books I was reading. In one letter that began with the languid declaration, "Any wit I ever possessed has left me, any eloquence I ever enjoyed has been used up," I reported that I had just read Dostoyevsky's *The Gambler*, Fitzgerald's *The Great Gatsby* and *The Beautiful and Damned*, Austen's *Pride and Prejudice* and *Northanger Abbey*, *The Paper Men*, by William Golding—and *Middlemarch*, "which is a brilliant novel and should be read," I offered airily.

I can hardly bear to read these letters, which my cousin saved and gave back to me a few years ago. The combination of egotism and insecurity they convey embarrasses the part of me that still feels represented in them, as well as paining the part of me that feels an adult pity for the emotional trials of my younger self. But the sheer weight of the packet in my hands reminds me how crucial the epistolary habit was in those days before e-mail and mobile phones, when the single telephone in my home was used only rarely, and never just for chatting on. Sitting at my desk and writing letters—on childish Snoopy notepaper I'd been given for Christmas, using a heavy, liver-coloured fountain pen with a gold cap that had belonged to my mother until I claimed it—was no less significant a part of my growing up than were the mild adventures I excitedly recounted: of underage pub-going at fifteen, at seventeen of spending an entangled weekend in London with a boyfriend, not visiting the Greenwich Hospital. Writing letters was one of the things there was to do while I was waiting for my life to start.

And so the letters that George Eliot wrote when she was Dorothea Brooke's age move me because of their dreadfulness, not in spite of it. She, too, was waiting for her life to start—not complacently, or resignedly, but anxiously and urgently. She had many more responsibilities than I had as a teenager: since her mother died she'd been running her father's household, making damson jam and supervising the dairy. But she knew she was not where she would end up. "My soul seems for weeks together completely benumbed, and when I am aroused from this torpid state the intervals of activity are comparatively short," she wrote at nineteen. She was troubled, she went on to say, that she did not make better use of her time in the service of God. "I feel that my besetting sin is the one of all others most destroying, as it is the fruitful parent of them all, Ambition, a desire insatiable for the esteem of my fellow creatures," she wrote. "This seems the centre whence all my actions proceed."

Ambition—"fastidious yet hungry," as she would later write to Mrs. Congreve—was what Mary Ann Evans felt seized by. She regarded it as if it were an external evil pressing upon her, rather than—that which is equally possible—a good rising within her. She admitted to it, and in doing so she gave voice to it. She knew she wanted something. She knew she wanted to *do* something. She didn't know what it was. She just knew she wanted, and wanted, and wanted.

ONE morning in late spring I caught the train from London to Nuneaton. I'd only been to the Midlands once before, when I was eighteen, on a weeklong school trip spent on a barge that wended its way through the area's network of canals. (Most of the time I lay on the roof of the barge, bored by the slow-passing scenery, bathing in the inconsistent sun and doggedly working my way through the Penguin edition of *Ulysses*.) The journey takes about an hour on the fast train, which further flattens the fields and pastures and turns the canals into leaden streaks alongside its tracks.

The Midlands are lacking in drama, topographically speaking, and George Eliot is the great advocate of the loveliness to be found in their modest plainness. In chapter 12 of *Middlemarch*, she paints a picture of the land in which she grew up that is as attentive to each facet and flaw of its subject as the portraits by Dutch masters she admired. "Little details gave each field a particular physiognomy, dear to the eyes that have looked on them from childhood," she writes. "The pool in the corner where the grasses were dank and trees leaned whisperingly; the great oak shadowing a bare place in mid-pasture; the high bank where the ash-trees grew; the sudden slope of the old marl-pit making a red background for the burdock; the huddled roofs and ricks of the homestead without a traceable way of approach; the grey gate and fences against the depths of the bordering wood; and the stray hovel, its old, old thatch full of mossy hills and valleys with wondrous modulations of light and shadow such as we travel far to see in later life, and see larger, but not more beautiful."

The countryside I saw through the train window wasn't at all like the coastal English landscape of my youth, where tumbling hills break off into chalk-white cliffs, but the note of nostalgia in

Eliot's description resonated with me. It was more than twenty years since I'd lived in England, and returning always induced a melancholy in me, a reminder of being a restless adolescent struggling with the likes of James Joyce. These days when I took the train from London to my hometown I was always struck by the understated beauty of the countryside. I'd failed to appreciate it when I'd been immersed in it, but now could see that it was no less lovely than any of the many places I had travelled far to see.

I first moved to New York to do a graduate degree in journalism, expecting to return to England after a year. Studying journalism in a classroom turned out to be mostly absurd. One instructor, a weary former city reporter, conducted pretend press conferences in which he would impersonate the whiny, petulant mayor of the city while we, his students, asked pretend questions. Another instructor aired her dispiriting opinion in our first class that most of us would end up in PR. Much of the time I felt like I was wasting time. But I also got a part-time job at a magazine where I did research for writers and answered the phones and even wrote a few short pieces, learning skills and gaining experience that only a real deadline and a real pay cheque could provide. When my course was almost over a job in the fact-checking department at the magazine opened up. I was offered it, and a few weeks before I was due to move home to England I decided that I wasn't going to move home after all.

I didn't feel at home in New York, exactly—it was too alien and disconcerting for that. But I enjoyed the sense of estrangement my new life offered me. I shared a small apartment that had sloping floorboards, exposed-brick walls, and an occasional rodent problem, four flights above a busy SoHo intersection. On summer nights when it was too hot to sleep I would sit on the fire escape, looking out over the water towers on the buildings opposite and down on the lively streets below, enjoying the exotic sensation of sultry air on my skin. Where I grew up it was always cool at night, even after the warmest of days. I found the abrasiveness of New York exciting, even glamorous. I liked being able to yell at someone who shoved me on the subway, rather than feeling obliged to fume silently.

After more than twenty years New York no longer felt exotic, and the abrasiveness had become less appealing. Now the mild, middle-class manners and gentle landscapes I found when I returned to England had an emollient quality. It was so soothing, this middling Englishness, that I had to be on my guard lest nostalgia slip into sentimentality. I was in danger of being too invested in my melancholic attachment to a half-remembered, half-idealized homeland. Even so, when I came back to England, I missed it more than I did when I was away.

My train arrived at Nuneaton, a market town ten miles north of Coventry. There's a bronze statue of George Eliot in the centre of town, where she sits on a low wall, awash in long skirts, thick hair resting on her shoulders, eyes cast down, a book at her side. Not far away, past slightly dilapidated chain stores, there's a pub named for her, the George Eliot Hotel, that is said to be the one upon which she modelled the Red Lion in *Scenes of Clerical Life*, a collection of three stories that marked her fictional debut. In Riversley Park, the town's spacious public gardens, there's an obelisk bearing her name at which members of a local literary society lay a wreath on her birthday.

Also within Riversley Park is the Nuneaton Museum and Art

Gallery, which owns a substantial collection of objects related to George Eliot, many of them acquired from local families. When I visited, the gallery in which the collection was usually displayed was being repainted, and Catherine Nisbet, the museum's manager, took me into an upstairs room where the objects were being stored. Wearing latex gloves, she drew items out of boxes one by one and carefully unfolded the tissue paper they had been wrapped in, as if they were the most precious and unexpected of Christmas presents.

Many of them probably had been presents once. Out came George Eliot's reticule, a leather-covered case that contained, embedded in blue velvet, a penknife, buttonhook, and crochet hook, all with delicate handles of mother-of-pearl. Out came a pair of ornamental china dogs, King Charles spaniels with superior looks on their faces, which were formerly owned by one of George Eliot's aunts, supposedly the models for the Dodson sisters in *The Mill on the Floss*, Eliot's second novel, published in 1860. Out came a soup tureen and four matching vegetable dishes in pale, creamy ceramic, which George Eliot and John Walter Cross received as a wedding gift, in 1880. And out came a portable writing desk, decorated on the outside with gilt and mother-of-pearl inlay, and lined inside with purple velvet.

I, too, was wearing latex gloves, and I gently ran my finger along the desk's lacquered surface. Nisbet said, "You'd feel you had to write something really good with this." I thought of a letter George Eliot wrote to Harriet Melusina Fay Peirce, an American activist on behalf of women's welfare, in 1866, just after the publication of her fifth novel, *Felix Holt, the Radical*. In the letter, she gave a surprisingly unguarded explanation of why she made a late start in fiction. "I was too proud and ambitious to write: I did not believe that I could do anything fine, and I did not choose to do anything of that mediocre sort which I despised when it was done by others," she wrote. I imagined her as a stiff, self-conscious, inhibited girl, warily examining herself for signs of greatness, too proud and too fearful to lay paper to desktop and try.

GEORGE Eliot's childhood home, Griff House, is on the outskirts of Nuneaton, and seen from the front appears much as it did when Mary Ann Evans lived there, from the age of a few months until she was twenty-two. It has a handsome Georgian facade of red brick, a steep slate roof, and well-proportioned windows that overlook a wide lawn edged with trees. In an engraving that appears in Cross's *Life*, the house is half obscured by an exuberant growth of ivy, picturesquely if inconveniently creeping into the rain gutters.

These days the ivy has been removed, and that is the least of the changes that have been made to the home that George Eliot loved. A few years ago Griff House was bought by Whitbread, the hospitality company, which appended a sprawling pseudo-Georgian hotel and surf-and-turf restaurant to the rear of the old farmhouse. In the Evanses' day Griff was in the countryside, on the edge of the Arbury estate, but now there is an incessant roar of traffic from the highway passing only a few hundred feet away. It could not be further from the sleepier atmosphere of the 1820s, when, as Eliot wrote in the opening pages of *Felix Holt*, "the morning silvered the meadows with their long lines of bushy willows marking the watercourses, or burnished the golden corn-ricks clustered near the long roofs of some midland homestead."

Taken out of context, such beautifully rendered passages can appear sentimental: Eliot's meadows were surely sodden with rain and dampened with mist far more often than they were silvered or burnished by sunshine. But the purpose to which Eliot puts her passages of natural description is anything but sentimental. They convey an authentic nostalgia—a melancholy homesickness of the sort that might be experienced by a journeying epic hero, if on a more modest scale. Eliot describes a landscape that was already vanishing when she was writing. During her childhood, Griff House looked out over fields, but within a few years a colliery was visible from its upper windows.

I'd gone to Griff with my notebook in hand, hoping, as a reporter does at the outset of a new assignment, to understand something about my subject by surveying the place in which she'd spent so many years. Visiting the former homes of famous writers tends to be a compromised and often unsatisfying endeavour; by contrast with a painter's studio, the nature of literary creativity is not easily suggested by the site of creation. While shuffling through such places I start thinking about how much has changed, rather than how much has stayed the same—wondering about how drafty the windows would have been, and whether indoor plumbing had yet been installed. Preservation tends to mean sanitization. "Stupidity of people tricking out and altering such a place instead of letting one see it as he saw it and lived in it," Eliot once wrote when she visited Friedrich Schiller's home, in Weimar.

But George Eliot's childhood home hasn't been preserved as a monument to her. It's been almost erased by the present. The ground-floor parlour has been converted into a bar, with an enormous flat-screen television tuned to a satellite sports channel over the fireplace. In what was once the dining room, there's a pool table instead of a dining table. Lurid slot machines have been installed on the flagstones of the entrance hall, where a wood-panelled nook that once served as Robert Evans's office is now a snug little retreat with upholstered armchairs and beer mats on the tabletop.

It felt ridiculous to be wandering these rooms, trying to ignore the glowing fire-escape signs and the soft rock on the sound system, and attempting to imagine the house as it was. But I tried anyhow, and saw glimmers of what Griff must have been. My first evening there, I sat with a beer at a trestle table on what would have been the lawn in front of the house. The sound of traffic carried over hedges, and someone's phone kept jangling with "The Entertainer," but there were bluebells flowering under the trees and daisies growing in the grass, as there must have been nearly two hundred years ago.

The upper floors of the house are now private, occupied by the hotel manager and his family, but I arranged to see the attic, to which the young Mary Ann Evans sometimes absconded in search of privacy. Later, she transferred her fondness for that elevated retreat to Maggie Tulliver, the heroine of *The Mill on the Floss*: "Here she fretted out all her ill-humours, and talked aloud to the worm-eaten floors and the worm-eaten shelves."

The attic had been converted into a bedroom since Mary Ann's day, with steeply sloping walls and uneven floors that were covered with carpet the colour and consistency of porridge. Sturdy wooden rafters were coated with chocolate-brown paint. A cobwebbed window overlooked parked cars and the main road and a light-industrial estate beyond. The room's most recent occupant had been the manager's daughter, who was now in her twenties and living elsewhere. A narrow bed was still covered with her pink bedspread, and on top of a laminated dresser stood a ceramic statuette of Tigger from *Winnie the Pooh*. Left behind along with the figurine and the bedding was a slightly melancholy atmosphere of half-formed hopes and enthusiasms. It was a room to look out from, and from which to hope for something more.

George Eliot did not write an autobiography, though she once said she wished she could, telling a friend—with what strikes me as an uncharacteristic overestimation of her abilities—that "she could do it better than anyone else, because she could do it impartially, judging herself, and showing how wrong *she* was." Her most straightforwardly autobiographical character is Maggie Tulliver, and as a grown woman Eliot discussed with a friend the ways in which *The Mill on the Floss* was inspired by her own history. Everything in the novel was softened, she said; her own experience was worse.

Maggie's is bad enough. She chafes against the complacency and conservatism of the bourgeois mill-owning family into which she has been born. Her relatives are obsessed with propriety: a great deal of attention is paid in Maggie's house to having the right linen on one's table while alive and the right comestibles at one's funeral when dead.

The child Maggie, meanwhile, is persistently improper. She chops off her unruly black hair in a fit of passion, and she runs away to join the gypsies—occasions for "that bitter sense of the irrevocable which was almost an everyday experience of her small soul." There is no book that I know of that better captures the frustration of being a little girl who feels she is not being taken seriously. The single page in which George Eliot recalls the small, penetrating miseries of childhood—when one is left out of a game by classmates, or denied sufficiently grown-up clothing when one's friends are all permitted it, or when, on a rainy day with nothing to do, one falls "from idleness into mischief, from mischief into defiance, and from defiance into sulkiness"—is worth a shelf of so-called parenting books on its own, so sharp is its delineation of this forgotten anguish. It concludes with this faultless recommendation: "Surely if we could recall that early bitterness, and the dim guesses, the strangely perspectiveless conception of life that gave the bitterness its intensity, we should not pooh-pooh the griefs of our children."

As a teenager, Maggie is tormented by the same urgent sense of longing that besets the heroine of "Miss Brooke," though she comes from a different class and has quite different expectations of life. "She thought it was part of the hardship of her life that there was laid upon her the burthen of larger wants than others seemed to feel, that she had to endure this wide hopeless yearning for that something, whatever it was, that was greatest and best upon this earth," Eliot writes of Maggie. In *The Mill on the Floss*, George Eliot presents a natural history of yearning. She shows how Maggie's longing to be elsewhere and otherwise originates. She shows the soil in which it grows; what nurtures it and what blights it.

When it comes to Dorothea Brooke, however, yearning is a condition for which no originating cause is given. One of the odd things about "Miss Brooke" is how little of the heroine's personal history is revealed. We learn that Dorothea is of privileged social background, without any "yard-measuring or parcel-tying fore-

fathers," and that she has an extremely comfortable if not exor-
bitant fortune of seven hundred pounds a year—the equivalent
of about half a million pounds today. But of the parents who left
her that fortune we know virtually nothing, except that they died
when she and Celia were "about twelve years old."

I stumble over this sentence every time I read it. How can
Dorothea and Celia, who are different ages, *both* be characterized
as "about twelve years old" when their parents die? And why is
nothing more said about such a significant loss? Dorothea herself is oddly untroubled by the absence of her parents: she barely
thinks of them. In the novel's first chapter, she consents to divide
the jewels that she and Celia have inherited from their mother,
and her disdain for what she considers the frivolousness of personal decoration is one of the ways in which George Eliot signals
her heroine's unusual priorities. ("'A cross is the last thing I would
wear as a trinket.' Dorothea shuddered slightly.") When Dorothea
finally is enticed by their beauty into accepting an emerald-and-
diamond ring and bracelet, she thinks of the poverty of the miners
who dug the gems out of the earth rather than of the presumably
once-beloved hand they last adorned. The deaths of the Brooke
parents are treated with barely more reverence in the pages of
Middlemarch than is the bereavement of Jack Worthing in Oscar
Wilde's *The Importance of Being Earnest*—whose loss of one parent, as Lady Bracknell points out, may be regarded as a misfor-
tune, but whose loss of two looks like carelessness.

Eliot's reference to the age at which the sisters lost their parents also looks like carelessness: I suppose they could be eleven
and thirteen, but then why be so confoundingly nonspecific?
(In fact the manuscript of *Middlemarch* reveals that the phrase

referring to these parental deaths was an afterthought, written in above the text.) But it soon becomes clear that the lack of a fuller biographical sketch is not an oversight. George Eliot doesn't need to provide Dorothea with a fleshed-out childhood, or a detailed history. She comes into the world of the novel fully developed, like a second Minerva.

Or rather, she comes into it partly developed. The only growth that matters is that which occurs within the novel's pages—the growth that turns her from a prematurely opinionated, occasionally priggish, alarmingly passionate, and inchoately ambitious young woman into something else.

Dorothea has this in common with her creator, though there are important differences between them. Nina Auerbach, of the University of Pennsylvania, has made the persuasive observation that for all Dorothea's purported longing to be learned she doesn't make much effort to educate herself, even though she has access to her uncle's no doubt well-stocked library. Mary Ann Evans, by contrast, was so fervently eager to expand her knowledge as an adolescent that Francis Newdigate, her father's employer, gave her access to the library at Arbury Hall. (She read up on ecclesiastical history, which she intended to condense into a chart: a *Key to All Mythologies* of sorts.) At nineteen, she told Maria Lewis that her mind was filled with disjointed specimens—"of history, ancient and modern, scraps of poetry picked up from Shakespeare, Cowper, Wordsworth, and Milton, newspaper topics, morsels of Addison and Bacon, Latin verbs, geometry entomology and chemistry, reviews and metaphysics." She set herself a fiercely demanding curriculum. A tutor, Signor Joseph Henry Brezzi, was hired to teach her Italian; he then started her on German. In another letter to Maria Lewis she recounted with excitement her discovery of the correct pronunciations of *sch* and *ö*, which she and her correspondent had previously been getting wrong. "Goethe, the German way of spelling which is Göthe, is pronounced as though the former vowel were the French eu in peu," she wrote, with palpable enthusiasm. Mary Ann Evans was so determined to learn German that she set about doing so without, in all possibility, ever having heard it on the lips of a native speaker. Within a few years she would be the first English translator of David Friedrich Strauss, the German theologian.

I find this diligent effort to become an educated person tremendously moving. In this acquisition of languages it is possible to glimpse the effort that would be required for Mary Ann Evans to turn herself into George Eliot. Years later, a friend from Geneva commented that she spoke French badly, but she knew it well. Once, when she was in her fifties, Eliot urged a German correspondent to write in that language. "I am as quick in reading foreign languages as I am slow to speak them," she said, wryly. Coming to languages too late for effortless fluency, she set about achieving what she could through resolution and determination. She found an outlet for her hungry ambition by reshaping herself into an intellectual. She turned her yearning into learning.

DOROTHEA Brooke does not make of herself what George Eliot did. The prologue to *Middlemarch*, which Eliot called the "prelude," compares the heroine we are about to meet with Saint Teresa of Ávila, whose "passionate, ideal nature demanded an epic life." Now an epic life is impossible, Eliot writes. Perhaps all that is available for "later-born Theresas" is "a life of mistakes, the off-spring of a certain spiritual grandeur ill-matched with the mean-ness of opportunity."

Saint Teresa fades pretty promptly from view once *Middle-march* begins, as a contemporary reader in particular may not be sorry to discover. But it seems that George Eliot had at one point intended that Dorothea would more actively seek a vocation, or at least identify a possible one. According to a schema Eliot sketched out for the novel in a notebook known as *Quarry for Middlemarch,* Dorothea, after being widowed and asserting that she would never remarry, was to declare an intention to "go on some heroic errand of carrying away emigrants etc."

That didn't happen. Dorothea's heroism, such as it is, turns out to be of a much smaller and more domestic kind. *Middle-march* offers what George Eliot calls, in a wonderfully sugges-tive turn of phrase, "the home epic"—the momentous, ordinary journey travelled by most of us who have not even thought of aspiring to sainthood. The home epic has its own nostalgia—not for a country left behind, but for a childhood landscape lost. It's a journey we may not even realize we are undertaking until we are halfway through its course.

When I first read *Middlemarch* as a provincial teenager chaf-ing against the provinces, beginning to discover for myself the difficulties of civilization, I was disposed to concur with the pro-logue and to believe that Dorothea's limitations lay outside her—"the meanness of opportunity"—rather than within her. As a young woman coming of age at a moment when legal equality had been won but social equality still seemed some distance off, I was indignant on Dorothea's behalf about her limited opportunities and appreciated Eliot's ironical commentary about women's lack of rights. (The novel can easily be mined for arch, feminist apopthegms, such as "A woman dictates before marriage in order that she may have an appetite for submission afterwards.")

But now, when I look at Dorothea again, I don't find myself regretting her lack of accomplishment, or not exactly. I care less about what she represents as a "later-born Theresa"—bound by her mean opportunities to remain unfulfilled—than I am impressed by the way in which she gives expression to what George Eliot refers to as "the common yearning of womanhood." This yearning seems to have changed little over the years, even if a girl's education no longer demands lessons on carriage descent.

As Miss Brooke, Dorothea remains for me the embodiment of that unnameable, agonizing ache of adolescence, in which burgeoning hopes and ambitions and terrors and longings are all roiled together. When I spend time in her company, I remember what it was like to be eighteen, and at the beginning of things. I remember going for my entrance interview at Oxford and meeting with the senior English literature tutor at what was to become my college—a forbidding-seeming Scotsman who, I learned much later, was possessed of a magnificently dry sense of humour and was particularly partial to bright, ambitious, state-school students from the provinces. His study was furnished with low-slung easy chairs upholstered in mustard-coloured corduroy; one could either perch on a chair's edge or sink into its depths. During my interview I shifted uncomfortably between one position and the other while talking passionately about *Middlemarch*. Afterwards I walked across the cobblestones of a narrow lane and stepped on to the wide, lovely sweep of the High Street in a state of exhilaration and anxiety. I felt as if my life were an unread book—the thickest and most daunting of novels—that I was holding in my hands. I didn't know what the story would be, or where it would lead, and I was almost too overawed to crack its spine and begin.

Chapter 2

Old and Young

*"We do not expect people to be deeply moved by
what is not unusual."*
—*MIDDLEMARCH*, CHAPTER 20

When Virginia Woolf described *Middlemarch* as "one of the few English novels written for grown-up people," what did she mean? The observation was made in an essay that appeared in the *Times Literary Supplement* to mark the centenary of George Eliot's birth, in November 1919. Before writing it Woolf immersed herself in Cross's *Life* and in the novels—"in order to sum her up once and for all," as she wrote to a friend, with a note of self-mockery.

The phrase she coined has become the one that is most often used to sum *Middlemarch* up once and for all, but Woolf's assessment of the novel was more qualified than is usually acknowledged. In the essay, she begins by describing the accomplishment of the early works, *Scenes of Clerical Life* and *Adam Bede* and *The Mill on the Floss*, which seem drawn from Eliot's own rural experience and are peopled with characters so true to life that readers forget they are fictional. "We move among them, now bored, now sympathetic, but always with that unquestioning acceptance of all that they say and do, which we accord to the great originals only," Woolf writes. "We scarcely wish to analyse what we feel to be so large and deeply human."

It is in contrast with this sure-handedness that Woolf makes reference to *Middlemarch*. Here is her full characterization: "It is not that her power diminishes [after the early novels], for, to our thinking, it is at its highest in the mature *Middlemarch,* the magnificent book which with all its imperfections is one of the few English novels written for grown-up people."

"With all its imperfections." What are these imperfections? Woolf gives few specifics, though she cites Eliot's unwillingness to let one sentence stand for many and contrasts it with the delicacy shown by Jane Austen in *Emma*. (" 'Whom are you going to dance with?' asked Mr. Knightley, at the Westons' ball. 'With you, if you will ask me,' said Emma; and she has said enough," Woolf writes. "Mrs. Casaubon would have talked for an hour and we should have looked out of the window.") She says that Eliot—the granddaughter of a carpenter, as she reminds us—is out of her depth when it comes to the depiction of higher social strata, and resorts to stock images of claret and velvet carpets. Eliot's hold on dialogue is often slack. Occasionally, she lacks taste. She suffers from "an elderly dread of fatigue from the effort of emotional concentration."

According to Woolf, though, these failings are more than compensated for by the pitiful truth that is revealed in Dorothea's thwarted aspirations. "The ancient consciousness of woman, charged with suffering and sensibility, and for so many ages dumb, seems in [Eliot's heroines] to have brimmed and overflowed and uttered a demand for something—they scarcely know what—for something that is perhaps incompatible with the facts of human existence," Woolf writes. This melancholy acknowledgement of limitation makes the book distinctively appropriate for "grown-up people," those who are old enough to appreciate the artistic representation of failure rather than success.

But what an interesting choice of phrase it is. "Grown-up people" is a juvenile expression. It's what children call adults, or how adults refer to themselves when talking to children. ("A merry day for the children, who ran and shouted to see if they could top the wind with their voices; and the grown-up people, too, were in good spirits, inclined to believe in yet finer days when the wind had fallen," Eliot writes in *Adam Bede*.) It's not how adults usually speak of themselves, at least not without irony. "Grown-up people" is an expression from the nursery.

In Woolf's case, this was a nursery on the third floor of a house on Hyde Park Gate, Kensington, where she grew up amid social privilege and intellectual sophistication. Her father, Sir Leslie Stephen, was the editor of the *Cornhill Magazine*, who had attended Eliot's Sunday salon at the Priory. Woolf's mother, Julia Stephen, had been a celebrated beauty since childhood and served as a model for Edward Burne-Jones, the Pre-Raphaelite painter, among other artists of the moment. The Stephen children's quarters lay above rooms filled with books and hung with art, frequented by cultured people who had an easy familiarity with claret and velvet carpets.

Downstairs, a small sunroom adjacent to the large double drawing room had been ceded to the younger generation. "From this room too we could spy on the grown-ups," Vanessa Bell, Woolf's older sister, once recalled. In this hideaway with a view over the garden Vanessa would paint while Virginia read aloud from the Victorian novelists. "I can still hear much of George Eliot & Thackeray in her voice," Vanessa wrote. *Middlemarch* may be a book for grown-up people, but it is also a book for precocious girls like the Stephen sisters; and to my mind, Woolf's use of this formulation has a touch of archness about it, a slight affectation of youthful arrogance. Woolf was thirty-seven when she wrote her Eliot essay and didn't any longer think of herself as young, but she certainly thought of herself as doing something new in fiction. She had published her first novel, *The Voyage Out*, four years earlier; her second, *Night and Day*, appeared in October 1919. In the essay Woolf expresses her admiration and respect for George Eliot—"We must lay upon her grave whatever we have it in our power to bestow of laurel and rose" is its swelling conclusion. But at the same time she positions herself as the clever child, watching quietly from the neighbouring room, ready to supersede her distinguished but fatigued elder.

Or perhaps I impute a youthful arrogance to Woolf because I remember what it was to be a young person chafing to compete with her professional elders, instead of being, as I was, subservient to them. In my first job, as a fact-checker at a weekly magazine, I worked with four other checkers, all of us in our early twenties. Our department amounted to a very small pen hemmed in by filing cabinets stuffed with old proofs and bookcases lined with reference books. This was well before the Internet, and we spent long hours on the phone to sources, or visiting libraries to find articles on microfilm. Our desks were jammed close together, piled high with newspapers and marked-up manuscripts of stories that it was our job to make sure were free of errors.

It was a demanding and stressful occupation. We were blamed if an article was published with a mistake, but, it seemed, rarely thanked when we prevented it. Often we would be there until late at night, long after more senior editorial staff had gone home, and we'd order dinner on expenses from the Italian restaurant across the street and make jokes at the expense of certain writers we worked with. How lazy they were, we'd complain; how badly they wrote. In truth, I was learning a lot from doing this work: seeing how to build a story, discovering where to find a fact. But still, I was eager for my chance to show how I could do it better.

"About his ordinary bearing there was a certain fling, a fearless expectation of success, a confidence in his own powers and integrity much fortified by contempt for petty obstacles or seductions of which he had no experience," Eliot writes of Dr. Tertius Lydgate in the opening chapter of Book Two of *Middlemarch*, "Old and Young," which was published in February 1872, three months after the first installment had appeared. Readers of the first volume, including the reviewer for the *Athenaeum*, predicted that "the tale is to centre around a woman's life." But they were in error. While *Middlemarch* opens with its focus upon the inward struggles of Dorothea Brooke as she becomes Dorothea Casaubon, it soon expands beyond her. Dorothea is only one element within a much wider social panorama.

Lydgate, at twenty-seven, is fresh from his medical studies in London, Edinburgh, and Paris, and determined to make the provincial town of Middlemarch the crucible of his own scientific advances. He holds this ambition notwithstanding the already established medical practices of Messrs. Wrench and Toller and Drs. Minchin and Sprague, who hitherto have tended to the health of the community without resort to suspicious modern methods. (Eliot's thumbnail sketch of Mr. Wrench is evidence of her ability to let one sentence stand for many if she wants to: "Mr. Wrench was a small, neat, bilious man, with a well-dressed wig: he had a laborious practice, an irascible temper, a lymphatic wife, and seven children." You could learn more about how to write from a description like that—its compression, its rhythm—than in a year's worth of classes.)

Lydgate brims with self-assured ambition and focus, determined to be above the petty politicking of his elders. A new hospital is opening in Middlemarch, underwritten by Nicholas Bulstrode, the rich, pious banker, and Lydgate hopes that the establishment of a medical school will one day follow. In this anticipated centre of scientific enterprise he aspires to identify the "primitive tissue"—the foundational building block of life. He is convinced, Eliot writes, "that the medical profession as it might be was the finest in the world; presenting the most perfect interchange between science and art; offering the most direct alliance between intellectual conquest and the social good." He seems to have found what Dorothea seeks—a cause and a passion to which to devote his life.

Unlike Dorothea, Lydgate has a history, some of it quite vivid, and several pages are devoted to his backstory. While in Paris, Lydgate became infatuated from afar with an actress who was married to a fellow actor; during a performance she stabbed her husband to death, apparently by accident. Lydgate rushed to the stage to tend to her, and an acquaintance began. When she upped and left Paris he traced her to Lyon, and rushed there with a proposal of marriage. She told him that the stabbing was no accident: her husband bored her, and she decided to dispatch him. "You are a good young man. But I do not like husbands. I will never have another," she informed the stunned Lydgate, who quickly fled back to his galvanic experiments upon frogs and rabbits, resolved to take a "strictly scientific view of woman," with ideas of marriage postponed until an indefinite future.

His resolution to remain a single man is thwarted, in Book Two of *Middlemarch*, by the force of Rosamond Vincy's wish to make a husband of him. Lydgate, an exotic stranger, strikes Rosamond as much more sophisticated and interesting than the prosperous young men of Middlemarch by whom she has already been courted, and even before they have been introduced Lydgate doesn't really stand a chance. He intends to be only an infrequent visitor at the Vincy home, where, in his lofty estimation, "the provision for passing the time without any labour of intelligence, might make the house beguiling to people who had no particular use for their odd hours." Lydgate plans to make better use of his odd hours, until Rosamond begins to exercise her charms upon him. ("Do you care about dancing at all? I am not quite sure whether clever men ever dance?" "I would dance with you, if you would allow me.")

Rosamond believes that they are as good as engaged, and Eliot conveys the irresistible force of her conviction in a remarkable metaphor. "Circumstances were almost sure to be on the side of Rosamond's idea, which had a shaping activity and looked through watchful blue eyes, whereas Lydgate's lay blind and unconcerned as a jelly-fish which gets melted without knowing it," she writes. When Lydgate's clumsy attempt to extricate himself ends up bringing tears to those blue eyes, his intentions to remain unattached are shattered. "That moment of naturalness was the crystallizing feather-touch: it shook flirtation into love." Eliot's delineation of the growing attachment between Lydgate and Rosamond is delicious if more than slightly horrifying to read. Rosamond is an eminently recognizable type, the fatally nubile pretty girl whose charms have never failed her, while Lydgate, who is clever about most things, is cloddishly dense about women. Watching them make their way towards marriage—she concertedly, he obliviously—has an appalling satisfaction for connoisseurs of romantic plots.

But it is another, much earlier, passion in Lydgate's life that makes him most compelling to me. Lydgate was a bright child— "it had already occurred to him that books were stuff, and that life was stupid"—and, one wet day during a school holiday, hunting to find a book he hadn't yet read, he stumbled across an encyclopaedia in his family's library. He opened the first volume to see an entry for "Anatomy," and his life was changed in an instant. He had found his vocation.

George Eliot gives a marvellous description of the dawning of an intellectual passion. "Most of us who turn to any subject we love remember some morning or evening hour when we got on a high stool to reach down an untried volume, or sat with parted lips listening to a new talker, or for very lack of books began to listen to the voices within, as the first traceable beginning of our love," she writes, in a direct address to the reader. It's a powerful evocation of the promise that learning can hold for a reader, and of the thrill of realizing what it might be to have an intellectually creative life—of the realization that one might find one's destiny in books.

And one need not have discovered one's precise vocation at an early age, as Lydgate did, to know something of the experience of developing a germinal passion by browsing in a library. Intellectual passion—a love for that "which must be wooed with industrious thought and patient renunciation of small desires"—is rarely accorded the attention that romantic love commands, as Eliot points out; but the reader whom Eliot addresses will likely recognize this other, overlooked passion, because the chances are that he or she has felt it, too. I didn't know what I wanted to do with my life when I was in my teens; but the solitary lunchtime hours I spent in my school library, looking at art books or reading literature, were both a discovery in their own right, and a taste of the pleasures of study and thought.

In this passage about intellectual passion, Eliot steps into the story to speak directly to the reader. (Or, as literary critics have pointed out, the contrived persona of a narrator steps into the story to speak directly to the reader.) This was a technique that Eliot used with some frequency, and one of the most celebrated examples of this kind of interjection appears towards the end of Book Two of *Middlemarch*, when the reader is reintroduced to Dorothea Brooke, now Dorothea Casaubon, on her honeymoon in Rome. Dorothea is alone in her boudoir, and is weeping. But, Eliot asks with a note of irony, is an extravagance of emotion so very unusual in a new bride? "That element of tragedy which lies in the very fact of frequency, has not yet wrought itself into the coarse emotion of mankind; and perhaps our frames could hardly bear much of it," she writes. "If we had a keen vision and feeling of all ordinary human life, it would be like hearing the grass grow and the squirrel's heart beat, and we should die of that roar which lies on the other side of silence. As it is, the quickest of us walk about well wadded with stupidity."

This kind of editorializing can strike today's reader as awkward and off-putting. We're wiser now, we think, than to believe in the authoritative inclusiveness of the first person plural; feminist or Marxist or post-colonial literary theory has made us conscious of perspectives that have been excluded by, or don't care to be encompassed by, its embrace. We may even be writing from one of those perspectives ourselves. (I humbly submit: when I write "we," I mean by it "I, and hopefully you.") The explicit intrusion of a narrator's voice in Eliot's fiction can strike the contemporary ear as old-fashioned. Today's realist novelists don't tend to step on to their pages, formally addressing the reader like a lawyer making a case before a courtroom.

Some contemporary critics of Eliot weren't particularly enamoured of the technique, either—so much so that Leslie Stephen, writing in the *Cornhill Magazine* immediately after Eliot's death, felt a need to defend the practice. Stephen argued that it was one of the ways in which Eliot, the most intellectual of authors, sought to include in her fiction the ideas and convictions that were crucially important to her. "We are indeed told dogmatically that a novelist should never indulge in little asides to the reader. Why not?" he wrote. "A child, it is true, dislikes to have the illusion broken, and is angry if you try to persuade him that Giant Despair was not a real personage like his favourite Blunderbore. But the attempt to produce such illusions is really unworthy of work intended for full-grown readers." In a foreshadowing of the formula his daughter Virginia Woolf would later use, Stephen suggests that Eliot's use of the magisterial authorial interjection is one of the things that make her novels suitable for grown-up people.

It's one of the techniques she feels most at home using. "You are like a great giant walking about among us and fixing every one you meet upon your canvas," John Blackwood, her publisher, remarked with approval after he'd read the manuscript of the second volume of *Middlemarch*. Blackwood's use of the first person plural isn't a slip. He means to include readers of Eliot's books among the diminutive characters whom George Eliot fixes on her canvas— the ones who gossip about Lydgate's unconventional unwillingness to dispense medicines, or about his bizarre request to conduct a postmortem on a patient, or about his unseemly closeness to Bulstrode. Bulstrode's ultimate downfall levels Lydgate, too, after the doctor accepts a loan that, when the fact of it emerges publicly, is taken by onlookers to be a bribe—and which may, indeed, hamper Lydgate's ability to judge Bulstrode's actions objectively. By directly addressing us, Eliot draws us deeper inside her panorama. She makes Middlemarchers of us all.

But Eliot does something in addition with those moments of authorial interjection. She insists that the reader look at the characters in the book from her own elevated viewpoint. We are granted a wider perspective, and a greater insight, than is available to their neighbours down in the world of Middlemarch. By showing us the way each character is bound within his or her own narrow viewpoint, while providing us with a broader view, she nurtures what Virginia Woolf described as "the melancholy virtue of tolerance." "If Art does not enlarge men's sympathies, it does nothing morally," Eliot once wrote. "The only effect I ardently long to produce by my writings, is that those who read them should be better able to *imagine* and to *feel* the pains and the joys of those who differ from themselves in everything but the broad fact of being struggling erring human creatures."

And this is one way in which *Middlemarch* is a book about young people for older people. This is one reason why Woolf's epigrammatic observation rings true. When I read of the boy Lydgate in his father's library, taking up a book and being seized by a passion, or I glimpse the newly-wed Dorothea, distraught in her Roman boudoir, unable to name the deficit she feels or to identify the nature of her disappointment, I am able not only to imagine their vivid, solipsistic experience but also to see them from Eliot's authorial perspective of heightened, mature sympathy. In viewing them I am invited to shed my wadded layers of stupidity, and to listen for the sound of growing grass.

My train rumbled into Coventry, and after I left the station I set off towards the city centre. I could see from my map that there was a park, Greyfriars Green, through which I needed to pass, but to reach it I had to navigate a tangle of roads and pedestrian walkways under and alongside a busy ring road that encircles the city. This ring road was built in the 1960s according to the latest urban-planning principles, as was much of the contemporary city centre. Coventry has a very old foundation—it is thought to have been the site of a Roman settlement, and then a Saxon nunnery, centuries before its most celebrated resident, Lady Godiva, endowed a monastery there in 1043. In the first decades of the twentieth century it became an important centre of car and then aeroplane manufacturing, which explains why, on the night of 14 November 1940, German air forces unleashed an incendiary bombardment upon it. More than five hundred people were killed and much of the city centre was destroyed, including the four-teenth-century cathedral, which was reduced to a charred shell.

I'm old enough for this piece of history not to feel altogether distant. I grew up in the 1970s hearing stories of the Blitz in London. My parents, who were eight and nine when the war began, both lived in a West London suburb. My mother's father worked as a panel-beater at a local automobile factory; as a boy he had been granted a scholarship to a grammar school, but his own father had recently died, and at fourteen he had to leave school and learn a trade. During the war, he made tail fins for Spitfire planes. They lived in a terraced house, where my grandfather installed an Anderson shelter, made from corrugated metal, in the front room, displacing the walnut-veneered cocktail cabinet that was among his most prized possessions. He built a brick wall inches from the bay window to protect the shelter against a blast, and moved the furniture out of the bedroom above. My mother was the eldest of three children, and she and her siblings used to sleep in bunk beds in the shelter, while my grandparents slept on a narrow mat-tress on the floor outside. It was a small house, and surrendering two rooms must have made it feel even smaller. Anti-aircraft guns were stationed in the streets at night, making a terrifying noise. During the safer daytimes my mother and the other neighbour-hood kids ran in the streets outside, playing a fantasy game they called "being evacuated to America."

My father's father, who worked as a commercial artist on Fleet Street, spent the nights of the Blitz as a fire-watcher at the Evening Standard building on Shoe Lane, and whenever I see the famous photograph of the dome of St. Paul's rising above the smoky devastation of the City, I imagine him on a roof nearby, in heroic pose like a figure from a Stalinist propaganda poster, holding a bucket. He belonged to a different generation to my maternal grandparents. Born in 1888, at the end of the Victorian era, he was old enough to have enlisted in the infantry in the First World War in 1915, and lucky enough to have seen the war's end, by which time he had been commissioned in the field as an officer. When I was young my father would sometimes bring out a precious relic: a yellowed map that my grandfather had carried in his pack, denoting the landscape of France cut through by the Somme. My grandfather was gregarious and charming, given to wearing a suit of green tweed, brightly coloured shirts, suede shoes. He was unafraid of the grand gesture. My father contracted measles at the age of four, and because there was a new baby at home he was sent to an isolation hospital for almost three months, his parents forbidden to visit. My grandfather went to the hospital anyway, and gained access to the ward by putting on a white coat and impersonating a doctor. He died of tuberculosis when my father, brokenhearted, was seventeen. I've spent forty years wishing I could have met him.

I found my way through the maze of footpaths and walked across Greyfriars Green. George Eliot and her widowed father moved to Coventry in 1841, when she was twenty-one; she would live there until his death, eight years later. Her brother Isaac had recently married, and Griff House was ceded to him and the new family that he was expected soon to produce. Father and daughter moved to Bird Grove, a large semi-detached house in Foleshill, then an affluent district a mile north of the city centre. Coventry was chosen over the countryside because if a husband was to be found for Mary Ann that was where he might most likely be encountered. She hated being nudged out of her home, not least because of the crude dynamics of the matrimonial marketplace upon which she, a complicated commodity, was being floated. "It is like dying to one stage of existence," she wrote to a friend.

Inasmuch as any place served as an inspiration for the town of Middlemarch, Coventry was it. Like the Coventry of the 1820s, Middlemarch is a prosperous provincial town with a thriving textile industry: Ned Plymdale, one of the would-be suitors of Rosamond Vincy, is the son of a textile manufacturer. Will Ladislaw attends a "meeting about the Mechanics' Institute," a centre of learning for working men like the Coventry Mechanics Institution, which opened in 1828. Caleb Garth and Fred Vincy encounter surveyors measuring the land around Middlemarch for the coming railway; Coventry's railway station, part of the London to Birmingham line, opened in 1838.

When Lydgate arrives in Middlemarch a new hospital has just been built; in Coventry, the pressing need for a new medical institution led in 1831 to the establishment of two of them. There was the Self-Supporting Dispensary, the users of which secured access to its services by means of a small weekly subscription, and the General Dispensary, which supplied medical services to the poor and relied upon charitable donations for its operating costs. The Coventry and Warwickshire Hospital, a larger institution, was founded in 1838, just before George Eliot moved to the city. It was located in "a building of considerable extent with an enclosed garden," writes Benjamin Poole, who published a history of the city in 1847—perhaps like the "laurel-planted plots" of the New Hospital in *Middlemarch*.

But if Middlemarch has a canal, or a ruined monastery, or an imposing fifteenth-century guildhall, as Coventry did during the reign of George IV, we do not hear about them. George Eliot does not map Middlemarch onto the physical contours of Coventry. In fact, the novel offers little physical description of the town of Middlemarch at all. We see the balcony of an inn, the White Hart, from which Mr. Brooke launches and simultaneously aborts his career as a political candidate, "which looked out advantageously at an angle of the market-place, commanding a large area in front and two converging streets." We know that the Vincys' dining room looks beyond iron palisading on to "that highly respectable street called Lowick Gate." We know something of the Green Dragon inn, with its billiard room and its archway giving on to the High Street; and we see a public house presided over by Mrs. Dollop, the Tankard in Slaughter Lane, where Lydgate's reputation is murdered by gossip. But a reader is left with very little sense of what the streets and buildings of Middlemarch look like, or how one location lies in relation to another.

This lack of physical description doesn't feel like a deficit, though. What Eliot most seeks to convey is Middlemarch as a state of mind—as the condition of consummate ordinariness, of absolutely middling Englishness. In her original plan for the novel, which she conceived in the first few months of 1869, it was to begin not with a woman named Dorothea Brooke, but deep within the town of Middlemarch, populated by Lydgate and the Vincys and other characters. "I am delighted to hear of a Novel of English Life having taken such warm possession of you," Blackwood wrote to her that February. She replied, "The various elements of the story have been soliciting my mind for years—asking for a complete embodiment." It was not until towards the end of 1870 that she began writing "Miss Brooke," and she only thought of knitting the two stories together in the beginning of 1871.

A clue as to what she means Middlemarch to represent is indicated by her choice of name for the town. Eliot's made-up place names—Broxton, Treby Magna, St. Ogg's—typically adhere closely to the conventions of actual English place names. But while there are many towns in England that begin with the word "middle"—Middleton and Middlesbrough and Middlewich and Middleham—there are no towns that end in the suffix "-march." There is a town called March, in Cambridgeshire, which is recorded in the Domesday Book as Merche; the name derives from the Old English word *mearc*, meaning boundary. And there are towns that end in "-marsh"—Michelmarsh, Saltmarsh, Widemarsh—deriving from the Old English word *mersc,* meaning marsh, of which there were plenty around Warwickshire when George Eliot was writing.

But the word "march" is suggestive of more than just boundaries or marshes. It implies that the book, with its subtitle, "A Study of Provincial Life," will be concerned with that which is absolutely pedestrian and ordinary. Provincialism—geographical, emotional—will be at its heart. "You will not like us at Middlemarch, I feel sure. We are very stupid, and you have been used to something quite different," Rosamond tells Lydgate, charmingly, on their first encounter. He replies, equally charmingly: "I suppose all country towns are pretty much alike, but I have noticed that one always believes one's own town to be more stupid than any other."

If one is from a provincial town, it's easy to assume that in the great elsewhere people are enjoying far more sophisticated and complex lives. I assumed it when I looked out from the town in which I was raised towards the tantalizing city of London, from which my parents had moved when I was three. (I was, I insisted, a city person forcibly removed to the provinces, even if I had only the sketchiest memories of London life, mostly involving playgrounds.) And there's some truth to the assumption, if by sophistication and complexity one means access to museums and arts and neighbours unlike oneself. But *Middlemarch* is not just concerned with the social consequences of geographical provincialism. It is also concerned with the emotional repercussions of a kind of immature provincialism of the soul—a small-minded, self-centred perspective that resists the implications of a larger view.

Eliot didn't think Coventry was stupid, not entirely, though she missed the "free range for walking" which she had enjoyed at Griff, she wrote to a friend. Rather than tramping widely through fields, she was now required to step daintily through drawing rooms, perhaps wearing the fancy pair of kid ankle boots decorated with ribbons that is in the Nuneaton museum's collection. (The boots are extremely narrow, with soles that are barely worn, as if they have only ever trodden on carpets.) Often, she chose to stay home with her books rather than to socialize. A couple of months after her move, she reported to Maria Lewis that she had failed to call on some acquaintances, "young ladies being the animals that would possess the minimum of attraction for me in a menagerie of the varieties of the human race."

She had a study upstairs at Bird Grove where she could escape the menagerie and the requirement to be a presentable specimen within it, and could devote herself to her books instead. "I have been rather humbled in thinking that if I were thrown on an uncivilised island and had to form a literature for its inhabitants from my own mental stock how very fragmentary would be the information with which I could furnish them," she wrote to Lewis. "It would be a good mode of testing one's knowledge, to set one's self the task of writing sketches of all subjects that have entered into one's studies, entirely from the chronicles of memory."

As I walked through Coventry, I thought about this serious-minded young woman stocking the chronicles of her memory for future use. Now an estate agent's office, 29 Warwick Row once housed the Miss Franklins' school, which George Eliot had attended in the first half of her teens and where she helped sew the baby's cloak that belongs to the Herbert museum. ("Her sewing is exquisite; it is the nicest thing I know about Mary," Rosamond says airily when she engages serious, plain, intelligent Mary Garth to sew items for her trousseau.) I wandered through the pedestrian shopping centre that was constructed after the Coventry Blitz obliterated most of George Eliot's Coventry, and progressed to Holy Trinity Church. Here, Robert Evans held the office of sidesman, passing along the aisles at the end of the service bearing a basket for contributions.

Holy Trinity survived the war mostly unscathed. It's a big church, largely built in the medieval era, and its most remarkable feature is a fifteenth-century doom painting high on a wall over the nave, depicting the Last Judgement. The painting, which was restored and unveiled in 2004, is aged and yellowed, and the lighting is kept deliberately dim. When I visited I had to crane my neck to look at it, and resort to souvenir postcards to see the details.

Even so, it was not hard to understand how it would have terrified churchgoers for generations. The painting shows Christ enthroned, surrounded by dozens of other figures. Some of them are saints ascending to heaven, including John the Baptist in a camel-skin robe, and a tonsured Saint Peter, the first pope. But many of them are ordinary-looking people, stripped naked and, in some cases, carrying the tools of their trade. Three alewives are chained together, bearing tankards with which they have tried to defraud customers. Some of these anonymous figures are going heavenwards, but others are being borne towards the mouth of hell, represented by a gaping mouth of a fanged beast with bloodshot eye.

There used to be paintings like this in churches all over England, but during the Reformation they were condemned as misbegotten church-establishment propaganda and painted over with whitewash, and many of them were lost. Coventry's is considered one of the finest surviving examples, though it, too, was covered up, until a piece of it was exposed in 1831 during repair work to the church, and a local artist was engaged to uncover it completely. When George Eliot lived in Coventry in the 1840s the restoration was quite new, though by the early twentieth century a coat of varnish the restorer applied had blackened and ob-scured it again.

It wasn't much to Victorian taste. "As a relic, it is interest-ing from its antiquity; but is otherwise less attractive," Benjamin Poole observed in his history of the city, noting the depiction of "unhappy spirits condemned to exclusion from the abodes of bliss . . . who, in the most unaccountable attitudes, are being removed by devils into the place of torment." The image of the ultimate judgement being delivered upon those ordinary, anony-mous people would have confronted Eliot every Sunday, when she entered the church on her father's arm.

UNTIL that Sunday when she didn't. On the second day of Janu-ary in 1842, not even a year after moving to Coventry, Mary Ann Evans declined to accompany her father to church. Two weeks later she again did not attend the service. "Went to church in the forenoon Mary Ann did not go to church," Robert Evans wrote in his diary.

She did not merely grow out of her religiosity, as one might grow out of some dwindling youthful enthusiasms. She thought her way out of it through study and enquiry—through industrious thought and patient renunciation of small desires. In Coventry, she had become acquainted with a group of young intellectuals who gathered at the home of Charles Bray, a ribbon manufacturer, and his wife, Cara; these friends would remain important to her for the rest of her life. The Brays lived at a house called Rosehill, not far from Bird Grove, which became a second home to Mary

Ann. The Brays were freethinking and enquiring people, and introduced her to novel ideas, including phrenology, the study of personality as revealed through the shape of one's skull. (Mary Ann had her head examined by George Combe, a prominent advocate of the pseudoscience, who was amazed at the size of her brain.) It was through the Brays that she later met Emerson, with whom she discussed Rousseau. Emerson said she had a "calm, serious soul"; she called him "the first *man* I have ever seen."

The Brays and their circle also introduced her to the latest ideas in liberal theology. Cara Bray's brother, Charles Hennell, was the author of a book, *An Inquiry Concerning the Origin of Christianity*, which argued that an account of the life of Jesus could and should be given without resort to supernatural or miraculous occurrences. Mary Ann read it, intending to formulate an argument against it; instead she was converted to Hennell's disbelief.

She became more or less agnostic—a term that was not coined until 1869 by her friend Thomas Henry Huxley, but which seems most accurately to apply to her rejection of the supernatural element of religion. Today atheists have claimed her as one of their own, with good reason, although she might have resisted a partisan alignment. But her relinquishing of religion was executed with a distinctly religious flavour. "I wish to be among the ranks of that glorious crusade that is seeking to set Truth's Holy Sepulchre free from a usurped domination," she wrote to a neighbour. But her loss of faith in the church was complete.

Her father was furious, and Mary Ann did what a writer does: she took up her pen to defend herself. One Monday morning she sat down in her study at Bird Grove, a south-facing room overlooking meadows and gardens towards the spires of Coventry, and wrote a long letter to her father, extending over two sheets of paper, with words filling the page to its margins. The letter—the only one she wrote to her father that survives—looks as if it were written swiftly, with thoughts put down as quickly as they came to mind; the words are elongated, as if her hand were rushing across the page in a force of passion. But she maintains clarity and legibility. Her mind is clear, as is her urgent wish to be understood.

First, she lays out her new beliefs. "I regard [the Bible] as histories consisting of mingled truth and fiction, and while I admire and cherish much of what I believe to have been the moral teaching of Jesus himself, I consider the system of doctrines built upon the facts of his life and drawn as to its materials from Jewish notions to be most dishonourable to God and most pernicious in its influence on individual and social happiness," she writes. She cannot join in with worship of which she disapproves—at least not without "vile hypocrisy and a miserable truckling to the smile of the world for the sake of my supposed interests."

Those supposed interests are her marital prospects. She goes on to say that she realizes her behaviour has, in the eyes of her father at least, rendered her unmarriageable. She also recognizes that her family at large—and her brother Isaac in particular—believe that the expense to which Robert Evans is being put to maintain a home in Coventry for the specific purpose of finding her a husband is now going to waste, and the money should rightfully be redistributed among her other siblings. "I could not be happy to remain as an incubus or an unjust absorber of your hardly earned gains," she writes, and the reader can feel the anger simmering. The true injustice, she clearly feels, is being done to her. She goes on to say that she would be just as happy to live in the country with her father, or anywhere else with him. "I fear nothing but voluntarily leaving you," she writes—unless he does not want her. In which case, she writes, "I must prefer to rely on my own energies and resources, feeble as they are."

The way she ends the letter is devastating. At the bottom of the second sheet of notepaper, the words contracting to fit the page, she writes, "As a last vindication of herself from one who has no one to speak for her I may be permitted to say that if ever I loved you I do so now, if ever I sought to obey the laws of my Creator and to follow duty wherever it may lead me I have that determination now and the consciousness of this will support me though every being on earth were to frown upon me." These impassioned, furious, heartbroken words could be those left unspoken by silent, faithful Cordelia, from whom King Lear imperiously commands a declaration of filial love, and then banishes for her failure to heave her heart into her mouth.

In 1869, the year she started writing the story that would end up being Book Two of *Middlemarch*, Eliot described her conflict with her father to Emily Davies, the founder of Girton College, the first women's college at Cambridge. She said that she regretted how she had conducted herself during those months, when tensions were so great between herself and her father that instead of speaking directly to him she was reduced to writing from her study upstairs to his office downstairs. Davies recalled that Eliot "dwelt a little on how much fault there is on the side of the young in such cases, of their ignorance of life, & the narrowness of their intellectual superiority."

Eliot's retrospective judgement of her younger self strikes me as too severe. Fidelity towards her father's memory comes at the expense of fidelity to her own wish to avoid hypocrisy—to avoid merely following custom when her intellectual convictions told her to do otherwise. I think she was justified in her opposition to her father, though I can also understand her mortification about how she expressed it. Being absolutely sure that one is right is part of growing up, and so is realizing, years later, that the truth might be more nuanced.

Lydgate is convinced that he has a superior knowledge in medical matters, an attitude that strikes others as arrogance. And his convictions are also justified. Lydgate has his failings: he has terribly mistaken ideas about women, and he also turns out to have devastatingly compromising expectations about what kind of domestic accoutrements are proper for a man of his birth and station, even when he can't afford to pay for them and has to take out a loan from Bulstrode to cover his expenses. But when it comes to medicine, Lydgate actually is as superior as he thinks he is.

Eliot is more forgiving of Lydgate's presumption in *Middlemarch* than she was of her own rebellion in Coventry. In the person of Lydgate, she shows how necessary youthful assertion is, and how inevitable is its expression, particularly in the case of a young person who has realized early on that books are stuff, and life is stupid. Lydgate is on the side of progress and open-mindedness; when it comes to science, at least, he stands against the creeping provincialism of the mind. Lydgate is undone not just by arrogance—he thinks he knows better than everyone else—but also by the fact that he expects everyone else to be better than they are. Being above pettiness, he expects others to be so also. And he expects to be judged fairly, by the patrons of Middlemarch's inns as well as the members of its boardrooms. His error, as it unfolds in the book, lies in not realizing what an immense and impossible expectation that is.

THE Foleshill Road has changed a great deal since George Eliot wrote her letter to Robert Evans. There are no longer meadows between it and the three spires of Coventry—which, improbably, still stand, despite the efforts of the Luftwaffe three quarters of a century ago. Instead, there are stores offering East Asian sweets and travel agents specializing in flights to Dhaka. The neighbourhood is home to a large Bangladeshi community, and Bird Grove is now the Coventry Bangladesh Centre, which provides employment advice and training to local residents.

The house is dilapidated now, its front door defaced with graffiti. There is a weed-infested car park where much of the garden used to be. When I went there in the company of John Burton, a retired teacher of English and the very dedicated chairman of the George Eliot Fellowship, a literary society devoted to the author, it wasn't clear how far we'd get over the threshold. But Muhammed Abdul, the young man who sat behind the reception desk in what would have been the spacious front hall, was kind and welcoming. He showed us the drawing room, which came with "window curtains, Blinds, and . . . Carpiting," according to Robert Evans's diary. (Evans's diary was a place for him to make shorthand notes about important matters; even so, the contrast between his written English and that of his erudite daughter is notable.) The room was now filled with computer terminals, incongruous beneath the high ceilings with decorative mouldings picked out in brown paint. We went up a curving formal staircase that had been painted in mud-brown gloss, and I thought how big the house was for a family of two, even with a full complement of servants. How excruciating it must have been for Mary Ann to be treading her way softly around that large, redundant space, at the most painful of odds with her most beloved of relatives.

We entered a small room that seems likely to have been the one she used as a study, facing south, looking towards the city. It was crammed with sewing machines and supplies: teaching materials. But the young Bangladeshi women who used them were not acquiring feminine arts as a necessary accomplishment for entry to the marriage marketplace. These women wished "to increase *Employability and Competence*," as a brochure for the centre put it. This was not sewing of the sort that the Miss Franklins taught. It was sewing as a skill, as a means of making a living—as a way for young women to rely upon their own energies and resources, and thereby be better equipped to bear the pressures imposed by fathers and brothers.

Mary Ann Evans was not turned out of her father's home, as she feared she might be after declining to go to church. Within a few weeks, a compromise had been reached. She would continue to accompany him on Sundays, but would be free to have her own opinions about the services she sat through. "I generally manage to sink some little well at church, by dint of making myself deaf and looking up at the roof and arches," she later wrote to a friend. She would be there but not there.

Near the front of Holy Trinity, in the pews reserved for more affluent residents, a carefully worded sign identifies the church as the place of worship that George Eliot attended during the years that she lived in Coventry, but it does not say that she worshipped there. As I stood in the deserted church when I visited, taking a last look around before a curate locked it up for the evening, I imagined her walking across the flagstones with her father, reconciled but still irretrievably separated, and looking up at the doom painting as she passed. There, as in the pews around her, she would have seen a varied collection of human creatures, and the images would have entered her imagination: the fraudulent alewives, those damned precursors of Mrs. Dollop of the Tankard; the figure of Jesus displaying his wounded hands and feet, risen by a miracle in which she no longer believed.

Robert Evans died in June 1849, and the day before his death she wrote to friends to say that she had stayed up until four the previous night holding his hand. "What shall I be without my Father?" she wrote, in anguish. "It will seem as if a part of my moral nature were gone. I had a horrid vision of myself last night becoming earthly sensual and devilish for want of that purifying restraining influence." She feared she was doomed without him.

But she wasn't, and her moral nature—an expression not much in fashion these days—wasn't destroyed. One of the things that makes *Middlemarch* a book for grown-ups—a book for adults, even—is Eliot's insistence upon taking moral questions seriously, and considering them in their complexity. The loss of faith that she underwent in Coventry was the beginning of a life-long intellectual process of separating morality from religion—of determining how to be a good person in the absence of the Christian God. The humanistic project of working out how best to understand one's fellow creatures, and how to behave towards them in the light of that understanding, underlay all her work. And with its wide panorama, its multiple characters, its interrelated plots, its intricate detail, *Middlemarch* is Eliot's doom painting without God.

As a young woman, Eliot greatly admired the novelist George Sand. "I should never dream of going to her writings as a moral code or text book," she wrote to a friend. It was, she added, sufficient for her "that I cannot read six pages of hers without feeling that it is given to her to delineate human passion and its results . . . so that one might live a century with nothing but one's own dull faculties and not know so much as those six pages will suggest."

I've never read the works of George Sand, but I think about this line, and what it has to say about the experience of reading *Middlemarch*. Eliot's novel is intensely moral—but it is not a moral codebook, and no one would want to read it if it were. Rather, through her delineation of human passions—romantic and intellectual—Eliot reveals her morality. *Middlemarch* demands that we enter into the perspective of other struggling, erring humans—and recognize that we, too, will sometimes be struggling, and may sometimes be erring, even when we are at our most arrogant and confident. And this is why every time I go back to the novel I feel that—while I might live a century without knowing as much as just a handful of its pages suggest—I may hope to be enlarged by each revisiting. Only a child believes a grown-up has stopped growing.

Chapter 3

Waiting for Death

"A change had come over Fred's sky, which
altered his view of the distance."

—*MIDDLEMARCH*, CHAPTER 23

Eliot's progress on her incipient Novel of English Life was interrupted in the spring of 1869 by the pressing demands of life itself. Thornton Arnott Lewes, George Henry Lewes's twenty-four-year-old son, who had spent the previous six years in the British colony of Natal, South Africa, arrived at the Priory, Eliot and Lewes's London home, dangerously ill.

"Thornie came home. Dreadfully shocked to see him so worn," Lewes wrote in his diary the evening that Thornton arrived. "A dreadful day—Thornie rolling on the floor in agony," he wrote the following day. Thornton, usually a muscular young man of thirteen stone, had lost nearly four stone and was "piteously wasted," as George Eliot wrote to Blackwood. Dr. James Paget, the foremost surgeon of the day who included Queen Victoria among his patients, prescribed morphine. A prone couch was set up in the drawing room near the piano, and whenever the sedatives wore off Thornton listened to Eliot playing, and was able to speak a little about his life in Natal, where he had purchased a tract of land and had built a farm. "In the evening he got excited talking about his African experiences and singing Zulu songs," Lewes wrote in his diary on 11 May. "Made anxious about him."

Thornie, as he was always known, was Lewes's middle child, born in 1844. An older brother, Charles, was born in 1842, and a younger brother, Herbert, called Bertie, in 1846. (Lewes's first child, a daughter, had been born in December 1841; she survived two days. A fourth and youngest son, St. Vincent, was born in 1848; he died when he was two years old.) Lewes had been separated from their mother, Agnes, since the children were quite young, but peculiar circumstances precluded a divorce.

The Leweses' situation was odd—even by the standards of the Victorian age, when divorce was rare and remained difficult to achieve despite the Matrimonial Causes Act of 1857. The couple married young: George Henry Lewes was twenty-three, and Agnes was nineteen. Within a decade, Agnes had become the lover of Thornton Leigh Hunt, a writer and an editor who was Lewes's close friend and co-founder with him of the *Leader*, a weekly magazine. A sketch made in 1844 by the novelist Thackeray depicts Agnes at the piano with Lewes by her side, mustachioed and singing; Hunt, a step or two away, looks on with a trace of a smile on his face, his thumbs tucked into his waistcoat. When in 1850 Agnes gave birth to another son, Edmund, the baby's father was Hunt.

Lewes seems to have condoned the liaison in principle, at least at first: he gave Edmund his last name, thus sparing the child the stigma of illegitimacy. But after the birth of Agnes's second child with Hunt, in 1851, there was a permanent rift between Lewes and Agnes. Lewes no longer thought of himself as her husband, although he gave his last name to all of the four children she bore Hunt. They separated, with no possibility of divorce.

Lewes first met Mary Ann Evans—or Marian, as she preferred to be known by then—in 1851, by which time she was living in London. Immediately after her father's death, in 1849, she had made her first trip to Europe, travelling for several weeks through France, northern Italy, and Switzerland with her friends the Brays, and then spending eight months in lodgings in Geneva. Upon returning to England she soon determined to settle in the capital. Having proven herself as a translator and begun to show her capabilities as a critic, she hoped to make a living sufficient to supplement the small annuity she had been granted in her father's will.

In London, she became one of several lodgers at the home of John Chapman, the publisher. Chapman's household, at 142 Strand, notoriously included not just his wife but also his mistress, who was governess to the Chapman children. Eliot and Chapman seem to have had a brief entanglement of some kind when she first moved in, though the extent of their intimacy is obscure; at any rate, their closeness was sufficient for both wife and mistress soon to demand that she move out. She did, for a while, returning to the Brays at Rosehill, but returned to Chapman's when his editorial need for her predominated over his womenfolk's objection.

It was in this unconventional milieu that she met Lewes and learned of his own unhappy and insoluble marital conundrum. Even so, it shocked many of their friends—if not the unshockable Chapman—when in 1854 she and Lewes set up home together. While it was generally understood that strict observance of marriage law was not necessary, open defiance of it was something else altogether. Soon, Eliot began calling herself Marian Evans Lewes, both for the sake of appearances (landladies were apt to be suspicious) and because she felt that they were married in every respect that really mattered. She called Lewes her husband. She laid claim to a family, even if she had come by it in an unusual manner.

She spoke of her new responsibilities with defiant conventionality. "We shall both be hard workers, for we have three little boys to keep as well as ourselves," Eliot wrote to her older, married half-sister, Fanny Houghton, in 1857, when she finally told her siblings of her relationship with Lewes. Of the boys, she explained, "Two of them are in Switzerland, at a delightful school there, and the youngest is at school in England."

No letter survives to tell us the immediate response of Fanny, who knew what it was to be an inconvenient stepchild: after her father's remarriage she had been sent out of the family home, when she was fourteen and Mary Ann was a baby, to serve as housekeeper to her brother, Robert, the oldest Evans child, on a neighbouring farm. Eliot clearly hoped for her sister's acceptance of the situation. "I am sure you retain enough friendship and sisterly affection for me to be glad that I should have a kind husband to love me and take care of me," she wrote. But Fanny did not prove to be tolerant of her half-sister's unconventional new household; like Eliot's siblings Isaac and Chrissey, she cut off correspondence.

If Eliot's relationship with Lewes was irregular, her relation to those "three little boys" of whom she spoke so intimately to Fanny was even more so. She had never laid eyes on them, and they had no idea that she existed. They had been packed off to boarding school at an early age, at least in part to keep them in ignorance of the Leweses' peculiar ménage with Thornton Hunt. It was nothing unusual for boys to be sent off to be educated and not to see their parents for months at a time—although the isolation of the Lewes boys from their family seems to have been extreme. Once installed at Hofwyl, a school in Bern that emphasized modern languages and outdoor activities, they did not come home to England for several years. They saw their father only once a year in the summer, and their mother never visited.

For their parents, as much as for Eliot, the Lewes boys seem to have existed largely as an abstract concern rather than a familiar presence. Lewes seems to have been, in absentia, a fond father, prone to none of the chilliness typically cultivated in the higher social classes in England. "I suppose you will be glad to hear from Papsy as he would be glad to hug you!" he once wrote to Charles and Thornie, offering them an ingenious substitute for paternal affection: "*Kiss each other* for me—the only way I know of sending a kiss so far."

The boys wrote letters home. Charles, who was studious and sensitive, mostly addressed his to Agnes; in them he recounted news of his academic progress and of the domestic arrangements at school. ("I have just finished my third lesson in music and am already further than several boys who have had several lessons more than me," he reported proudly, at the age of fourteen.) Thornie addressed his letters to Lewes, and if Eliot read them over his shoulder—as surely she did—she would have come to know this middle boy as an exuberant correspondent, full of passions and interests. He collected butterflies and botanical specimens, and at twelve he wrote, "I love natural History above all things, and when I grow up, it is my desire to become a naturalist." He was a budding philatelist, and some of his letters are half composed of what must have been wearying requests for stamps of foreign nations. There are affectionate enquiries after Lewes's health and his travels—"I hope your head is quite well, and that you had a good passage home"—and occasional nods towards Lewes's work, which all three boys must have taken to be the sole reason for their father's unavailability. "I hope your book will sell well, though I don't know which it is," he writes in one letter. His valedictions to Lewes are florid: "I remain Dear Pater meus Filius affectionatus Thorntonius Arnottus Ludovicus Ranarum Rex."

Eliot knew all about the likes and dislikes of young boys from Isaac, her nearest sibling in age. As a child she adored Isaac, though, as is sometimes the case with little sisters, the adoration was not reciprocated. He is usually taken to be the inspiration for Tom Tulliver, Maggie's domineering sibling in *The Mill on the Floss*. She began writing that novel in March 1859, by which time Thornie's letters would have immersed her once more in the typical preoccupations of boyhood. He gave accounts of murdering insects (215 mayflies in twenty minutes on one occasion), defying schoolmasters (one "punishes me now for any little thing he can possibly find out, if for example, I smile in a lesson"), and playing at soldiers. In one letter he recounted the discovery in a school storeroom of a range of weaponry from an earlier incarnation of the institution: "a real gun but with the lock broken, a splendid standard, eight or ten swords, a cannon, cartouche boxes, drums, horns for the officers, etc. Yesterday afternoon we had a grand parade, the cannon was loaded and fired nearly twelve times, if not more even; I am the guard of the cannon." He developed a keen interest in taxidermy, which complemented his passion for shooting. "I have got two nice lizards for you, which however cannot be forwarded by the post," he wrote to Lewes. "One has got a bullet shot in his side through which a *pistolbullet* from my *pistol* went."

I feel sure that Eliot felt a degree of disorientation as she absorbed this material. She was in her mid thirties, and before she met Lewes she had probably expected to remain childless. She and Lewes chose not to have children together; she told one friend they practised birth control. Possibly they felt that while they had voluntarily chosen cohabitation in spite of social censure, it would be unjust to visit the stigma of illegitimacy upon a child. Equally likely, Eliot preferred to devote her energies to her work without the distractions and dangers of childbearing and child rearing. And Lewes may have felt, with eminent justification, that caring for his boys as well as supporting the children Agnes had borne with Hunt was paternal responsibility enough.

But now there were children in her life, at least in a manner of speaking. "We are all very good puppies and wag our tails very merrily," Thornie told Lewes. Eliot liked dogs, but had not thought to adopt three human ones. Nor had she done so quite yet. The three boys she described assertively to her sister as part of her family—and for whom she became, along with Lewes, financially responsible—existed for a long time not as flesh-and-blood children, but as conceptual ones, elements in a new way of domestic life she was just beginning to build, just as she was building her new imaginative life as a novelist.

"My life has deepened unspeakably during the last year," she wrote at the close of 1857, the year that *Scenes of Clerical Life* was serialized in *Blackwoods Magazine*. "I feel a greater capacity for moral and intellectual enjoyment, a more acute sense of my deficiencies in the past, a more solemn desire to be faithful to coming duties, than any I remember at any former period of my life." Amid those duties and that depth came the unknown Lewes boys. Long before she heard heavy footsteps clattering up and down her staircase, or listened patiently to indefatigable accounts of various armaments and their uses, or caught the sweet but slightly rank scent of a young head of hair that has gone too many days without washing, she had imaginary children, boys she had begun to try to love before they knew she was in the world.

I JUGGLED a paper cup of coffee and a bag full of books as I made my way through Grand Central Station, then climbed aboard the commuter train to New Haven and looked for a window seat from which I could watch the grey streets of the South Bronx melt into the wooded suburbs of Connecticut. It had been years since I'd taken this train, but in my mid twenties I spent hundreds of hours on this line, journeying back and forth to see a man I loved.

It was a situation both complicated and simple. He had a young daughter whom I had yet to meet, and for months as I fell in love with him I heard about her and took her into my imagination. I would sit on this train, staring out of the window and trying to picture an obscure future in which I would take on a domestic role unlike any I had so far played, or had imagined myself playing: one in which I would commit myself not just to one person, but to two.

No longer a fact-checker, I was now a regular contributor to the magazine where I worked, producing often acerbic profiles of prominent cultural figures, which is one way for a young writer to get attention. I lived alone, in a tiny rented apartment in downtown Manhattan, where I had hardly any furniture beyond a futon bed that I only occasionally folded up into a couch. I didn't even have bookshelves, and my books, hundreds of them, were stacked against a wall in precarious piles, their orange and black and grey spines abutting each other like bricks in an uneven wall that has been foolishly and irrevocably constructed without foundations. Alone in that apartment after a long day at the magazine's offices I often dwelled on the responsibility I was close to assuming, wondering if I had come far enough from childhood to open myself to a child.

I could recall nothing in the books ranged against the wall that seemed to speak directly to my situation, and I longed for the simplicity of direct comparison. *Middlemarch* had a lot to say about falling in love; it even had something to say about falling in love with a learned scholar much older than oneself, not that I saw my own love affair in that unflattering light. But it had nothing, I thought, to tell me about falling in love with someone who came with such prior emotional commitments and practical obligations. I didn't understand how to navigate this paradigm, and *Middlemarch* didn't seem to give me any answers—not, at least, beyond the alternative of escaping into a different kind of love affair, one with a figure more like Ladislaw, who has his own legal complications (a codicil to Casaubon's will means Dorothea forfeits her fortune if she marries him) but does not come trailing a custody agreement.

I often dreamed about the daughter. She became part of my life without my being any part of hers; and it was difficult to be invisible to her when she was so vivid to me. Circumstances demanded maturity of me, and I strove to be as grown up as was required; and yet circumstances also conspired to make me feel as if I were the one who was young and powerless. Eventually, I did meet her, and when that day arrived I discovered that she was smaller than she had become in my imagination: a little human animal with soft nut-brown hair and bright eyes and an open expression. Eventually, too, I came to love her—not out of a sense of responsibility, nor out of love for her father, but for her, in herself, her sweet nature and good humour and irresistible intelligence. In all my imaginings about what it would mean to have her in my life, I had forgotten to include the prospect of joy.

I SETTLED into the peaceful, sunlit reading room at the Beinecke Rare Book & Manuscript Library at Yale, opened a file, and began paging through the lightweight sheets of writing paper fit for the international mail. These were letters written by Thornton Lewes, including the first he ever wrote to Eliot in August 1859. "For the first time do I seize the pen to begin a correspondence which is to be lasting," it begins, with kinetic flourish. His father had travelled to Hofwyl that summer to tell his sons, finally, that he was separated from Agnes, and that they had a new mother: the celebrated author of *Adam Bede*, which had been published to great acclaim that year. "They were less distressed than I had anticipated and were delighted to hear about Marian," Lewes wrote in his journal.

However distressed or delighted the boys really were when out of the wishful sight of their father, Thornie's letters to Eliot brim with an affection ready to be spent on a likely object. "We received your letter at St. Moriz in the canton of the Grisons, some three hours walk from Italy," Thornie wrote in that first letter, which was a response to an introductory one from her. "You can imagine how glad we were to get it, as being the first from you. It put a touch to our happiness on the journey." He told her that both he and Charles liked *Adam Bede* very much, Lewes having brought them a copy when he visited. And he clearly had conceived of one bonus of having a famous author as a stepmother: "If you happen to have many letters, stamps from foreign countries, I shall be very glad if you send me them for my collection."

As I sat in the library and looked through Thornie's early letters, written in a surprisingly careful and elegant hand, I found myself utterly enchanted by this lively, mischievous boy. I also wondered if his letters horrified Eliot at least as much as they amused her. Eliot wrote to tell him that she and Lewes had acquired a dog, Pug; Thornie responded, "I am not afraid of him as a rival, as he is not very dangerous, but when I come home, if he still lives and is impudent, I warn you beforehand, that I shall shoot him through the head, which will make a very good end for the Biography of Pug Pugnose, Esq."

He was bold and saw the possible advantages to be gained through triangulation. He asked her to pressure Lewes to give him a raise in his pocket money. He dared to enquire whether he and his brothers were to be included on a trip to Italy—a trip that Lewes and Eliot had planned to be very much à deux. "It is understood that we three imps should go with you, is it not?" Thornie wrote. Cost should not be an issue, he observed cheekily, "considering you are to get about 1,000,000 pounds for your next book."

The imps did not go to Italy, though Lewes did send Thornie some Italian stamps for his collection, a fact that makes me think irresistibly of the souvenirs sold in holiday resorts like the one I grew up in: "My Parents Went to ___ and All I Got Was This Lousy T-Shirt." For a year, Eliot corresponded with the Lewes boys without meeting them, though she knew the day was approaching when they would materialize. "At Easter our eldest boy will come home from school," she wrote to a friend in December 1859, using what was always her preferred formulation: "our boys" rather than "my husband's sons" or "my stepsons." She said that it would "make a new epoch" in their domestic life, for until then she and Lewes had lived alone.

The prospect was daunting. For all her confident references to her theoretical family, she knew she did not know what she had got herself into, and she was anxious about the transformation of the abstract into the concrete. "I hope my heart will be large enough for all the love that is required of me," she admitted.

Eliot's heart was evidently large enough for Charles Lewes. "It is very sweet as one gets old to have some young life about one," she wrote to a friend, after the two elder boys arrived at the Priory for the first time, in the summer of 1860. "He is quite a passionate musician, and we play Beethoven duets with increasing appetite every evening." But her tolerance for having young life about her does not seem to have extended so easily to the ebullient Thornie, who was swiftly dispatched to Edinburgh to complete his education. From there, he continued to write to her, affectionately if sometimes slightly challengingly. He told her, upon his arrival, that he was "celebrated through Edinburgh and Leith" for his academic potential, "but please don't be jealous of my reputation, it doesn't equal yours yet."

Whatever her private worries about the effect of boisterous boys upon her working and domestic life, Eliot seems to have inspired a real fondness in Thornie. He wrote her intimate, warm letters, at once confiding and ostentatious. He told of theatrical visits, flirtations, japes. He made her a present of a preserved chaffinch, with strict instructions that it was to be kept under a glass shade, "for it is a moral and physical impossibility that a *small* bird should not spoil in 2 months, if not covered by a shade." He sent her copies of poems he had composed: "I have no doubt of producing something superfine," he wrote. When in 1861 she sent him *Silas Marner,* the story of a reclusive, crabbed weaver redeemed by the unexpected adoption of a child, he declared it better even than *Adam Bede,* and told her, "when I had come to the last page I almost got angry at there being no more of it."

Thornie remained at a physical distance, even during holidays. In one letter he recounted spending a jolly Christmas and New Year in Edinburgh with family friends, kissing the girls under mistletoe which he had bought for the occasion. Blackwood, who lived in Edinburgh, occasionally served in loco parentis; in one letter Thornie gave the menu of a dinner he attended at Blackwood's house, which sounds ideal for a hungry adolescent boy: "Soup, Fried Soles, mutton, fowls, oyster patties, pheasant, blancmange, omelette, dessert, etc. Wine in abundance i.e. 8 glasses of sherry and 1 of port, which small quantity of course had not the slightest effect upon my nervous system." Eliot and Lewes were glad to have the publisher keeping an eye out for Thornie, of whom Lewes wrote, "The young bear wants licking into shape, but there is real power in him."

In one letter to Lewes, the young bear enclosed a photographic portrait, advising his father to "admire the singularly beautiful features and expression, the powerful biceps, the broad chest, the iron legs, the never failing gun of your 'second' son Thornton." The photo is reproduced in *George Eliot's Family Life And Letters*, by Arthur Paterson, a book from the 1920s whose author tends to sentimentalize Eliot in his effort to depict her as "an affectionate woman telling domestic news about herself and 'Pater.'"

This, though, is not a sentimental photograph. Thornie doesn't seem to be especially tall, though he looks well built, with a firm chin and a strong gaze; around the eyes in particular he bears a strong resemblance to George Henry Lewes as he appears in a portrait that was drawn when he was twenty-three. (Thornie reports that the photo is said to be "just like father in the good old days of yore.") He appears to have been carefully groomed for the camera, and is wearing a formal coat and bow tie, with his hair smoothed down in a manner incompatible with roving the hillsides looking for wildlife to massacre. Held proudly in his hands is a gleaming rifle.

FRED Vincy, the eldest son of the mayor of Middlemarch, is being groomed for the clergy—an improbable social costume for the unhappy Fred, who wishes to find another career. "I don't like divinity, and preaching, and feeling obliged to look serious," he tells the kindly Mr. Farebrother, whose own clerical collar causes him some discomfort. "I like riding across country, and doing as other men do. I don't mean that I want to be a bad fellow in any way; but I've no taste for the sort of thing people expect from a clergyman."

Fred expects to receive an inheritance from an uncle, old Mr. Featherstone, a rich, ailing, childless misanthrope. Anticipating the receipt of a fortune without the exertion of effort beyond the expression of his familial charm, Fred is careless with his own resources and with the resources of others. At the outset of Book Three, "Waiting for Death," he borrows money from Caleb Garth, expecting to make it and more back on a horse-trading deal, and convinced that "by dint of 'swapping' he should gradually metamorphose a horse worth forty pounds into a horse that would fetch a hundred at any moment."

Unsurprisingly, his scheme fails, and he is unable to repay Caleb Garth, who can ill afford to subsidize him. Mrs. Garth must give up her hope of having her son Albert apprenticed; and Mary Garth must surrender the money she has earned by taking care of sick, grumpy Mr. Featherstone. It is upon visiting the Garths at home with the news and realizing the harm he has done to them that Fred first begins to understand the implications of his recklessness. "He had not occupied himself with the inconvenience and possible injury that his breach might occasion them, for this exercise of the imagination on other people's needs is not common with hopeful young gentlemen," Eliot writes. "But at this moment he suddenly saw himself as a pitiful rascal who was robbing two women of their savings."

His shame is all the greater because Fred hopes that Mary will one day consent to marry him. Fred, for all his fondness of gambling and horses, is essentially a domestic creature who is looking forward to the comforts and pleasures of married life. Unlike his sister, Rosamond, who has cast her eye over all the young men of Middlemarch and found them lacking, Fred has fixed his sights on Mary, the childhood playmate with whom he once enacted a pretend wedding using a ring taken from an umbrella. But he is not entirely confident of winning her. "I suppose a woman is never in love with anyone she has always known—ever since she can remember, as a man often is. It is always some new fellow who strikes a girl," Fred grumbles to Mary, his conviction conditioned by his sister's preferences. "Let me see," Mary replies, archly. "I must go back on my experience. There is Juliet—she seems an example of what you say. But then Ophelia had probably known Hamlet a long while."

Mary, who is beloved by Fred not in spite of but because of her sharp, sometimes wounding, intelligence, is a quiet heroine of *Middlemarch*, and may be particularly appealing to the kind of female reader whose own girlhood has been coloured by the dawning knowledge that while her face is not as pretty as that of other girls, her mind is quicker than theirs. Mary is light and funny and serious at the same time, and while she loves Fred, she will not promise herself to him until he has determined what kind of a man he is going to be.

He insists that he needs licking into shape, and that only she can accomplish it. "I never shall be good for anything, Mary, if you will not say that you love me—if you will not promise to marry me—I mean, when I am able to marry," he tells her. Far from being won over by his declarations, Mary is tart and riddling in response. "If I did love you, I would not marry you: I would certainly not promise ever to marry you," she replies. Fred tells her that she is wicked to say so: if she loves him, she ought to promise to marry him. "On the contrary, I think it would be wicked in me to marry you even if I did love you," she replies.

In this exchange, Mary reminds me not so much of Juliet or Ophelia—pretty girls, both, and look where it got *them*—as of Rosalind, the clever, irresistible heroine of *As You Like It*. The play is set in the Forest of Arden, a re-imagined version of the region in Warwickshire that was the birthplace of both Shakespeare and George Eliot, and Rosalind spends most of it in the guise of a boy, Ganymede. In a wonderful comic conceit, Rosalind-as-Ganymede impersonates *herself* as the love object of the smitten Orlando. "Love me, Rosalind," Orlando begs. "Yes, faith, will I, Fridays and Saturdays, and all," Rosalind replies. "And wilt thou have me?" Orlando asks. "Ay, and twenty such," counters Rosalind. "Are you not good?" she says. "Why then, can one desire too much of a good thing?"

Rosalind shows that it is possible for a woman to be both intelligent and passionate. She is, of course, in love with Orlando even as she tests him. "O coz, coz, coz, my pretty little coz, that thou didst know how many fathom deep I am in love!" she tells Celia, her cousin. "But it cannot be sounded; my affection hath an unknown bottom, like the Bay of Portugal." Her aching, secret, high-spirited confession conjures all the thrilling urgency of falling in love under complicated circumstances.

Rosalind, clever Mary's ancestor, is cherished by clever girls everywhere. Fred cherishes Mary for her cleverness—he brings her books when he visits—and this is one of his most admirable qualities. Whatever his other failings, he isn't intimidated by a woman with a brain. (He also admires and respects Mary's mother, Mrs.

Garth, who teaches her children history in the kitchen while baking jam puffs.) But cleverness is not the only quality that Fred cherishes in Mary. Mary is what Americans call homely: unhandsome, even ugly at an unfortunate angle. But she also inspires in Fred that familiar, comforting, easy sense of rightness that is what the English mean when using the word "homely" to describe a house.

"A homely place with an orchard in front of it, a rambling, old-fashioned, halftimbered building, which before the town had spread had been a farm-house, but was now surrounded by the private gardens of the townsmen," is how Eliot describes the Garths' house, where Fred goes to make his confession of fiscal irresponsibility. Mary, a girl from the borderlands of the Forest of Arden, is home to Fred. But she is much more than home, too—as is Rosalind, with her glorious admonition to Orlando on behalf of clever girls, and the women they grow up into: "Make the doors upon a woman's wit, and it will out at the casement; shut that and 'twill out at the key-hole; stop that, 'twill fly with the smoke out at the chimney."

"No fear of *my* marrying," Thornie wrote to Lewes the summer after he turned twenty, not long after his older brother Charles had announced his engagement. "I am to be the bachelor as Charlie is not, that's clear, and I made up my mind to it a long while ago."

Thornie would miss his brother's wedding, to a young woman called Gertrude Hill. In the autumn of 1863 he had set sail on the two-month voyage to Durban, South Africa, arriving there just before New Year. "Well, our poor boy Thornie parted from us today and set out on his voyage to Natal," Eliot wrote to Sara Hennell, the sister of Cara Bray and of Charles Hennell, with whom she had been close friends since the Rosehill days. "I say 'poor' as one does about all beings that are gone away from us for a long while," she added. "But he went in excellent spirits with a large packet of recommendatory letters to all sorts of people, and with what he cares much more for—a first rate rifle and revolver."

Thornie's departure for Natal came after several months during which his career had been worryingly undecided. Lewes and Eliot had hoped that he would go to India to join the civil service there, but, as they belatedly discovered, he had failed to study sufficiently for the necessary examinations. Charles Lewes, meanwhile, had become a civil servant closer to home, in the Post Office, thanks to the intercession of Anthony Trollope, a family friend, who, as well as being a successful novelist, was a career postal official. Lewes and Eliot were determined to find Thornie a post abroad. "He is of an active adventurous temperament, fond of Natural History, and of roving about in search of 'specimens,' so that a life of London work would not suit him at all," Eliot wrote to a friend. It would not suit her to have him there, either: in a letter written while all three boys were home, she wrote that she was "up to the ears in Boydom," a condition in which she was unable to be productive.

One idea was that Thornie and his younger brother Bertie might go together to Algiers to establish a farm. Thornie, however, had other intentions: he wanted to join Polish insurgents fighting the Russians. Lewes and Eliot were horrified, and feared for what they called his moral nature. "The idea of his enlisting in a guerrilla band, and in such a cause was too preposterous, and afflicted us greatly," Lewes wrote in his diary. "But for some time we feared that he would set us at defiance and start."

Instead, he left for Natal with "a very sanguine expectation of shooting lions," Eliot told a friend. Every element of the adventure seemed to delight Thornie, who managed to make even the privations of the long voyage aboard the *Damietta* sound entertaining—among them the fact that his trunk, which was packed at the bottom of the hold, proved impossible to retrieve. "I have given up sleeping in bed, it is too hot," he wrote from his cabin, where it was 30°C. "Keep in my clothes *on* bed, get up at 6:30, strip, air my clothes, get a ducking of salt water & am prepared for a large breakfast at 8:30." He and his shipmates had the thrill of deep-sea fishing—"we had some shark steak for breakfast, rather tough and strong but quite palatable"—and bagging albatross. He published his own shipboard newspaper, the *Damietta Blunderbuss*. (A sample headline: "'No Monopoly' as the Cockroach said when he drove the blowfly off the seed cake.") He defended Darwinism among his fellow passengers. "I have consequently been set down as an atheist and a fool, but that does not matter as it furnishes subjects for chaffing me, and as I stand it of course, you know how, I am very popular," he reported. He joined in dramatic productions, including one in which he appeared as the devil, wearing blue tights and a tail—"to the horror of the children and many of the females, and to the intense disapprobation of the parson," he reported with glee.

South Africa itself proved thrilling. The colony of Natal had been established twenty years earlier, on the southeastern coast of the continent, and encompassed rugged mountains and expansive grasslands, which "have very much the character of the higher

moors of Devonshire," a contemporary author noted, though unlike Devonshire, Natal was populated with hippopotamuses and
hyenas and innumerable rare and beautiful butterflies. Upon arriving Thornie laid plans to join an interpreter going on the court
circuit around the townships, to be followed by an excursion as-
sisting a French trader for which he was to be paid three pounds
a month. "Won't that be glorious!" he wrote to Lewes. "I would
have gone willingly for nothing at all, as the shooting and butter-
fly catching will be quite enough payment."

Thornie's recreational expectations were not all so benignly
pastoral. In the same letter he joked blithely of his intentions
of shooting "Bushmen," "who are almost the same as Chimps
or gorillas . . . still, there is worse game no doubt, than Lions,
Leopards, & Bushmen." Eliot transcribed extended passages of
Thornie's letter to her friend Barbara Bodichon, who had written
introductions for him to Durban society, but she omitted those
lines. Thornie's crude racism was embarrassing to Eliot: it suggested his moral nature was not after all as pure as she and Lewes
would have liked to believe.

But it was hardly unusual for the time and the context. In
her last novel, *Daniel Deronda*, which was published in 1876,
Eliot would allude to the ugliness and hypocrisy that characterized contemporary attitudes towards colonized populations, with
her hero, Deronda, as the pointed voice of reason. In that book,
at a gathering of gentlefolk, discussion turns to the West Indies.
"Grandcourt held that the Jamaican negro was a beastly sort of
baptist Caliban; Deronda said that he had always felt a little with
Caliban, who naturally had his own point of view and could sing
a good song," Eliot writes. "Mrs. Torrington was sure she should

never sleep in her bed if she lived among blacks; her husband corrected her by saying that the blacks would be manageable enough if it were not for the half-breeds; and Deronda remarked that the whites had to thank themselves for the half-breeds."

The satire and contempt here are evident, but even so, looking back from today's perspective, one can't help wondering how Eliot managed to square her generous-minded humanism and her insistence on the need for sympathy with one's fellow men and women with her own support of the colonial endeavour in Natal. Possibly, as she packed Thornie off to Africa, she made an intellectual case to herself for the virtues of colonialism, which was after all widely culturally sanctioned. Possibly, also, she was clueless as to what else the Lewes boys might do with themselves now that they were men. The colonial adventure presented itself as a convenient option, especially if one could edit out its more problematic aspects.

Thornie doesn't seem to have given a thought to larger questions of justice: he was in his element. He visited coffee plantations and hunted leopard. He wrote to Lewes, offering to procure him a baboon. He went into Durban society, such as it was, attending the small theatre and becoming a regular visitor at the home of Mr. John Sanderson, an editor and avid amateur naturalist. "His wife is a charming creature about 30, no children, and immensely fond of music," Thornie wrote. "So you may imagine the evenings we have together, sonatas, symphonies etc, while I howl German songs." Thornie seemed to have found his course in life. "The wild, free and easy, independent life suits me wonderfully," he wrote. "If you could only see me you would say it agreed with me."

THE congenial young man who charms the wife of his friend with song and sophisticated attention figures in *Middlemarch*, too. "Mr. Orlando Ladislaw is making a sad dark-blue scandal by warbling continually with your Mr. Lydgate's wife, who they tell me is as pretty as pretty can be," Mrs. Cadwallader, the parson's wife, tells Dorothea. "It seems nobody ever goes into the house without finding this young gentleman lying on the rug or warbling at the piano."

Like Fred Vincy, Will Ladislaw is another iteration upon a theme: that of the young man seeking to determine his course in life. While Fred seems endowed with Thornie's outdoorsy tastes and with his amiable good nature, Ladislaw shares Thornie's restlessness and his quest for adventure. At the outset of the novel, Will Ladislaw is introduced as a young man without any fixed career, but with a desire for travel and discovery. The reader learns that he elected not to go to an English university, but studied instead in Heidelberg; when we first meet him, he is leaving for Rome for the vague purpose of exposing himself to culture. His cousin, Mr. Casaubon, has supplied him with funds for a year of exploration, although Casaubon considers Ladislaw self-indulgent and lacking in application. "I shall let him be tried by the test of freedom," Casaubon loftily tells Dorothea and Mr. Brooke. Dorothea has a more compassionate perspective upon the frailties of a young person who has not yet determined what to make of him- or herself. "People may really have in them some vocation which is not quite plain to themselves, may they not?" she asks. "They may seem idle and weak because they are growing. We should be very patient with each other, I think."

In Rome Ladislaw studies painting, though he quickly recognizes the limitations of his talents for that art, or for poetry, Thornie's amateur pursuit. "To be a poet is to have a soul so quick to discern, that no shade of quality escapes it, and so quick to feel, that discernment is but a hand playing with finely ordered variety on the chords of emotion—a soul in which knowledge passes instantaneously into feeling, and feeling flashes back as a new organ of knowledge," Ladislaw tells Dorothea, with self-important authority. "But you leave out the poems. I think they are wanted to complete the poet," she points out in earnest reply.

Back in England, Ladislaw makes rushed assaults on more prosaic careers. For a while, he becomes the editor of a local newspaper, the *Pioneer*, and he contemplates entering politics, now that the Reform Bill is about to open the field: "He could go away easily, and begin a career which at five-and-twenty seemed probable enough in the inward order of things, where talent brings fame, and fame everything else which is delightful." Like Thornie, Will imagines the world bending to his irrepressible will.

As *Middlemarch* progresses the reader sees Ladislaw repeatedly declaring that he is about to leave town to seek his fate, although he finds it hard to get moving. Thornie, on the other hand, was in a new field of experience altogether, and his adventures grew more lurid as time passed. He volunteered for battle against the Basotho resisting colonial rule whose land lay on the eastern edge of Natal, and set off with an Enfield rifle and a sabre. "By tomorrow we hope to have 2,000 men here to start for Basuto land, to wreak vengeance on their heads," he wrote home. "Of course I volunteer, and hope to have the pleasure of potting a few Basutos before I have done with them. Who would have thought, that by my coming out here, instead of going to Poland, I should have fallen from the frying pan into the fire, and instead of fighting an enemy I hate, I should have to fight one I despise."

He sent missives home with some details of his experiences, which must have shocked Lewes and Eliot. The horrors could no longer easily be edited out. "We soon arrived at the scene of the murder of the Boers," he wrote in one. The dead men "had been buried by a party from Harrismith, or rather had had some branches and earth strewn over them, and their legs were sticking through." But Thornie maintained his usual jaunty tone, describing the weevil-infested biscuits that were among their supplies at camp, and the stewing in butter of a whole sheep. "I composed a Frontier Guard Song for the occasion, which though very mediocre, was welcomed with great applause," he wrote.

In spite of this violent turn, Lewes and Eliot were evidently not ready to retreat from the colonial opportunity. When the fighting died down, Bertie Lewes, Thornie's younger brother, joined him in Natal. (Bertie's own letters to Lewes, which are also collected at the Beinecke, are few and seem laboriously written.) Thornie was glad to have Bertie there, but their adventures continued to be perilous. The brothers established a farm; it burned down, igniting their gunpowder and causing twenty pounds' worth of damage. They resorted to living in a hut constructed by their African employees, "something like a large beehive, in which we are very comfortable," Thornie wrote. The loss of books, at least, was compensated for by new ones sent from home. "We should be miserable without books, and our old lot has been read and reread times out of number," Thornie wrote to Lewes, in thanks for a shipment. "I can tell you that *good* novels bear rereading."

On a tip, the brothers undertook a trading adventure. They purchased blankets which—like Fred Vincy and his horses—they aimed to transform by dint of swapping into a valuable quantity of ivory. Thornie hoped to use the proceeds to fund a trip home, but they were no more successful in this than Fred and his horse-trading. "We are on our last legs," Thornie wrote to Lewes.

Worse, Thornie was suffering from what he thought were kidney stones, which were causing him paroxysms of pain. "I can hardly stoop to touch the ground, I can't sit up for half an hour, all I can do is lie down, then get up and walk about for half an hour, then lie down again," he wrote in October 1868. "In fact if I were 50 instead of 24, I should have quietly walked some fine day over our waterfall; but while there is youth there is hope." Within seven months, he was in agonies on the couch at the Priory.

When Thornie arrived at home, leaving Bertie behind in Africa, George Eliot's slow progress on *Middlemarch* temporarily halted. She and Lewes were absorbed in looking after him. By June tuberculosis of the spine had been diagnosed, and the only prescription was rest, cod-liver oil, and morphine, which induced Thornie, who was subsisting on a diet of mainly fruit and milk, to long periods of sleep.

He was sweeter than ever, Eliot wrote to a friend. His moral nature was uncorrupted even by experience of warfare, she insisted. "There is nothing that we discern in his character or habits to cause us grief," she said. Perhaps Eliot was attempting to reassure herself that she had not failed Thornie by sending him overseas. And perhaps, too, the sweetness that had always been there was more poignant to her now, with the rambunctiousness wasted away.

That month, Eliot began writing an introduction to *Middlemarch*, and "meditated characters" for the novel, as she noted in her diary. Otherwise, she sat by Thornie with her books, absenting herself quietly on the few occasions that Agnes Lewes came to visit. On 1 August as she sat by his bedside she read through all of Shakespeare's sonnets, making notes on them in the small leatherbound notebook that is now in the New York Public Library. She marked down individual lines she admired: "Looking on darkness which the blind do see"; "My grief lies onward & my joy behind." And she remarked upon the "wearisome series about leaving posterity"—the sequence of sonnets in which the poet urges another man to father a child, so his beauty might live on in his son.

Thornie died at six thirty in the evening of 19 October 1869, in Eliot's arms. "Nurse and I raised him and his last breathings were quite peaceful," she wrote to Cara Bray in Coventry. To Barbara Bodichon Eliot wrote, "It has cut deeper than I expected—that he is gone and I can never make him feel my love any more. Just now all else seems trivial compared with the powers of delighting and soothing a heart that is in need." In her diary, she wrote, "This death seems to me the beginning of our own."

"She had lavished almost a mother's love on my dear boy, and felt almost a mother's grief," Lewes wrote to Blackwood a few weeks later. He revised the formulation slightly for a letter to Thomas Trollope, the brother of the novelist, omitting the second modification of Eliot's maternal sensibility: "She had lavished almost a mother's love on the dear boy, and suffered a mother's grief in the bereavement."

Eliot was conscious of the ambiguity of her maternal status. In a letter to Harriet Beecher Stowe written a few months before Thornie's death, just as he returned to London, she begged the American novelist's forgiveness for the fragmentary nature of her note. She added that she had little anxiety that Stowe would misinterpret her, "for you have had longer experience than I as a writer, and fuller experience as a woman, since you have borne children and known the mother's history from the beginning."

The question of what it might mean for a woman to be a mother, or not, recurs throughout Eliot's books. In an early work, "Janet's Repentance," one of the *Scenes of Clerical Life*, she describes the power of motherhood, which "turns timidity into fierce courage, and dreadless defiance into tremulous submission; it turns thoughtlessness into foresight, and yet stills all anxiety into calm content; it makes selfishness become self-denial, and gives even to hard vanity the glance of admiring love." When she wrote those words she was still of childbearing age, and I wonder what she felt about forgoing that intensity of experience herself, as the years of its possibility melted away. (In the case of Janet Dempster, who is cruelly bullied by her husband and becomes an alcoholic, childlessness constitutes "half [her] misery.") But Eliot's books are also filled with women for whom motherhood has produced more problems than satisfactions. In *Felix Holt* there is the haunting Mrs. Transome, who, shockingly, longs for the death of her elder son so that her younger son, the offspring of a long-past affair, can inherit her estate. Daniel Deronda is abandoned as a child by his mother, the Princess Halm-Eberstein, an opera singer who goes by the stage name of Alcharisi. This is in part so that Daniel will grow up as an English gentleman in ignorance of his Jewish heritage, which his mother despises, but it is also so that she will be free to pursue her vocation unencumbered. "Every woman is supposed to have the same set of motives, or else to be a monster," the Princess tells him, when they finally meet in Deronda's adulthood. "I am not a monster, but I have not felt exactly what other women feel—or say they feel, for fear of being thought unlike others."

The Princess is an extreme example of a woman who forgoes motherhood for her art, and while she is personally unsympathetic in many ways she presents a conflict that Eliot would have shared, to some degree. (Deronda's mother tells him: "You can never imagine what it is to have a man's force of genius in you, and yet to suffer the slavery of being a girl.") Eliot believed that in spite of not ever bearing a child she had the emotional capacity for a maternal relation. But she recognized the contradictions inherent in her situation. In a letter to a friend written during Thornie's illness she remarked that, "in proportion as I profoundly rejoice that I never brought a child into the world, I am conscious of having an unused stock of motherly tenderness"—a formulation that both pushes away and embraces the role of mother.

WHEN my love affair with the man in New Haven came to an end, my sense of loss was twofold. The end of things with him was explicable, if acutely painful. But the end of things with his daughter hurt differently, because the severing of that bond felt arbitrary. I had felt her close, and now she was gone—as distant as if she had sailed from me across the equator to inhabit a strange new land. Bereft, I told myself that I would never, ever, get involved with someone who already had children—not because they were too hard to love, but because they were too hard to lose.

But a few years later I met a man who had three sons, not very different in age than were the Lewes boys when George Eliot met George Henry Lewes. I hoped my heart would be large enough for all the love that was required of me; my hope turned into trust, and we married. As a younger woman I had not anticipated having a marital home instantly filled with half-grown boys, and if sometimes in the years of their adolescence I found it helpful to recall Dorothea's words about the need for patience with young men—who may seem idle and weak because they are growing—more often I have been impressed by my stepsons' resourcefulness and moved by their varied good natures. Before long another small brother was added to the fraternity, and it is one of the great joys of my life to see my son playing with his adored older brothers, and to recognize the ways in which my unexpected family has brought me an increase of love, not a diminution of it.

"I feel very full of thankfulness for all the creatures I have got to love, all the beautiful and great things that are given to me to know, and I feel, too, much *younger* and more hopeful, as if a great deal of life and work were still before me," Eliot wrote to Charles, the oldest Lewes boy, in 1861, a few months after he had moved home to London. As the scholar Rosemarie Bodenheimer has pointed out, it was around the time that the Lewes boys came into her life that Eliot and Lewes began speaking of her books as her children. She referred to *The Mill on the Floss* as "my youngest child" as she was writing it, and the metaphor seems to have been adopted by the Lewes boys as well. In 1861, on reading a newspaper announcement of a forthcoming work by her, Thornie wrote from Edinburgh, "What is its name, or is the Baby work not yet christened?"

Eliot spoke of the labour of producing her books as a form of parturition, and of them existing as independent lives once produced. She once told a correspondent that her experience of finishing a novel was not exultant or triumphant. "What comes after, is rather the sense that the work has been produced within one, like offspring, developing and growing by some force of which one's own life has only served as a vehicle, and that what is left of oneself is only a poor husk." However apt a description that might be of writing a book, I can't help feeling that Eliot misses something about motherhood in her choice of metaphor. When I was the mother of a newborn I felt the opposite of dried up and used up. Though I was exhausted, I had never felt more alive and vital and necessary. Books are less like babies, perhaps, than they are like adolescents: nurtured by motherly tenderness but very much their own person, then launched into the world to stand on their own.

In her novels, though, Eliot is a one-woman refutation of the canard that only writers who are parents can write well about parenthood. One of the comic threads running through *Middlemarch* is the myopic delight that Celia, Dorothea's younger sister, takes in her firstborn son, baby Arthur. It's a painfully accurate caricature; after my son was born, I giddily wrote to a friend, a professor of English literature, "All these years I've thought I was Dorothea, and now I've turned overnight into Celia."

Elsewhere in the novel, her perceptiveness about how anguishing a mother's experience can be is so acute that I can hardly bear the sense of recognition I feel in reading it. Fred is adored by his mother, the mild, good-natured, silly Mrs. Vincy, whose imagination is limited to the most restricted precincts of Middlemarch, and who sees only nascent promise in her eldest son's dilatoriness. There is a great deal of comic value in this, but in Book Three of *Middlemarch*, Eliot grants Mrs. Vincy a moment of gravitas. Fred has been taken sick, and Dr. Lydgate has diagnosed typhoid fever. Mrs. Vincy is distraught. "Her brightness was all bedimmed; unconscious of her costume which had always been so fresh and gay, she was like a sick bird with languid eye and plumage ruffled," Eliot writes. "She went about very quietly: her one low cry was to Lydgate. She would follow him out of the room and put her hand on his arm moaning out, 'Save my boy.'"

Eliot's characterization of Mrs. Vincy's distress as her first-born son lies in mortal danger is profoundly compassionate, and subtly captures a harrowing truth. "All the deepest fibres of the mother's memory were stirred, and the young man whose voice took a gentler tone when he spoke to her, was one with the babe whom she had loved, with a love new to her, before he was born," she writes. Eliot locates even silly Mrs. Vincy's dignity and depth. She finds it in Mrs. Vincy's motherhood, and in her terrible fear of the worst that can befall a mother.

CHARLES Lewes was the only stepson who would survive her. Six years after Thornie's death, Bertie was afflicted with similar wasting symptoms and died, leaving a widow and two small children. Bertie didn't even make it back to England in his illness; he died in Durban, at the home of John Sanderson, Thornie's old friend, and his charming musical wife, Marie.

"He came into our house, looking like the ghost of his former self, quite suddenly one day and I shall never forget the shock it gave me," Marie Sanderson wrote in a letter to Eliot. Bertie had been in good spirits, under the circumstances. He was gaining weight, and expected to recover. "We used to have pleasant talk about different things—Middlemarch for instance," Mrs. Sanderson went on in her letter. In reading this, I ask myself what they said about the book, and what they recognized in it, and whether they spoke of Rosamond and Ladislaw spending their evenings in careless song.

Charles Lewes grew to become a pillar of George Eliot's life, as she was of his. When the *Times* suggested in its obituary of Agnes Lewes that George Henry Lewes had abandoned her and the Lewes children for George Eliot, Charles came to the passionate defence of Eliot, whom he always called *Mutter*, the German word for mother. "George Eliot found a ruined life, and she made it into a beautiful life," he said. "She found us poor little motherless boys, and what she did for us no one on earth will ever know."

Charles and his wife, Gertrude, had only daughters, the youngest of whom, Elinor, married Ernest Carrington Ouvry, a lawyer. In her will, Elinor left the copyright to the works of George Eliot to one of her grandsons, Jonathan Ouvry. Jonathan is also a custodian of a few family relics, most of Eliot and Lewes's possessions and papers having been sold at auction in 1923, after Gertrude Lewes died.

Now in his seventies, Jonathan is theatrical in demeanour.

A former solicitor and a keen amateur singer, he is animated and twinkly of eye, the kind of person you can imagine, in his younger years, wearing a tail and tights and playing Mephistopheles. I visited him and his wife, Marjorie, at their home in London one warm afternoon in late summer, and while Marjorie prepared dinner, Jonathan showed me his family treasures: a portrait of another ancestor, Frederic Ouvry, who was a solicitor of Dickens's; a book about Octavia Hill, the sister of Gertrude Lewes, who was a prominent activist on behalf of women; a memoir published by Charles Lee Lewes, George Henry Lewes's grandfather, who was a well-known comic actor in the eighteenth century and who, Jonathan told me, originated the role of Young Marlow in Oliver Goldsmith's play *She Stoops to Conquer*. It was exciting to discover these strands and traces of literary life married unexpectedly together and surviving, not in a museum, but in the comfortable domesticity of a London home.

Over dinner we talked about Jonathan's children—Marjorie's stepchildren—and my children, and the complicated bonds of family. After dinner we sat in the living room, where, on the mantelpiece, was a small leather wallet with the initials G.H.L. and the date of 1874 embossed upon it, a gift from Eliot to Lewes. Next to it was Eliot's pen. It had a slim handle made from what looked like bone, and a tarnished metal nib. I asked if I could hold it, and when Jonathan said I could, I gingerly picked it up.

It felt heavier in my hand than I expected, and I thought of the labour it must have demanded. "Have you known the misery of writing with a *tired* steel pen which is reluctant to make a mark?" Eliot once wrote to a friend. I imagined her holding this pen, dipping it over and over into an inkstand, taking care against blotting or smudging, and I wondered which of her works she had written with it.

Jonathan's older brother, David Ouvry, is quieter and less ebullient. He is a retired teacher of English and a devoted musician; when I visited him and his partner, Daphne, in their home in the Cotswolds he showed me his workshop, where carefully shaped pieces of wood waited to be assembled into a violin. The beautiful, rambling house, which was largely built in the sixteenth century, had an imposing fireplace in the dining room, large enough to stew a whole sheep in butter. In the living room, David showed me objects he had inherited. A lamp stood on a side table that had belonged to George Eliot, and on the wall near the grand piano hung a portrait, a pencil drawing, of a beautiful young woman.

She was Blanche Lewes, the eldest daughter of Charles and Gertrude, who was born in the summer of 1872, as George Eliot was finishing *Middlemarch*. After the birth, which followed Gertrude's loss of a stillborn baby a year earlier, Eliot wrote with quiet exultation to her friend Maria Congreve. "This morning came the joyful news that Gertrude has a fine healthy baby—a daughter," she wrote. "We have just been saying in our walk, that by the end of this century our one-day-old grand-daughter will probably be married and have children of her own, while we are pretty sure to be at rest." Eliot added, "We have longed for more continuous warmth and brightness, and to-day may perhaps be the beginning of that one wanting condition." She seems to be talking both about the weather—there has been "delicious sunshine" that day—and about the larger brightness offered by the baby's new life: a granddaughter, unmodified by the qualifier "step," fully claimed as family, promising continuation.

David and I ascended the stairs and passed a framed portrait of George Henry Lewes, drawn by a friend, Rudolf Lehmann, in 1867, when Lewes was fifty. It was a copy of one that is in the collection of the British Museum, and I had seen it reproduced many times before. In it, Lewes has thinning hair and extravagant beard; his brow is furrowed and his eyes are intense, like Thornie's in his schoolboy portrait. "Every time I look at it I see different things," David told me. "I think I see a more sensitive face than I used to."

Upstairs, David led me to a bookcase, and I stooped down to look at the volumes ranged upon it: first editions of all of George Eliot's novels, inscribed by the author to Charles Lewes and Gertrude. David pulled out *Middlemarch*. He'd reread the novel recently, he said, and then astonished me by saying that rather than using a battered paperback he'd read Charles and Gertrude's copy. "It was very nice to do that," he said, with a quiet note of satisfaction. Thornie had written that "*good* novels bear re-reading." The book that Eliot had given Charles hadn't become a relic after all: it was a useful thing, still being used.

David handed *Middlemarch* to me, and I opened it at the inscription. "To Charles & Gertrude Lewes," it read. "Their loving Mutter gives this book of hers, which was coming into the world and growing along with their little daughter Blanche." The inscription to Charles and Gertrude was deeply touching, tying the cherished birth of the girl in the portrait downstairs at David's house with the labour Eliot had spent on her own literary off-spring.

But *Middlemarch* also grew as Thornie was dying, and now when I read about Fred Vincy and his unformed hopefulness and Will Ladislaw and his chafing restlessness—and when I am up to my ears in boydom, as three big and one small clatter on the stairs of my house, or spiritedly recount their adventures over the dinner table—I see Thornie Lewes inscribed within its pages, too. I was wrong in my twenties, when I thought that *Middlemarch* had nothing to tell me about being a stepparent—and not just because I was being too literal-minded about what was represented in the book and what wasn't, and failed to see how Eliot's intelligence might illuminate situations she had not explicitly described.

A book may not tell us exactly how to live our own lives, but our own lives can teach us how to read a book. Now when I read the novel in the light of Eliot's life, and in the light of my own, I see her experience of unexpected family woven deep into the fabric of the novel—not as part of the book's obvious pattern, but as part of its tensile strength. *Middlemarch* seems charged with the question of being a stepmother: of how one might do well by one's stepchildren, or unwittingly fail them, and of all that might be gained from opening one's heart wider.

Chapter 4

Three Love Problems

*"A man is seldom ashamed of feeling that he
cannot love a woman so well when he sees a
certain greatness in her: nature having intended
greatness for men."*

—MIDDLEMARCH, CHAPTER 39

In a review that appeared in the *Athenaeum* on 30 March 1872, in advance of the publication of "Three Love Problems," the fourth book of *Middlemarch*, the writer suggested that towards the end of the third book "a riddle is put" which "ought to be the hinge of the tale."

The reviewer does not elaborate, nor return to the idea in later reviews. (*Middlemarch*, being published serially in eight five-shilling parts, was also reviewed serially in some periodicals.) But the reference must have been to a charged exchange that takes place between Dorothea—now Mrs. Casaubon—and Lydgate. The doctor has been called to Lowick Manor, the Casaubon residence, because Mr. Casaubon has suffered what appears to be a heart attack.

Lydgate and Dorothea withdraw to the library. The shutters

are closed, and as they sit in the gloom Lydgate suggests to Dorothea that, although her husband seems to be recovering, ongoing vigilance against overexertion is required. He must not work as hard as he has done, nor may he restrict his occupations so exclusively. Perhaps, Lydgate suggests, they might go abroad. "Oh, that would not do—that would be worse than anything," Dorothea responds. As tears roll down her cheeks she tells Lydgate that nothing will be of any use to Casaubon that he does not enjoy. Lydgate is deeply touched, yet wonders what her marriage must be like: "Women just like Dorothea had not entered into his traditions."

Then Dorothea begs Lydgate to advise her. "You know all about life and death," she tells him. "He has been labouring all his life and looking forward. He minds about nothing else. And I mind about nothing else." Eliot underlines the importance of this exchange not by showing the reader how Lydgate responds in the moment, but by telling how he sees it later, in retrospect. "For years after Lydgate remembered the impression produced in him by this involuntary appeal—this cry from soul to soul, without other consciousness than their moving with kindred natures in the same embroiled medium, the same troublous fitfully-illuminated life," she writes.

Lydgate, Eliot suggests, recognized this moment as a hinge upon which his life might turn. And in the mind of the reviewer for the *Athenaeum*, a seed was sown for what might be coming in *Middlemarch*: the notion that Dorothea and Lydgate—who at this point in the story is still unmarried—might end up marrying each other.

It's easy for me to forget that there was ever a time when I did not know how the love problems presented in the novel would be resolved. But in the spring of 1872, no one at all beyond Eliot knew how the novel would conclude, and the whole reading public was on tenterhooks to discover what would happen next. "'Have you read the last Book?' is an almost inevitable question in the haunts of men," the *Daily Telegraph* noted in its review of Book Four. The Archbishop of Dublin, Richard Chenevix Trench, hid his copy inside the clerical hat on his lap at the opening of the Dublin Exhibition, so that he could read it surreptitiously during the speeches—a delicious detail of a churchman's human weakness that might have come from the pages of a novel by George Eliot.

"We all grumble at 'Middlemarch,'" a reviewer for the *Spectator* said. "But we all read it, and all feel that there is nothing to compare with it appearing at the present moment in the way of English literature, and not a few of us calculate whether we shall get the August number before we go for our autumn holiday, or whether we shall have to wait for it till we return." With Book Four, we are approaching the very middle of *Middlemarch*—and even though I know well how the novel concludes, the riddle posed in chapter 30 always beguiles me with its suggestion of alternative fates, of different love matches, of other possible endings.

Certain genres of fiction derive their satisfactions from the predictability of their conclusion. The reader knows where things are going to end up: in a romance the lovers are united; in a detective story the murder mystery is solved. There is a pleasure in the familiarity of the journey. But a successful realist novel necessarily takes unpredictable turns in just the way real life predictably must. The resolution of *Middlemarch*, even as seen in prospect halfway through the book, cannot possibly be completely tidy. (An example: Mary Garth has two possible suitors, Fred Vincy and Mr. Farebrother. Both have qualities to recommend them, but at least one is bound to be disappointed.) *Middlemarch* permits the reader to imagine other possible directions its characters might take, leading to entirely different futures, and as so often in life, love is the crossroads.

"I HAD two offers last night—not of marriage, but of music—which I find it impossible to resist," Eliot wrote spiritedly to Cara Bray, her Coventry friend, in March 1852. She was thirty-two years old, living in London, and working as a journalist—the editor in all but name of the *Westminster Review*, a lively monthly periodical published by John Chapman. And marriage was on her mind, as her joke to Cara let slip. Dancing around the corners of her consciousness was the possibility that she might wed Herbert Spencer, the issuer of one of the musical offers, who took her to see *William Tell* at the Royal Italian Opera house in Covent Garden on the first of April that year.

Spencer was an appropriate match for Eliot in many respects. Born within a few months of her, also in the Midlands, he was her equal in intellectual power and unconventionality. Though nowadays his name is less immediately familiar than that of contemporaries like Charles Darwin or Matthew Arnold, he was to become the most significant social philosopher of the Victorian era. In the 1850s Spencer was working at the *Economist*, where among other duties he covered the arts. He had also just published his first book, a theory of ethics with the encompassing title *Social Statics; or, the Conditions Essential to Human Happiness Specified, and the First of Them Developed*. Eliot had read and admired it.

Eliot had met Spencer through Chapman, her boss and her landlord at 142 Strand. The Strand was London's longest and most important thoroughfare, connecting the City in the east with Westminster and Parliament in the west. Rosemary Ashton, a biographer of both Eliot and George Henry Lewes, gives a sense of its character in her book *142 Strand*: "Here are shoemakers, watchmakers, tailors, wax chandlers, tobacconists, umbrella makers, cutlers, linen drapers, pianoforte makers, hatmakers, wigmakers, shirtmakers, mapmakers, lozenge manufacturers, and sellers of food of all sorts, including shellfish, Italian oil, and Twining's famous tea." There were more than twenty newspapers and magazines along its length, as well as book publishers and printers. There were cigar clubs and supper rooms and a resort with the suggestive name of the Coal Hole, at which nude or seminude women arranged in *tableaux vivants* were only one of the entertainments.

Eliot's dark but quiet rooms were at the rear of the house. "I can see her now, with her hair over her shoulders, the easy chair half sideways to the fire, her feet over the arms, and a proof in her hands," William Hale White, a fellow resident of the establishment, recalled after her death, providing a physical description that seems startlingly modern. This is not the upright Victorian woman of popular imagination, trussed in corsets and composed with hairpins. She could be any single, metropolitan woman of today, curled on a couch until late at night, poring over a book or typing on a laptop, completely absorbed in the concentrated pleasure of satisfying work.

Her life was intellectually thrilling, with many leading writers and thinkers of the day contributing to the publication. There were discussions of whether Charlotte Brontë should be sought to write an article about modern novelists: "She would have to leave out Currer Bell, who is perhaps the best of them all," Eliot observed. In the first issue that she edited Eliot also wrote an admiring re-view of *Life of Sterling*, by Thomas Carlyle, whom Chapman had unsuccessfully wooed as a contributor. (Like all her journalism, it was unsigned. The only work that was ever published under the name Marian Evans was a translation of "The Essence of Christianity," by the philosopher Ludwig Andreas Feuerbach, in 1854. She did not adopt the pseudonym George Eliot until the publication of her first work of fiction in what seems to have been a bid for it to be judged independent of the reputation of its notorious author.) In her review she described the kind of biography that was prevalent at the time—"the dreary three or five volumed compilations of letter, and diary, and detail, little to the purpose"—and outlined her conception of an alternative. She called for "a real 'Life,' setting forth briefly and vividly the man's inward and outward struggles, aims, and achievements, so as to make clear the meaning which his experience has for his fellows"—a characterization fit to inspire, and perhaps also intimidate, any would-be chronicler of Eliot's life. Eliot called for a biographer to have the imaginative talents of a novelist: what she described as "a loving and poetic nature which sees the beauty and the depth of familiar things, and the artistic power which seizes characteristic points and renders them with life-like effect." And her own writing, too, had started to show a confidence and flair—a voice—beyond that of the dutiful translator.

"I am training myself up to say adieu to all delights, I care for nothing but doing my work and doing it well," she wrote to a friend, gleefully. Eliot took much better advantage of London than she had done when she visited as a pious teenager and disparaged it as the great Babel, though her proximity to its turbulent immoralities, including the domestic arrangements at her own place of residence, was now much greater. She went to see the Crystal Palace, walked in Greenwich Park, and had her first, oblique encounter with Charles Dickens, at a meeting called at Chapman's house to discuss publishing copyright. "Dickens in the chair—a position he fills remarkably well, preserving a courteous neutrality of eyebrow, and speaking with clearness and decision," she reported to Cara and Charles Bray, with the barely suppressed excitement of a neophyte city dweller spotting a celebrity across a restaurant dining room.

Her letters to the Brays, her closest friends, frequently have a quality of nervous energy about them—flashes of a bright, brittle cleverness that seems to mask anxiety. She provides vivid vignettes that indicate the novelist in the making, though she does not yet manifest the large, perceptive generosity that characterizes the authorial voice of *Middlemarch*. She was sometimes satirical, as in her secondhand report of Dickens's house on Tavistock Square: "Splendid library, of course, with soft carpet, couches etc. such as become a sympathizer with the suffering classes," she wrote. "How can we sufficiently pity the needy unless we know fully the blessings of plenty?" And she was sometimes scathingly unkind.

"We met that odious Mrs. Richard Greaves at Miss Swanwick's," she wrote. "She is fearful—her whole organization seems made for the sake of her teeth—if indeed they are not false."

Within a year or two, she would be writing withering analyses of revered public figures, like Dr. John Cumming. He was a well-known Evangelical preacher—a profession, she noted, which makes it possible "to reconcile small ability with great ambition, superficial knowledge with the prestige of erudition, a middling morale with a high reputation for sanctity." With her youthful priggishness outgrown, her critical judgement could be astringent, even snarky, and she enjoyed the professional attention she got through exercising it. If one is accustomed to think of George Eliot as she ended up—the novelist famous for the generosity of her comprehension—it's shocking, and not a little thrilling, to read these earlier essays and discover how slashing she could be. I wouldn't exchange the large, sympathetic capacities she later uncovered for these lesser dagger blows, but there's something very satisfying about knowing she once had it in her to land them. It's oddly reassuring to know that before she grew good, George Eliot could be bad—to realize that she, also, had a frustrated ferocity that it gratified her to unleash, at least until she found her way to a different kind of writing, one that allowed her to lay down her arms, and to flourish without combativeness or cruelty.

Beyond the pages of the periodicals, too, she could be acid and spiky, defensive in anticipation of attack. "Treating people ill is an infallible sign of special love with me," she wrote to a friend. New acquaintances were not sure what to make of her. "I don't know whether you will like Miss Evans," Bessie Rayner Parkes, who became Eliot's good friend, wrote to Barbara Bodichon, who became an even better one. "At least I know you will *like* her for her large unprejudiced mind, her complete superiority to most women. But whether you or I should ever *love* her, as a friend, I don't know at all. There is as yet no high moral purpose in the impression she makes, and it is that alone which commands love. I think she will alter. Large angels take a long time unfolding their wings, but when they do, soar out of sight. Miss Evans either has no wings, or, which I think is the case, they are coming, budding."

I WALKED along the Strand one day in early autumn. Number 142 is no longer standing: the site is now home to Strand Bridge House, an unlovely office building that houses the United Nations Refugee Agency and the Centre of Flexible Learning in Dentistry. (Eliot could have used that—she was plagued by toothache throughout her life.) Next door was a down-at-heel hotel and a pungent Indian restaurant celebrating the last days of the Raj. The establishments Eliot knew had been replaced by contemporary ones: a shoe repairer and a travel agent and a hairdresser and a Pizza Hut. A few steps away lay Somerset House, the site of a royal palace from the reign of Elizabeth I until that of George III—the last vestige of the era when the Strand was lined with riverfront mansions. The Baroque church of St. Mary-le-Strand stood islanded by traffic lanes thronging with helmeted cyclists and lurching double-decker buses.

From the Strand it was a short walk to the National Portrait Gallery, my destination for the morning. There, I hoped to come face-to-face with George Eliot—or at least with several pictures of her. When she moved to 142 Strand there was no National

Portrait Gallery, but its establishment was under discussion. Its founder, Philip Henry Stanhope, described the projected museum in the House of Lords in 1856 as one devoted to images of "those persons who are most honourably commemorated in British history as warriors or as statesmen, or in arts, in literature, or in science." It finally opened in 1859, on Great George Street, in Westminster, which is where Eliot visited it in the 1860s.

Now it has a permanent home on St. Martin's Place, and I walked there along Duncannon Street, which runs through what once was the graveyard of St. Martin-in-the-Fields, to the corner of Trafalgar Square. I have photographs of myself taken in the square as a three-year-old in a blue sundress, warily perched on the rim of a fountain. Fifteen years later, when I would come up to London from my hometown, I would walk this way from Waterloo Station—in those days there were homeless people living under the arches, where now there are fancy wine bars—across a footbridge over the Thames, past Charing Cross. Sometimes I'd go to the National Gallery, which flanks the northern side of the square, and in an effort at self-education I would stand before works by Titian or Caravaggio and try with only modest success to make sense of them. (Dorothea does the same thing when she and Casaubon go to Rome on their honeymoon. "I am seeing so much all at once, and not understanding half of it," she tells Ladislaw, who happens to be in Rome at the same time. "That always makes one feel stupid. It is painful to be told that anything is very fine and not to be able to feel that it is fine—something like being blind, while people talk of the sky.")

Sometimes I would go beyond Trafalgar Square to Soho, to

a restaurant with chequered tablecloths and wine-bottle candle-sticks, which struck me as inordinately sophisticated. There, a boyfriend introduced me to spaghetti vongole, well beyond the culinary range of my provincial town. That boyfriend was five or six years older than me, which seemed a lot at the time. He had a dramatic mane of hair, black with a blond streak, and wore charity-shop suits over satin pyjama shirts. He was part of my education, too. He introduced me to the works of Oscar Wilde and Leonard Cohen; he took me to charity shops, which I scoured for vintage silk dresses and velvet coats, musty remnants saved for fifty years by someone lately departed. We sometimes went to the Tate, on Millbank, where we would stand before the purple and grey Rothkos or gaze at works by Turner, who painted the Battle of Trafalgar when it was still recent news.

In 1851, the year in which Turner died and George Eliot arrived in London, Trafalgar Square was newly laid out, and the National Gallery building was only thirteen years old. What seemed to me as if it had always been there was modern and new to Eliot: the energy and industry of her age, rendered in marble and stone. Much of the National Portrait Gallery's first floor is devoted to portraits of Victorian eminences and as I wandered the galleries I encountered many of Eliot's friends and acquain-tances. There was a bronze bust of Florence Nightingale, Eliot's exact contemporary. Nightingale called on Eliot not long after she had arrived at 142 Strand; in later years, the novelist owned a ceramic bust of the nursing reformer, which is now on display at the museum in Coventry. There was a marble bust of Herbert Spencer as he was in his sixties, with a bald head and magnificent muttonchop whiskers—both of which he already had when Eliot first knew him in the 1850s, though then the head was slightly less bald and the whiskers slightly less pronounced.

In a gallery devoted to the arts in the early Victorian era there was a portrait of a sprightly looking Charles Dickens, painted in 1839 when he was only twenty-seven and already the creator of Oliver Twist and Nicholas Nickleby. Nearby was the remarkable triple portrait of the Brontë sisters, made by their brother, Branwell, that had been thought lost until the second wife of Charlotte's husband discovered it folded up on top of a cupboard. On the wall opposite the Brontës and Dickens was a glass case, and inside it was a small portrait in oils of George Eliot. If I hadn't been looking for it, I might easily have missed it.

François D'Albert Durade, an artist in whose Geneva home Eliot lodged in 1849 on the European trip she took after her father's death, made this painting, which is the only image that gives us an idea of how she must have looked when she lived at 142 Strand. Her thick, heavy hair is light brown, almost blonde, and is fastened in a simple bun. Her pale grey-blue eyes are large and limpid; her nose is long, her chin slightly dimpled. Her cheeks are very ruddy, and she's smiling faintly. She wears a blouse of delicate lace under a simple black dress that laces up the front. She's personable but not pretty, especially not in comparison with Jenny Lind, the opera singer known as the Swedish Nightingale, whose russet hair and creamy shoulders are displayed in a portrait on another wall. Nor does she have the dramatic intensity of Elizabeth Barrett Browning, whose portrait by Michele Gordigiani hangs nearby. Eliot's is not a great portrait by any means, and when the artist's son first sought to sell it to the museum, in 1905, there wasn't much urgency among the trustees to acquire it. (Alphonse D'Albert Durade first sought two hundred pounds for the work; he ended up accepting forty.) The painting looks like something one might find in a good antique shop, or hanging in a home as the only remembrance of a great-great-great-aunt. Eliot looks intelligent and modest and slightly straitlaced: the kind of woman whom you might happily hire to teach your children German and Latin, but from whom you wouldn't necessarily expect an intimate acquaintance with, or understanding of, the most intense human passions.

The portrait is generally held to be flattering. Eliot's plainness has been a subject of fascination to her biographers for generations. "It must be a terrible sorrow to be young and unattractive: to look into the mirror and see a sallow unhealthy face, with a yellowish skin, straight nose and mouse-coloured hair," wrote Anne Fremantle, an early biographer, in 1933, while Brenda Maddox, a twenty-first-century biographer, begins her own portrait of Eliot with a paradoxical reversal that takes her plainness to be the spur to her achievement: "Her face was her fortune." For visitors who paid Eliot court at the Priory in her later years, coming up with a novel way to characterize her looks seems to have been an almost obligatory exercise. The prize has gone by popular acclaim to Henry James, who called on her in 1869. "She is magnificently ugly—deliciously hideous," James, who at the time was twenty-six and handsome, wrote in a letter to his father. "She has a low forehead, a dull grey eye, a vast pendulous nose, a huge mouth, full of uneven teeth and a chin and jaw-bone *qui n'en finissent pas*." One wishes that Eliot had sat for a portrait as revealing as that which John Singer Sargent painted of James, in 1913, which shows the author, then seventy years old, corpulent and superior in all his penetrating, intelligent authority. (It hangs in the National Portrait Gallery, too.) She did, in 1860, sit for Samuel Lawrence, a noted portraitist of the time. For years Lawrence's drawing hung in Blackwood's office, but near the beginning of the last century it was moved and went astray; perhaps it will show up one day on top of a cupboard in Edinburgh. A sketch that survives in the collection of Girton College, Cambridge, is tantalizing and suggestive: in it Eliot looks dark-eyed and sombre, like a mournful Madonna.

Henry James happened to call on Eliot the day that Thornton Lewes had returned from Natal, a moment at which she can be excused for not looking her best, but as well as delivering a tour de force of disparagement, James described something else about Eliot's looks. A first impression of her hideousness, he said, soon gave way to something else entirely. "Now in this vast ugliness resides a most powerful beauty which, in a very few minutes steals forth and charms the mind, so that you end as I ended, in falling in love with her," he continued. "Yes behold me literally in love with this great horse-faced bluestocking."

Others noticed the same effect, including Sara Jane Lippincott, an American author who met her at Chapman's in June 1852, not long after Eliot had arrived in London. Lippincott listened as Eliot, Chapman, and others—they may well have included Spencer—discussed science and ethics. "Miss Evans certainly impressed me at first as exceedingly plain, with her aggressive jaw and her evasive blue eyes," she wrote. "Neither nose, nor mouth, nor chin were to my liking; but, as she grew interested and earnest in conversation, a great light flashed over or out of her face, till it seemed transfigured, while the sweetness of her rare smile was something quite indescribable." Ivan Turgenev, a friend of Eliot's, said that she made him understand that it was possible to fall in love with a woman who was not pretty.

I can't pretend to be above caring about Eliot's physical features; so much attention has been paid to the subject that one longs to know what she looked like, if only to find the words to repudiate Henry James. I feel defensive on her behalf: plain women, after all, have always found partners to love and to be loved by, else there would be far more solitary people in the world. They have even, on occasion, been sought out. George Eliot turned down a marriage proposal when in her mid twenties, from a young man who was an artist and a restorer of paintings. She was introduced to him while she was still living in Coventry, and after just three days' acquaintance he proposed, via her brother-in-law, Henry Houghton, Fanny's husband. The young man told Houghton that he found Miss Evans the most fascinating person he had ever met, and that he hoped it was not too bold of him to seek to marry a woman of such superior intelligence. After the proposal Eliot came to see the Brays, Cara reported in a letter, "so brimful of happiness;—though she said she had not fallen in love with him yet, but admired his character so much that she was sure she should." Within a few days, however, Eliot's impressions of the young man had changed, and she wrote to him to break it off. In Cara's paraphrase, "She made up her mind that she could never love or respect him enough to marry him and that it would involve too great a sacrifice of her mind and pursuits."

She chose her as-yet-unformed career over marriage—and whether or not she thought she might have another chance of marrying, she knew that anyone she did go on to marry would, like the portrait painter, have to appreciate her for her mind and pursuits, rather than for more conventional feminine attributes. Eliot met few of the expectations of women in her age, or in our own for that matter. The public continued to refer to her as "George Eliot" long after her true identity was revealed, as if she were a hybrid creature, neither properly female nor male. She wasn't mannish—when describing her, her contemporaries insisted on emphasizing her femininity—but she wasn't an ordinary woman, either. Bessie Rayner Parkes, whose father, Joseph Parkes, a lawyer and politician, was sufficiently impressed by Eliot in the early 1850s that he often invited her to dinners, described how she appeared in those early years in London. "She used to wear black velvet, then seldom adopted by unmarried ladies," wrote Parkes, who recalled that her father would escort Eliot down the great staircase of their house on Savile Row, "the only lady, except my mother, among the group of remarkable men, politicians, and authors of the first literary rank. She would talk and laugh softly, and look up into my father's face respectfully, while the light of the great hall-lamp shone on the waving masses of her hair, and the black velvet fell in folds about her feet." It's an evocative description of Eliot as a distinguished young woman holding her own among distinguished older men, an equal to the company, in full possession of herself.

The National Portrait Gallery's Public Study Room is in an annex behind the museum, and when I went there, a selection of its holdings had been brought out at my request. I settled down at a large table with a magnifying glass in hand and began my necessarily compromised attempt to set eyes on Eliot. One image showed her much as she must have looked when she met the picture restorer—a small watercolour painted by Cara Bray in 1842, when Eliot was twenty-two. She had fair curls, a long nose, a firm mouth, and intelligent eyes. "I am glad to hear that you approved dear Mrs. Bray's picture," an ironical Eliot wrote to Sara Hennell. "I should think it is like, only that her benevolence extends to the hiding of faults in my visage as well as my character."

There was a photograph for which she sat in 1858, the year she turned thirty-nine—after the publication of *Scenes of Clerical Life* but before the revelation that the well-known journalist Marian Evans was the George Eliot who had authored them. I could see why in her later years, Eliot told admirers who requested her photograph that she didn't have one to give. Her face is disproportionately long, with a substantial nose and a heavy chin that isn't at all concealed by the hand she is resting it upon. Her lips are open in a forced smile, revealing a glimpse of craggy teeth. Whenever I'd seen this photograph before, in reproduction, it had made me cringe to imagine the session during which it was taken, with the photographer requesting that she adopt a pose of simpering femininity. But there in the museum's archive I thought I could detect a merry spark in her eye, and I imagined her in the studio with Lewes, sharing their delicious secret as she posed for what would, in later years, be reprinted as a portrait of the novelist George Eliot.

More appealing, though no more flattering, was a pen-and-ink drawing of Eliot in profile, sketched by Lowes Cato Dickinson when he spotted her at a concert at St. James's Hall in London in 1872. This was the closest I could get to seeing what Eliot looked like when *Middlemarch* was published. I looked hard at the bump on her nose, the lower lip drawn up over her teeth, and the faintest play of amusement at the corners of her mouth. In this drawing, she looked like someone it would be good to talk with.

The Frederic Burton chalk drawing, the one that had gone over the fireplace at the Priory, had been laid out for me on a table in its gilt frame. It showed her at forty-five, close to my own age, and was more or less life-size. I leaned over it and scrutinized it as I might scrutinize my own reflection in an unfamiliar mirror, examining the incipient droop of the eyelids and the trace of a line emerging on the right cheek. This is what it is like to look at one's face in middle age—to see teeth that were painstakingly realigned in youth stubbornly shifting back to their origins; to see the encroaching furrow on the brow, no longer erased by a subtle muscular relaxation. To me, George Eliot's face looked kindly and not remarkably unattractive, Henry James notwithstanding, though perhaps I am predisposed to find her less than classically beautiful features sympathetic. "You'll be a good-looking woman when you are grown-up," the mother of a pretty, blue-eyed friend told me when I was ten or so—with, I suppose, the best of misplaced intentions—and I have never forgotten it. "To be called an ugly thing in contrast with that lovely creature your companion, is apt to produce some effect beyond a sense of fine veracity and fitness in the phrase," Eliot writes in *Middlemarch*.

William Hale White, her fellow resident at Chapman's, said that the likeness by Sir Frederic Burton was good, "but it gives permanence to that which was not permanent in her face. It lacks the generality combined with particularity which we find in portraits by the greatest masters." In *Middlemarch*, Will Ladislaw characterizes the deficiencies of painting, as compared to description. "The true seeing is within; and painting stares at you with an insistent imperfection," he tells Adolf Naumann, his artist friend, after they have spotted Dorothea in a gallery in Rome. "I feel that especially about representations of women. As if a woman were a mere coloured superficies! You must wait for movement and tone. There is a difference in their very breathing: they change from moment to moment.—This woman whom you have just seen, for example: how would you paint her voice, pray? But her voice is much diviner than anything you have seen of her." I looked at the insistent imperfection of the Burton portrait of Eliot for a long time, trying to imagine the animating spark, the light of intelligence and comprehension flashing from her brow, trying to hear her voice.

IN those days in the early 1850s when William Hale White got to know Eliot, she made repeated references in her letters to her looks: "I am getting as haggard as an old witch under London atmosphere and influences," she wrote to the Brays. This self-consciousness coincided with her budding friendship with Herbert Spencer. "I am going to the Opera tonight to hear the *Huguenots*. See what a fine thing it is to pick up people who are short-sighted enough to like one," she wrote. She and Spencer saw each other almost every day, and it became a common assumption among their circle that they would marry. "All the world is setting us down as engaged," Eliot told the Brays, though she reported the fact without pleasure, calling the gossip "a most disagreeable thing if one chose to make oneself uncomfortable."

Spencer was made extremely uncomfortable by such gossip. He had advanced views about marriage, and in his recently published book he had argued for the necessity of equality of rights between husband and wife, and imagined a future in which "women shall have attained to a clear perception of what is due to them, and men to a nobility of feeling which shall make them concede to women the freedom which they themselves claim." Under such circumstances, Spencer argued, married life "will not be characterized by perpetual squabbles, but by mutual concessions." Spencer recognized that in terms of intellect and sensibility, Eliot made him a good partner, but there was also an element of marital attraction less easily theorized. He later wrote in his autobiography that "physical beauty is a *sine quâ non* with me; as was once unhappily proved where the intellectual traits and the emotional traits were of the highest."

After Eliot's death, Spencer gave an account of their quasi-courtship in those early months of 1852, in an exculpatory letter to E. L. Youmans, his publisher in America. He had liked her company very much, Spencer explained, and since he had free tickets to the theatre and concerts, she had become his regular partner. However, he began to have qualms about what the frequency of their excursions might imply to Eliot, since, he told Youmans, "I could not perceive in myself any indications of a warmer feeling." He wrote to Eliot in an attempt to head off trouble, delicately suggesting that he was afraid she might be falling in love with him, and advising against it. "Then, afterwards, perceiving how insulting to her was the suggestion that while I felt in no danger of falling in love with her, she was in danger of falling in love with me,

I wrote a second letter, apologizing for my unintended insult," he continued. Eliot "took it all smilingly," he reported, and forgave him his rudeness.

I find it impossible to read Spencer's apologia, issued thirty years after the fact, without feeling pity for his bumbling ineptitude. The greatest thinker of his generation was less gifted in the sphere of the emotions, and the pile-up of embarrassing letters and conversations belies the dignity of expression that is rendered in the marble bust in the National Portrait Gallery. He was a clueless young man, and she was a proud young woman. To the extent that Eliot took his preemptive rejection "smilingly," it must have been a rueful smile. "We have agreed that we are not in love with each other, and that there is no reason why we should not have as much of each other's society as we like," she wrote to Charles and Cara Bray, and there is an unnatural brightness in her tone, a forced good humour. She gave a more bitter, prickly response to Spencer himself. "I felt disappointed rather than 'hurt' that you should not have sufficiently divined my character to perceive how remote it is from my habitual state of mind to imagine that any one is falling in love with me," she wrote.

The handful of letters that Eliot wrote to Spencer that spring and summer were considered by the trustees of his estate to be so incendiary that when they were given to the British Museum in the 1930s a prohibition was put upon publishing them, or even acknowledging their existence, for fifty years. They were finally published in full a few years early, in 1976, and they make for extremely painful reading. It is possible to see in them the unravelling of Eliot's hopes, such as they were, of marriage to Spencer, and the expression of her conviction, at thirty-two, that she was unlikely to find anyone else to whom she would be more than just a convenient companion for theatrical outings.

That summer, when temperatures had risen to 32°C in London and Eliot had escaped to the seaside resort of Broadstairs, she acidly countered a suggestion from Spencer that she had taken the cooler weather with her. "No credit to me for my virtues as a refrigerant," she wrote. "I owe them all to a few lumps of ice which I carried away with me from that tremendous glacier of yours." Still, she attempted to persuade him to join her on the coast, where she was spending several weeks. "I have had a loathing for books—for all tagging together of sentences since I came," she said in appeal. "You see I am sinking fast towards 'homogeneity' "—a reference to Spencer's theories—"and my brain will soon be a mere pulp unless you come to arrest the downward process."

She seems to have reneged on her side of their agreement that they were not in love. "I know this letter will make you very angry with me, but wait a little, and don't say anything to me while you are angry," she wrote that July, in a letter free from ironical jabs. "I want to know if you can assure me that you will not forsake me, that you will always be with me as much as you can and share your thoughts and feelings with me. If you become attached to some one else, then I must die, but until then I could gather courage to work and make life valuable, if only I had you near me. I do not ask you to sacrifice anything—I would be very good and cheerful and never annoy you. But I find it impossible to contemplate life under any other conditions."

Her abjection is deeply upsetting, even more than a century and a half after the fact. How could she—the remarkable young woman who was the intellectual equal of the celebrated politicians and writers at Joseph Parkes's dinner parties—have thought so little of herself? Yet her despair is also utterly recognizable, particularly to anyone who has pursued a demanding career and lived alone into her early thirties, and has wondered if she might always be alone.

And Eliot's letter is not all abjection. At the end there is a remarkable turn, in which she regains her self-possession and issues what now reads like an ultimatum to posterity. "I suppose no woman ever before wrote a letter such as this—but I am not ashamed of it," she writes. "I am conscious that in the light of reason and true refinement I am worthy of your respect and tenderness, whatever gross men or vulgar-minded women might think of me."

This last letter she sent from her exile on the coast is a pitiful grasp at an inadequate object. But it seems to me that it's more than that, too—that it's also a deliberate plumbing of the depths of self-abnegation. The glacial Spencer may have been unable to "perceive in myself any indications of a warmer feeling" towards Eliot, but Eliot sought to experience even her rejection at full emotional volume. I know which of them I would rather be. The price of the experience of love is the pain that love can cause, but that pain's dividend is a wider range of emotional knowledge and comprehension—an understanding that might, in the future, be recalled and relived, transformed in the pages of a book.

"Plain women he regarded as he did the other severe facts of life, to be faced with philosophy and investigated by science," Eliot writes of Lydgate early on in *Middlemarch*. For Lydgate, like

Spencer, beauty is a *sine qua non*, but for him beauty must also be accompanied by charm and subservience. "He held it one of the prettiest attitudes of the feminine mind to adore a man's pre-eminence without too precise a knowledge of what it consisted in," Eliot writes. Even a beautiful woman like Dorothea doesn't meet his standards, being altogether too enquiring and thought-ful: "The society of such women was about as relaxing as going from your work to teach the second form, instead of reclining in a paradise with sweet laughs for bird-notes, and blue eyes for a heaven."

And what is Lydgate's ideal woman? "An accomplished crea-ture who venerated his high musings and momentous labours and would never interfere with them; who would create order in the home and accounts with still magic, yet keep her fingers ready to touch the lute and transform life into romance at any moment; who was instructed to the true womanly limit and not a hair's-breadth beyond—docile, therefore, and ready to carry out behests which came from beyond that limit." He believes the beautiful Rosamond Vincy to be the embodiment of these virtues, but after marrying her discovers that she is the very opposite of compliant. Having been instructed to the true womanly limit but not beyond it, she is incapable of imagining herself living in any other fashion than that for which Mrs. Lemon's school has prepared her.

Her implacable expectation leads Lydgate to rent a house beyond his means and equip it with furniture and tableware he cannot afford, and if it's easy today to decry Lydgate's assump-tions about women's purpose in the world, it's altogether less easy to condemn his fiscal miscalculations. One of the ways in which the world of *Middlemarch* seems disconcertingly familiar is in its depiction of the dangers presented by ready credit: Henry James called Lydgate's story "a tragedy based on unpaid butchers' bills, and the urgent need for small economies." Rosamond's social aspiration leads her to ingratiate herself with Captain Lydgate, one of Lydgate's well-born but personally inconsequential cousins. (She and the Captain go riding after Lydgate has expressly forbidden it; as a result Rosamond miscarries her first child.) She tells Lydgate she wishes he had been something other than a doctor—concerned with "skeletons, and body-snatchers, and bits of things in phials, and quarrels with everybody, that end in your dying miserably." With prettily expressed contempt, Rosamond reveals her utter incompatibility with what is essential about Lydgate. "To say that you love me without loving the medical man in me, is the same sort of thing as to say you like eating a peach but don't like its flavour," he tells her, with mournful, resigned humour.

Eliot endowed Lydgate with her own intellectual vigour, but she also gave him a vein of petty-minded prejudice which she had encountered in others, to her own detriment. It's no wonder that he is so vividly drawn—nor that readers, halfway through *Middlemarch*, clutched at the glimmer of hope that he might be redeemed by a woman like Dorothea belatedly entering his traditions. A different writer might have staged that redemption, as readers of the finished book observed. "Had the author consulted the properties of romance and the fitness of things, [Lydgate] should have married Dorothea," is how the *Times* reviewer drily put it.

Eliot had expertly dissected the properties of romance in an essay called "Silly Novels by Lady Novelists," which appeared in the *Westminster Review* in 1856, immediately before she began writing her own fiction. It's an acid taxonomy of terrible popular novels and their predictable heroine, of whom Eliot writes, "her eyes and her wit are both dazzling; her nose and her morals are alike free from any tendency to irregularity." Men in such novels are similarly lacking in complexity; their role is to accompany the heroine "on her 'starring' expedition through life. They see her at a ball, and are dazzled; at a flower-show, and they are fascinated; on a riding excursion, and they are witched by her noble horse-manship."

Who read novels like these? Women like Rosamond Vincy. The reading of fiction is one of the feminine accomplishments Rosamond cultivates in anticipation of a proposal from Lydgate. Along with sketching landscapes and practising her music, "she found time also to read the best novels, and even the second best." Rosamond doesn't just read novels; she imagines herself at the centre of one of their overwrought plots: " 'If I loved, I should love at once and without change,' said Rosamond, with a great sense of being a romantic heroine, and playing the part prettily." Rosamond is inexperienced enough to see herself as starring at the centre of an implausible story with an inevitable happy ending.

In his *Life* of George Eliot, John Walter Cross gave an intriguing account of Eliot's creative method. "She told me that, in all that she considered her best writing, there was a 'not herself' which took possession of her, and that she felt her own personality to be merely the instrument through which this spirit, as it were, was acting," Cross wrote. Of all the characters Eliot attempted, "she found Rosamond's the most difficult to sustain." That is easy to believe. For most of *Middlemarch*, Rosamond is an exercise in beautiful triviality, with her blonde plaits and her graceful neck and her dress "of a fit and fashion so perfect that no dressmaker could look at it without emotion," a characterization that shows Eliot at her most cuttingly epigrammatic. (Dorothy Parker could not have put it better.) Rosamond is so dreadful that to channel her spirit for long would tax the most resilient of mediums, and Lydgate's awful realization of what he has committed himself to in his marriage—his recognition that "life must be taken up on a lower stage of expectation, as it is by men who have lost their limbs"—is an authentic, everyday tragedy.

Some readers have felt that Eliot hates Rosamond, and that she denies her the sympathy that she shows her other characters. But I don't think that's quite right. Eliot does not make Rosamond stupid—she is "clever with that sort of cleverness which catches every tone except the humorous," Eliot writes. "Happily she never attempted to joke, and this perhaps was the most decisive mark of her cleverness." But she clearly shows that Rosamond has been stunted by an education and upbringing that have prepared her for a life of pettiness and conventionality, and readied her for no vocation beyond marriage. Eliot repeatedly refers to "poor Rosamond," and these references are not ironic: Rosamond also deserves the reader's pity. Lydgate's understanding of her before their marriage was as paltry as her comprehension of him. His suggestion for resolving their economic crisis—that she surrender their house to her one-time suitor Ned Plymdale and his new bride—is asking her to give up everything to which she has ever aspired. It is saying he likes a peach without liking its flavour. Lydgate has no more access to Rosamond's emotional reality than she does to his. He is unable "to imagine fully what this sudden trial was to a young creature who had known nothing but indulgence, and whose dreams had all been of new indulgence, more exactly to her taste."

Eliot had never been indulged as a young woman, but she knew what it was to be in the unbearable situation of wanting the impossible, and trying to find any way to postpone a reckoning with reality. "I find it impossible to contemplate life under any other conditions," she had told Spencer, after begging him to allow her to live under impossible conditions, with the absence of reciprocal love. She brings her own stubborn insistence on the impossible to an understanding of Rosamond's tearful recalcitrance.

This isn't to suggest that Eliot is generous towards Rosamond. Near the end of the novel she stages a harrowing attack on Rosamond by Ladislaw, about whom Rosamond has been indulging in misplaced romantic fantasies. After that, Rosamond has a humbling encounter with Dorothea, in which she comes as close as she ever does to empathizing with another individual's crisis. But even then, Rosamond's fractional insight is limited and fleeting. Eliot punishes Rosamond—or punishes women like her, through her—in granting her only the view of the world surrounding her own image in a mirror, a circumscription that cannot be overcome unless she steps away from the looking glass.

Eliot does not allow Rosamond to grow into anything beyond the beautiful bloom from which her name derives, with its irresistible fragrance and its concealed thorns. (In *Daniel Deronda*, the novel that came after *Middlemarch*, Eliot would challenge herself to draw a more nuanced portrait of a self-involved beauty, Gwendolen Harleth, who may be the most complicated heroine in her fiction.) At the end of *Middlemarch*, Rosamond is as self-centred and as conventional in her convictions as she ever was, with the added savour of self-righteousness earned through what she regards as her sacrifice. "She simply continued to be mild in her temper, inflexible in her judgment, disposed to admonish her husband, and able to frustrate him by stratagem," Eliot writes. Lydgate calls her his basil plant, because "basil was a plant which had flourished wonderfully on a murdered man's brains." And to the end Rosamond insists on seeing the world as if it were governed by the rules of conventional romance, responding to this barbed endearment by asking Lydgate why, then, he had married her rather than Dorothea, "whom he was always praising and placing above her."

Elizabeth Malleson, an educator with whom Eliot was acquainted, once recalled an occasion during the serial publication of *Middlemarch* when she ran into Eliot and Lewes as they walked arm in arm along Regent Street, in London. "We stopped in the busy street to talk—I to utter lamentations for Lydgate in his relation to Rosamond, she smilingly to insist upon the inexorable fate dramatically necessary for her story," Malleson wrote afterwards. As always, though, with Eliot, Lydgate's fate is not imposed upon him. "Character too is a process and an unfolding," Eliot writes of Lydgate in an early chapter of the book, when what will become of him is still uncertain. He builds his fate for himself, through his words and his actions and his inactions, until there is no other story that can be told about him.

HERBERT Spencer never married. He outlived Eliot, dying in 1903 at the age of eighty-three. In his seventies he decided that he would like to experience some semblance of family life, and so he rented a house near Regent's Park that he shared with a pair of sisters, procured for him by a friend. The sisters, genteel ladies who had fallen on hard times, took care of his housekeeping in exchange for the home he supplied them.

After his death they wrote a memoir titled *Home Life with Herbert Spencer.* The book is a quirky mix of gossip and homage, and it paints Spencer as a decidedly odd bird. He blocked his ears with custom-made stoppers when parlour-room conversation became too trying. He insisted on his bed being made with a pleat down the centre of the upper sheet, so that he could move more freely in the night. He liked to wear what sounds like an oversize knitted onesie—"compounded in such a way that he only had to step into it and with one pull was fully clad in boots, trousers, and coat"—which the sisters called his "woolly bear." They recount his objection to a plain woman whom they once invited to visit: he ate alone in the drawing room rather than having to face someone "so ugly" over the dining table. Having Spencer in the house was interesting in the way that having a baby in the house is interesting, they say: one cannot but remark upon "the last thing 'it did,' the last thing 'it said,' and the last thing 'it ate.'"

On one occasion one of the sisters tactlessly remarked to Spencer that it was a shame he had never had children or grandchildren himself. She then tried to compensate for her rudeness by saying that if he had become a father the world would have been denied his most important work, *A System of Synthetic Philosophy.* "No, but there might have been a *'sympathetic'* philosophy," he replied—a reference to the sister's earlier garbling of the name of his book. Spencer spoke with "a whimsical laugh for the old joke," the sisters write, "and yet with a touch of pathos in his voice, as he seemed for a moment to realise what he had lost by giving up his whole life to the completion of his work." At the end of his life, Spencer must also have wondered what his work had lost through his domestic and romantic renunciation.

When, after her rejection by Spencer, Eliot began living with George Henry Lewes, she and Spencer forged a friendship on new grounds. She sometimes adopted a faintly patronizing, teasing tone towards him, the gentle revenge of the rejected upon the rejecter. Sofia Kovalevskaya, who would become Europe's first female professor of mathematics, at the University of Stockholm, remembered being introduced to Spencer at a gathering in the Priory in 1870, when she was nineteen. "I must warn you that he denies the very possibility of the existence of a woman mathematician," Eliot archly told Kovalevskaya. "He admits that from time to time a woman might appear who equals the average level of men in intellectual capacity, but he argues that an equal woman always directs her intellect and insight to the analysis of her friends' lives and would never chain herself to pure abstraction."

Eliot's own analysis of the lives of others has far outlasted Spencer's abstractions, with *Middlemarch* her masterwork of sympathetic philosophy. With hindsight, it seems obvious that Eliot had a fortunate escape from life as Mrs. Herbert Spencer, encumbered by a crotchety spouse in earplugs and a woolly bear. (What becomes of the brilliant young woman who knowingly forfeits reciprocal love, after disillusionment with her spouse sets in? There's a subject for a novel.) And while it's impossible to know for sure, it seems likely that had Marian Evans become Marian Spencer, she would not also have become George Eliot. Though Spencer later claimed that he had early on encouraged Eliot to write fiction, she did not find her fictional voice until she was loved by someone who saw beyond her capacity for brittle cleverness—in whose company she did not feel the need to be on her emotional guard. Even so, her experience with Spencer informed her understanding. He was part of her education, as Dorothea was part of Lydgate's education, and as all our loves, realized or otherwise—all our alternative plots—go to make us who we are, and become part of what we make.

Chapter 5

The Dead Hand

*"The memory has as many moods as the temper,
and shifts its scenery like a diorama."*
—*MIDDLEMARCH*, CHAPTER 53

I woke early and looked out of my hotel window to see pigeons alighting on the roof of the Examination Schools on Oxford High Street. More than twenty years earlier I'd entered that building for my final exams, wearing an academic gown and carrying a mortarboard, and I'd barely been back to Oxford since. A lot had changed. The boutique hotel I was staying in used to be a pub, appointed in oak and brass and reeking of beer and cigarette smoke. Patisseries had multiplied on the High Street. Leaving my hotel to walk outside, I tried to turn down Logic Lane to peer up at the window of what had once been my room, dark, narrow quarters in an unglamorous modern block, not the airy eighteenth-century chamber I'd hoped for. But there was a security gate blocking my way, and I was no longer entitled to the code.

I walked along the narrow pavement of Merton Street, past huddled stone cottages and knots of students with exactly the same jagged haircuts and black clothes that my friends and I had worn, and there was something disconcerting about seeing the fashions of my youth revived in the site of my youth. I remembered my own circuits around this city: wandering through Christ Church Meadow, from which Oxford always looked more like a landscape by Constable than a place one actually got to live in; or rushing across the cobblestones of Radcliffe Square to get to an Anglo-Saxon tutorial. Translating Anglo-Saxon was laborious, but I could glimpse the strange beauty of the poetry, with its bifurcated lines and internal alliteration. We read accounts of battles written in the late ninth century during the reign of Alfred the Great, who, according to legend, both burned cakes and founded my college. I remember the thrilling realization that I was seeing English literature being born—witnessing an author trying to invent prose narrative. The syntax was often confusing, so that it was hard to tell who did what to whom—the text dissolved into repetitions, "and then," "and then," "and then," like a child's early attempts at composition—but there was a sustained, urgent striving to tell a story. I realized with a sense of wonder that the books I loved were a later expression of this same effort. This history of reading and writing was my cultural inheritance, a centuries-long chain of readers and writers in this centuries-old city.

I was studying English literature because I loved books, a common enough motivation among students of literature, but I soon discovered that love didn't have much purchase when it came to our studies. It was the mid 1980s, the era of critical theory—an approach to literature that had been developed at Yale, among other distant and exotic locales. I'd never heard of critical theory before I got to Oxford, but I soon discovered that it was what the most sophisticated-seeming undergraduates were engaged by.

Scholars applied the tools of psychoanalysis or feminism to reveal the ways in which the author was blind to his or her own desire or prejudice, or they used the discipline of deconstruction to dispense with the author altogether. (Thus, J. Hillis Miller on George Eliot: "This incoherent, heterogeneous, 'unreadable,' or nonsynthesizable quality of the text of *Middlemarch* jeopardizes the narrator's effort of totalization.") Books—or texts, as they were called by those versed in theory—weren't supposed merely to be read, but to be interrogated, as if they had committed some criminal malfeasance.

Oxford was hardly a crucible of high theory, but theory was in the air, and it was intriguing. Knowing which books to read or which lectures to attend was like knowing which clubs played the best music, and reading Michel Foucault on the history of sexuality seemed a lot more exciting than reading Alexander Pope. I once went to a seminar in the college rooms of a don who was well known in Oxford and beyond for his application of Marxist theory to literature. ("Splendid library, of course, with soft carpet, couches, etc. such as become a sympathizer with the suffering classes," as Eliot wrote of Dickens.) I don't recall which author was the object of that particular inquisition, but I do remember the way the room was crowded with the don's acolytes. Monkish-looking young men with close-shaven heads wearing black turtlenecks huddled with their notebooks around the master, while others lounged on the rug at his feet. It felt very exclusive—and, with its clotted jargon, wilfully difficult. Under such influences I wrote, for part of my finals, an extended feminist critique of Spenser's *The Faerie Queene*, which, appropriately enough, clogged a friend's printer, like a lump of undigested food.

GEORGE Eliot visited Oxford for the first time in May 1870. She and Lewes travelled up from London by train in the morning, then had lunch with their hosts, Mark Pattison, the Rector of Lincoln College, and his wife, Emily Francis Pattison. Afterwards they took a walk through the city—which, Eliot wrote in her journal, "on this first view was rather disappointing to me."

Eliot had a habit of being unimpressed on a first encounter with places that were generally considered worthy of admiration. Ten years earlier, she and Lewes had gone to Rome and been initially underwhelmed. "A weary length of dirty uninteresting streets had brought us within sight of the dome of St. Peter's which was not impressive, seen in a peeping makeshift manner, just rising above the houses; and the Castle of St. Angelo seemed but a shabby likeness of the engravings," she wrote. "We wandered farther among narrow and ugly streets and came in to our hotel again, still with some dejection at the probable relations our 'Rome visited' was to bear to our 'Rome unvisited.'"

In the end Eliot found plenty to approve in Rome, though she found Trajan's Forum dreary, and was persistently irritated by the exterior of St. Peter's as well as being appalled by what she described as "the hideous red drapery" with which its interior had been decked for Easter. Eliot drew on her distaste for Rome when depicting Dorothea, on her honeymoon, chilled at St. Peter's by the sight of "the red drapery which was being hung for Christmas spreading itself everywhere like a disease of the retina."

To Dorothea, Rome seems to consist of "ruins and basilicas, palaces and colossi, set in the midst of a sordid present, where all that was living and warm-blooded seemed sunk in the deep degeneracy of a superstition divorced from reverence." The city is incomprehensible, a jumble of disconcerting impressions and experiences: "All this vast wreck of ambitious ideals, sensuous and spiritual, mixed confusedly with the signs of breathing forgetfulness and degradation, at first jarred her as with an electric shock, and then urged themselves on her with that ache belonging to a glut of confused ideas which check the flow of emotion." Eliot is necessarily elliptical about the intimacies of Dorothea's newlywed experience, but in passages like this one the city itself becomes a metaphor for Dorothea's disastrous induction into conjugal relations—the tremendous disparity between marriage unrealized and marriage realized.

What could have disappointed Eliot on that first walk in Oxford? She was staying in the very heart of the city, at Lincoln College, on Turl Street. Perhaps she was put off by the proximity to the covered market, which had been constructed a hundred years earlier and would have been busy with the trade of butchers, grocers, and fishmongers. (The stalls selling fish had been moved from one corner of the market to the other in 1850, after the owner of the Mitre Hotel complained about "the putrefaction of the entrails and scales thrown down some drain sewer or cesspool.") But in all likelihood, Eliot and Lewes would have headed in the opposite and more inviting direction, down the High Street. "One of the finest in England; not only for its width and regular arrangement, but for the beauty and magnificence of the churches and collegiate edifices lining it on both sides," is how *M'Culloch's Universal Gazetteer* described it in 1855.

They would have seen St. Mary's Church, with its ornate

fourteenth-century spire, and the Gothic grandeur of All Souls College, the church's neighbour. They might have walked around the gorgeous neoclassical rotunda of the Radcliffe Camera, opposite All Souls, and entered the austere quadrangle of the Bodleian Library, with its high, fortress-like walls. They would have passed the Divinity School, perhaps glimpsing its Gothic vaulted ceiling through large leaded windows, and a few steps later approached the Sheldonian Theatre, designed by Sir Christopher Wren. Perhaps if one has been disappointed by St. Peter's this would be an unimpressive circuit; otherwise, it's hard to imagine how one could find nothing here to admire, or to feel elevated by.

In later years, Eliot would come to enjoy visiting Oxford: she became good friends with Benjamin Jowett, the Master of Balliol College, who invited her and Lewes to the weekend parties he hosted. There she talked easily with scientists and classical scholars despite the limits of her formal education, "filling with wonder all who listened," in the words of one young observer, William Wordsworth, the grandson and namesake of the poet. And even on this first visit to Oxford there were a number of fascinating diversions. She and Lewes saw a brain being dissected at the newly opened museum of natural history; they walked in Christ Church Meadow and watched Oxford's rowing team race against one from Cambridge; and they mingled with undergraduates at Balliol—among whom, one student later suspected, she gathered material for the character of Fred Vincy.

But perhaps a dispiriting mood had been established at lunch on that first day. The Pattisons were relatively new friends of Eliot and Lewes; they had attended Sunday salons at the Priory, and Mrs. Pattison in particular had formed a close and confiding relationship with Eliot. Dr. Pattison, a native of Yorkshire who was six years older than Eliot, had first gone to Oxford at eighteen, as a student, and had become a fellow at Lincoln. In 1851, at the age of thirty-eight, Pattison had expected to be made rector—or head—of the college, but was sidelined by colleagues, to his great disappointment. A decade later he finally ascended to that coveted position, and swiftly did what university rules had prevented him from doing while a fellow: he got married. His wife, Emily Francis Strong, was twenty-one at the time, twenty-seven years his junior.

It's not recorded what the friends discussed during lunch together that first day in Oxford, but perhaps the rector asked after George Eliot's work. If so, she might reluctantly have mentioned her new novel: *Middlemarch*. A few days before going to Oxford, she'd met with Blackwood, her publisher, and discussed her progress with him. "It promises to be something wonderful," he reported afterwards. She, though, felt her progress was sluggish. "My novel, I suppose, will be finished some day: it creeps on," she had written to Blackwood a few weeks earlier. What Eliot discussed with Blackwood during their meeting would have been the introduction of Lydgate and the Vincy family. It was not until the end of that year that she would conceive of the story of Casaubon and Dorothea, writing the section that became the beginning of Book One and reanimated her progress on the novel.

But perhaps the conversation didn't turn at all to her writing. Eliot did not much like to discuss her works in progress: "Talking about my books, I find, has much the same malign effect on me as talking of my feelings or my religion," she once wrote. They could instead have discussed university politics. Eliot was once asked what the difference in her impressions was between Cambridge and Oxford, and she replied that at Cambridge they all seemed to speak well of each other, whereas at Oxford they all criticized each other. That afternoon as she walked around the city she may have been thinking of the pettiness of the scholars cloistered within the college walls.

In all likelihood Eliot and Lewes would have described their recent visit to Berlin, a city in which Pattison had spent some time after his first disappointing effort to become rector. The garrulous Lewes might have bragged about the eminences among whom they had hobnobbed, including Frederick VIII, Duke of Schleswig-Holstein. ("Altogether his Highness was as agreeable an acquaintance as if he had been Mr. Smith with a first rate education," Lewes had written afterwards in a letter.) Lewes would surely have described how at a grand party Eliot had been feted as a celebrity, surrounded by crowds of adoring women whose attentions she privately likened to being pecked at by flocks of birds. Eliot herself would likely have explained that her response to her fans had been coloured by the sore throat and headaches from which she had been suffering. "I felt my heart go out to some good women who seemed really to have an affectionate feeling towards me for the sake of my books," she had written to a friend. "But the sick animal longs for quiet and darkness."

Mrs. Pattison had been ill recently, too, and not long before the visit to Oxford Eliot had expressed her concern in a letter. "It saddens me to think of the trouble and the bodily suffering that you have undergone. Can severe troubles ever be said to have quite passed away?" Eliot had written. "I think it alters all one's tissues, enlarging life perhaps by bringing new susceptibilities, but often dulling even the wish for personal pleasure." Perhaps there was still a cloud of suffering hanging over the lunch table, a sense of troubles that were not of the transient kind.

CONSIDERABLE scholarly energy has been expended over the decades upon the question of whether the Rector of Lincoln and his wife inspired the characters of Edward Casaubon and Dorothea Brooke, about whom Eliot began writing a few months after this visit. Certainly the identification with the Pattisons was made almost immediately upon the novel's publication: in 1879 the novelist Margaret Oliphant described Pattison as "a curious wizened little man" who was "supposed to be the Casaubon of 'Middlemarch.'" The identification was repeated enough to become common currency. In 1895 *Outlook* magazine ran a brief article noting that Mrs. Pattison, who was widowed in 1884, had been remarried a year later, to Sir Charles Wentworth, Lord Dilke, a radical politician who had once been an art student. The writer observed that Mrs. Pattison had gone from Casaubon to Ladislaw, wryly noting that "as the novel was written, of course, long before the actual occurrence [of the second marriage], it has been cited as a remarkable example of George Eliot's insight into the characters of her friends."

Mrs. Pattison had grown up in Oxford, where her father was a banker. She showed early promise as an artist, and John Ruskin, a family acquaintance, advised her to go to London to study at the National Art Training School in South Kensington, which was eventually to become the Royal College of Art. There she was a brilliant student, impish and vivacious. She had advanced social views, but was also fanatically religious. Lord Dilke, her future second husband, was among her fellow students, and in a memoir of her that he wrote after her death he said she had presented a striking figure. "Miss Strong used to horrify her ordinary Church friends by her studies in dissection and anatomy and by her fearless advocacy of the necessity of drawing from the nude: but at the same time, still more greatly to shock them by her habit of doing penance for the smallest fault, imaginary or real, by lying for hours on the bare floor or on the stones, with her arms in the attitude of the cross," Dilke wrote.

After marrying Pattison, Francis, as she was always known, became a pupil to her much older scholar-husband. She learned Latin, German, and French sufficient to read the important works in the literatures of those languages. (Pattison loved reading classical Latin authors, and could himself write in a beautiful fluent Latin.) "Of all the periods of her life when, to judge by results, she worked with the most Benedictine application, that of the first years of her marriage with Mark Pattison must be pronounced supreme," Dilke wrote. She maintained her own interests—and her own income—by writing for the *Saturday Review* and other periodicals, and eventually she became an accomplished art historian. Dilke points out that she signed herself "E. F. S. Pattison," "the S . . . being introduced by her to mark her wish for some recognition of the independent existence of women." But, he added, "there was no personal resistance to the influence over her of her husband. His mind and learning deserved the surrender of the educational direction of a young girl, however gifted, to his mental and philosophical control; and he obtained it."

The presence of a young new wife would have made quite a change in Pattison's established way of life, and it could not have been entirely an easy adjustment for him. Francis was a beauty, with red-golden hair and a taste for flowing dresses worn without crinolines; she smoked cigarettes, a rarity among women at the time, and was lively and sociable. She must have been a vivid presence in an institution populated almost entirely by unmarried men.

Pattison's manner was very different from hers. In a memoir that was published posthumously in 1885, he characterized himself as prone to morbid depression, and wrote of how he needed to be alone to work. He recounted a telling incident from his youth, when a friend was visiting for the summer. Pattison described the "serious inconvenience" this genial young man caused by entering Pattison's bedroom, book in hand, while Pattison was trying to study. "Solitude was necessary to me; I had not—I have never had—the power of commanding my attention properly in the presence of another," Pattison wrote of this unhappy situation. Pattison was "morose and disagreeable," and eventually the young man got the message and retired to the guest bedroom. "I had gained my point, but, as so often since, with the uncomfortable consciousness of having done so in a wrong way," Pattison wrote, adding, "I mention this trifling incident because it is typical of my way of doing things all my life."

It does not seem to have been a contented marriage. Apart from the obvious differences in manners and personality, Francis would later complain of their sexual incompatibility. "You cannot forget that from the first I expressed the strongest aversion to that side of the common life," she wrote to the rector, after fifteen years of marriage. While plenty of nineteenth-century marriages did not conform to modern-day expectations of sexual harmony—as, for that matter, plenty of modern-day marriages also do not—that failure of compatibility seems eventually to have led both husband and wife to feel aggrieved and disappointed in other dimensions, too. If their marriage was outwardly harmonious when Eliot and Lewes came to visit, in 1870, within a very few years a rift was evident. Francis started spending a great deal of time abroad, with the fragility of her health as justification, and she rekindled her friendship with Sir Charles Wentworth, her former fellow art student. She came to feel put-upon by the demands of her gloomy, disappointed husband. In a letter sent in 1875 from a German spa, she wrote, "It distresses me to find that you are so depressed, and grieves me to think of you all alone, you must pluck up your courage and give me a little. . . . Do trust me a little! I'm not perhaps the sort of person you quite approve, but I have *some* feelings and *some* sense of duty."

For his part Pattison felt excruciatingly lonely, and considered himself wronged and abandoned. In the latter years of his life he found some consolation in the company of a young woman named Meta Bradley. She was the niece of the master of University College, and formed with Pattison what historians think was probably not a sexual but was certainly an emotionally intense relationship, serving as a comfort and a confidante to him, in the stead of his often-absent wife. He once told Bradley that the date of his wedding was "an anniversary which depresses me to the lowest depths of misery."

In the Casaubons, George Eliot portrayed one of the most inharmonious marriages ever concluded. The nature of their incompatibility is first suggested by the contrast between Casaubon's arid proposal letter, in which he outlines Dorothea's fitness "to supply aid in graver labours and to cast a charm over vacant hours," and Dorothea's full-hearted response to the proposal, in which she thanks him for his love—a declaration of which, the reader cannot but notice, he has failed to make.

Things only get worse from there. During the short period of their engagement Casaubon discovers that the depths of emotion in which he expected to be immersed seem to have run dry. Having determined to "abandon himself to the stream of feeling," he has been surprised to discover "what an exceedingly shallow rill it was." Though he can hardly bear to admit it to himself, Casaubon enters marriage in a state of anxiety about his insufficiency, rather than in pleasurable anticipation of his impending fulfilment.

Dorothea's disillusionment begins almost immediately after the wedding, while she is still on her disorienting, distressing honeymoon in Rome. She has anticipated that the world will widen for her under her husband's tutelage; instead, she discovers that she is excluded from his intellectual labours. Worse, it begins to dawn on her that his labours are far pettier than she had imagined when she believed her husband-to-be was another Locke or Milton. A lowering miasma settles upon Dorothea, Eliot writes. "How was it that in the weeks since her marriage, Dorothea had not distinctly observed but felt with a stifling depression, that the large vistas and wide fresh air which she had dreamed of finding in her husband's mind were replaced by ante-rooms and winding passages which seemed to lead nowhither?"

Casaubon, for his part, is as unhappy a newlywed as is Dorothea. He shrinks frigidly from her expressions of physical affection: "Having made his clerical toilette with due care in the morning, he was prepared only for those amenities of life which were suited to the well-adjusted stiff cravat of the period, and to a mind weighted with unpublished matter," Eliot writes. Casaubon is as rigid as his neckwear, and it is not difficult to imagine the lack of intimate congruity between Dorothea's affection—"she had ardour enough for what was near, to have kissed Mr. Casaubon's coat-sleeve, or to have caressed his shoe-latchet"—and her husband's flinching repulsion.

To members of Dorothea's circle at Tipton, her attraction to Casaubon makes no sense at all. He is regarded with unapologetic disgust. "No better than a mummy," is the verdict of Sir James Chettam. Mrs. Cadwallader, the rector's wife, sardonically jokes that his blood when viewed under a microscope is "all semicolons and parentheses." Will Ladislaw insists that Casaubon has done Dorothea a grievous wrong in marrying her. "If he chose to grow grey crunching bones in a cavern, he had no business to be luring a girl into his companionship," Ladislaw thinks.

The reader may feel inclined to agree with these judgements, at least in the earlier stages of the relation between the characters, when Casaubon's coldness and narcissism are clear to everyone except his hopeful bride. But as the novel progresses, Eliot will not allow the reader easily to dismiss Casaubon. Rather she insists that we also comprehend his frailties and weaknesses, and understand what she calls his "small hungry shivering self." She spells it out clearly, in the arch, authoritative voice she often assumes as narrator. "Mr. Casaubon, too, was the centre of his own world," she writes. "If he was liable to think that others were providentially made for him, and especially to consider them in light of their fitness for the author of a *Key to All Mythologies*, this trait is not quite alien to us, and, like the other mendicant hopes of mortals, claims some of our pity."

"But why always Dorothea?" Eliot famously interjects at one point in *Middlemarch*. It is central to Eliot's novelistic intention that the reader understand the unfolding of events from the perspectives of multiple characters, and there is a great deal of technical skill in the way she illustrates the dawning disillusionment of both Dorothea and Casaubon. Repeatedly, Eliot lulls the reader into an emotional complicity with Dorothea, and then subverts that sense of complicity by insisting that the reader also comprehend Casaubon.

Dorothea's first crisis and confusion in Rome is described in acute, inward detail. If Dorothea had been asked to describe what was going on, Eliot writes, she could not have done so: "To have been driven to be more particular would have been like trying to give a history of the lights and shadows; for that new real future which was replacing the imaginary drew its material from the endless minutiae by which her view of Mr. Casaubon and her wifely relation, now that she was married to him, was gradually changing with the secret motion of a watch-hand from what it had been in her maiden dream." For several pages, Eliot examines Dorothea's emotions under her microscope, as if she were dissecting her heroine's brain, the better to understand the course of its electrical flickers. But then she moves quickly and just as deeply into the inward movement of Casaubon's emotions and sensations. "In Mr. Casaubon's ear, Dorothea's voice gave loud emphatic iteration to those muffled suggestions of consciousness which it was possible to explain as mere fancy, the illusion of exaggerated sensitiveness," Eliot writes. "And this cruel outward accuser was there in the shape of a wife—nay, of a young bride, who, instead of observing his abundant pen scratches and amplitude of paper with the uncritical awe of an elegant-minded canary-bird, seemed to present herself as a spy watching everything with a malign power of inference." The oppressive intimacy implied by Eliot's choice of metaphors—the ticking watch, the muffled whispers, the scratching pen—suggest a rising, claustrophobic sense of emotional panic. One can imagine how Hitchcock would use the same material to similar psychological effect.

"The greatest benefit we owe to the artist, whether painter, poet, or novelist, is the extension of our sympathies," Eliot wrote in 1856, in an essay entitled "The Natural History of German Life." She went on: "Art is the nearest thing to life; it is a mode of amplifying experience and extending our contact with our fellow-men beyond the bounds of our personal lot." The notion of sympathy was a very important one for Eliot, as it had been for the Romantic poets before her. "Sympathy" was a far more resonant term in the Victorian era than it tends to be today, when it is often understood to mean no more than "feeling sorry for." When Eliot and her peers used the word, they meant by it the experience of feeling with another person: of entering fully, through an exercise of imaginative power, into the experience of another. In a letter Eliot wrote to John Blackwood in early 1857, after completing the first of the *Scenes of Clerical Life*, she gave a very early draft of what would become an artistic manifesto. "My stories always grow out of my psychological conception of the dramatis personae," she wrote. "My artistic bent is directed not at all to the presentation of eminently irreproachable characters, but to the presentation of mixed human beings in such a way as to call forth tolerant judgement, pity, and sympathy." Generating the experience of sympathy was what her fiction was for.

In *Middlemarch*, Eliot shows her reader that marital incompatibility is not simply a matter of one person being misunderstood by another—which is certainly how it can feel, when one is aggrieved and resentful—but that incompatibility consists of two people failing each other in their powers of comprehension. To Casaubon, Dorothea's expressions of solicitude about the progress he is making in his work sound like the most painful of critiques, as if she, no less than the "leading minds of Brasenose," considers all his efforts to be futile and worthy only of contempt. There's no doubt that Casaubon treats Dorothea horribly—first he leaves her blundering around the ruins of Rome, overwrought and overwhelmed, while he sequesters himself in the chaste, cold corridors of the Vatican; then he repeats the pattern in miniature when they return to boudoir and library in Lowick. But, Eliot insists, Dorothea has also failed to comprehend him. "She had not yet listened patiently to his heart-beats, but only felt that her own was beating violently."

This notion—that we each have our own centre of gravity, but must come to discover that others weigh the world differently to how we do—is one that is constantly repeated in the book. The necessity of growing out of such self-centredness is *the* theme of *Middlemarch*. In one of the most memorable editorial asides in the novel, Eliot elaborates upon this idea of how necessary it is to expand one's sympathies. "We are all of us born in moral stupidity, taking the world as an udder to feed our supreme selves," she writes. "Dorothea had early begun to emerge from that stupidity, but yet it had been easier for her to imagine how she would devote herself to Mr. Casaubon, and become wise and strong in his strength and wisdom, than to conceive with that distinctness which is no longer reflection but feeling—an idea wrought back to the directness of sense, like the solidity of objects—that he had an equivalent centre of self, whence the lights and shadows must always fall with a certain difference."

For Dorothea marriage provides a crash course in emotional sympathy, and by Book Five of *Middlemarch*, "The Dead Hand," she has begun to achieve it. She thought she would learn from Casaubon; instead what she learns is to feel with him. It's a difficult lesson, not least because Casaubon is so resistant to her sympathy. He continues to recoil from her, even when her gestures are ones of compassionate attention rather than affectionate need. In an episode at the end of Book Four, Dorothea approaches Casaubon as he walks along an avenue of sombre yew trees, like those one can find in so many English formal gardens. (They always seem to prompt sober contemplation, as the walled flower garden invites lighter distractions.) Casaubon has just met with Lydgate, who has told him that his heart condition may prove fatal at any time. "When the commonplace 'We all must die' transforms itself suddenly into the acute consciousness 'I must die—and soon', then death grapples us, and his fingers are cruel; afterwards, he may come to fold us in his arms as our mother did, and our last moment of dim earthly discerning may be like the first," is Eliot's magnificent summation of that awful, crystallizing realization.

Faced with the prospect of death, Casaubon remains embroiled in his stubbornly mortal obsessions of failure, his prevision of being judged by his academic peers. Dorothea, knowing what

Lydgate has told him, attempts to slip her arm through that of her husband; but he keeps his arm rigid, hands clasped behind his back. A more sentimental novelist might have made Casaubon bend his elbow slightly to accommodate her gesture, his confrontation with his own mortality a spur to understanding what comfort Dorothea could give him. Instead, Eliot gives a chilling representation of a deadly, unbridgeable distance in marriage: the absolute failure of sympathy.

Dorothea is outraged at his treatment of her, and spends several hours raging in her boudoir. Eliot writes that another woman in this situation might start to hate. But Dorothea struggles against that impulse and approaches Casaubon again, catching him off guard as he is ascending the staircase, taper in hand, heading for bed. He tells her, "Come, my dear, come. You are young, and need not to extend your life by watching." The "kind quiet melancholy of that speech," as Eliot calls it, is enough to move Dorothea's sympathy back to him. In a gesture of resignation and submission, she slips her hand into his, and the reader can imagine the cold inadequacy of his hand's responding touch.

Casaubon is not without his emotional intuitions—he accurately anticipates the inevitability of Dorothea and Ladislaw falling in love, and attempts through the codicil to his will to manipulate their futures with his dead hand. But his sympathies are never enlarged. He cannot feel with Dorothea—even if the meeting on the stairs does surprise him into a fleeting moment of kindness and reciprocity. (Great art "surprises even the trivial and the selfish into that attention to what is apart from themselves," Eliot writes in "The Natural History of German Life.")

But if Casaubon is incapable of emotional enlargement the

reader of *Middlemarch* is not, and Eliot sows the seeds of sympathy for Casaubon early on. Ladislaw steams inwardly at his prematurely elderly cousin marrying Dorothea, convinced in his own mind that "a man was bound to know himself better than that." But Casaubon, crucially, does *not* know himself better than that, and there is one moment in his proposal letter where pathos breaks through the pomposity. He has outlined the ways in which he considers Dorothea a suitable handmaiden to his labours; he has assured her that there is nothing in his past to cause her bitterness or shame. Then he tells her that if she were to refuse him he cannot help but feel that resignation to solitude will be more difficult now that his hopes have been raised. "But in this order of experience I am still young," he writes.

Casaubon may be in his mid forties, well into middle age, but he is still as inexperienced and fearful as he was as a young man, with the added burden of knowing that all that he expected to have accomplished by this point in his life is still undone. Dorothea fails to see that while Casaubon is by far her senior, he is still beset by the confusions of earlier years. "I mention this trifling incident because it is typical of my way of doing things all my life," Mark Pattison wrote of his clumsy teenage quest for solitude. Casaubon may have grey hair and a lined face, but when it comes to love, he's at least as unsophisticated as Dorothea, and maybe more.

At Dorothea's age it can be very hard to realize that a middle-aged person, who seems so very much older, has not necessarily achieved wisdom and self-mastery. When I was in my twenties it came as a surprise to me to learn that a person a generation older than I was might not feel him- or herself to be the experienced elder that he or she seemed to me, but might still be a green, anxious youth, at least in his or her self-perception. Looking back from the vantage point of forty-five, though, twenty doesn't look quite so far away. We are still recognizably ourselves, with many of the same confusions, even if experience has abated them, and granted us some self-awareness. We can hope, at best, that grow-ing older has given us some degree of emotional maturity, and a greater understanding of the perspectives and the projections of others. This greater understanding should, ideally, include a com-prehension of the errors of the young—precisely what Ladislaw suggests Casaubon lacks when he permits Dorothea to join him crunching bones in a cave. But then again, older men have often found it difficult to turn away idolizing young women.

When I read *Middlemarch* at Dorothea's age, and reread it in my early twenties, I did not react against Casaubon as violently as do Ladislaw and the others at Tipton. There was enough of Dorothea in me to understand her initial infatuation with what he represented to her, a person of knowledge and experience who could lead her out of the oppressive narrowness that had charac-terized her life thus far. Dorothea's hopes were misplaced, but they did not seem entirely unfounded. As I grew a little older with the book, though, I developed a greater scorn for Casaubon—for his undeserved self-importance and his intellectual pettiness, and for his ungenerous, withholding behaviour towards his young wife, who deserves so much better from him. By my thirties, it was easier to look down on Casaubon, to regard him as contemptible and repellent.

But having reached the age of Casaubon, I realize that it would take a great deal of self-regard on my part not to feel a tender sense of kinship with that sad, proud, desiccated man. In middle age, it becomes considerably harder to maintain a superior sense of distance from his preoccupations: his timid fear of professional judgement, hindering him from ever producing the work upon which he has staked his life; his quietly devastating discovery that, having deferred domestic intimacy for so long, he is incapable of entering into it; his perverse conviction that Dorothea's ardour and submissiveness amount to a cruel, deliberate undermining of all he has aspired to be. Casaubon is crippled by caution and undone by closed-heartedness. He is a frail creature tortured by his own sense of his insufficiencies, whose soul was "too languid to thrill out of self-consciousness into passionate delight; it went on fluttering in the swampy ground where it was hatched, thinking of its wings and never flying." Once Eliot was asked whom she had in mind as the original for Casaubon; in response, she silently tapped her own breast. And as I read *Middlemarch* in middle age, his failures and fears no longer seem so remote or theoretical to me as they once did, when I was in my Dorothea youth.

THE wife of the Rector of Lincoln met me in the porter's lodge at the college, wearing a burgundy-coloured suit and greeting me with the energetic manner of a Girl Scout leader. Margaret Langford's husband, Paul Langford, a historian, was appointed to the post in 2000, and while the rector no longer lives in the college's main quadrangle, a less cramped, more private neo-Georgian residence having been built farther along Turl Street eighty-odd years ago, Mrs. Langford had agreed to show me around the rooms in which the Pattisons had entertained Eliot and Lewes.

First, though, we stopped in the college's fifteenth-century hall to see a portrait of Mark Pattison that was hanging over the high table, where faculty are seated to dine. In it, Pattison has a reddish beard traced with grey, and deep lines are etched in his melancholy face. He looks down at a book in his lap, though it's impossible to tell what the book is. Perhaps, Mrs. Langford suggested with a note of conspiracy in her voice, it is one by Isaac Casaubon, the Renaissance scholar, about whom he wrote an influential book in 1875. Or perhaps it is one by John Milton, about whose works and life, including his devastatingly unsatisfying first marriage, Pattison published a volume in 1879. The rector's wife knew quite a bit about her predecessor, and about the speculation over whether the Pattisons inspired the Casaubons. "I don't think it was a match made in heaven," she said, with understatement.

Lord Dilke, Francis Pattison's second husband, publicly disavowed the identification, and said that his wife had always found the comparison odious. But in the memoir Dilke wrote of Francis after her death, he contradicted himself, claiming that Eliot had in some respects been drawing from life. Dilke wrote that Eliot had been thinking of Francis when she wrote of Dorothea knowing Pascal and Jeremy Taylor by heart, staying up all night to read theological books, and fasting; and he said that Book One of *Middlemarch* was to some extent drawn from the courtship of the Pattisons. Dorothea's expectations of marriage, he implied, were like those experienced by Emily Strong, while Casaubon's hopes for marriage bore a relation to those of Mark Pattison. In unpublished diaries Dilke wrote that he had it on the authority of George Eliot herself that she had based Casaubon's proposal letter upon the very one that Pattison wrote to Francis, though scholars are sceptical of this claim.

Gordon S. Haight, Eliot's pre-eminent biographer and the editor of nine volumes of her letters, thought that the identification was utterly wrong-headed. "There could hardly be greater contrast in moral character between the sophisticated worldly-minded Mrs. Pattison and the serious, naïve Dorothea Casaubon—unless it was that between the foolish pedant of Lowick and the energetic and learned Rector of Lincoln," is how Haight, who spent more than forty years studying Eliot, dismissed the case in one essay. Haight argued, reasonably enough, that Eliot had no motive to offend the Pattisons by exposing the difficulties of their marriage, and the fact that the friendship continued only makes clearer the absurdity of the identification.

But not everyone who reviewed the evidence agreed with Haight. John Sparrow, the conservative warden of All Souls College for a quarter of a century, provided an alternative version of events in a series of lectures he gave at Trinity College, Cambridge. Sparrow argued that when it came to Francis Pattison and Dorothea Casaubon, "it was only in inessentials that the two women differed." He acknowledged that, unlike Edward Casaubon, Mark Pattison was a man of true intellectual accomplishment. But he argued that there were none the less remarkable similarities between them—"the prematurely aged appearance, the stilted utterance, the selfishness about the larger things in life, the meanness about the little ones." Sparrow suggested that Eliot must have heard of the Pattisons' marital unhappiness from Francis, and then had chosen to reproduce it. The fact that both Pattisons continued to be on good terms with Eliot after the book was published is evidence of Eliot's shrewdness, Sparrow argued. "Pattison was not so vain as to be blind to the odious resemblance, but he was too proud to admit by any public gesture that a resemblance existed."

Sparrow's essays on Pattison are great fun to read. They have the fluid assurance of a barrister making a well-honed case before a courtroom, as well as a delicious insider's flavour of Oxford past. But perhaps the most nuanced engagement with the question of the Pattison/Casaubon identification is that of another Oxford scholar, A. D. Nuttall, in a book with the irresistible title *Dead from the Waist Down: Scholars and Scholarship in Literature and the Popular Imagination*. In it, Nuttall makes the persuasive observation that, while it is entirely possible that George Eliot was not intending to describe Francis Pattison in the character of Dorothea Brooke, it is certainly possible that Francis afterwards modelled herself upon Dorothea, and came to see her experience of marriage as similar to that of Eliot's heroine. Nuttall goes on to argue that just as Francis may have identified with Dorothea, Pattison may have seen himself in Casaubon, pointing out that Pattison's great projected work—a history of scholarship built around the figure of Joseph Scaliger—was never written.

Nuttall bases this contention on his reading of Pattison's *Memoirs*, which the rector wrote when he was in his seventies, and close to death. It is a remarkable work. A ruthless, scrupulous self-examination, it reveals Pattison's insecurities and his sense of his own personal failures—although it ends before he reaches the period of his marriage, so he doesn't have to examine whatever failures lay there. In it, Pattison told of falling short of his original intellectual goal, to produce "the history of learning from the Renaissance downwards." As he wrote in the *Memoirs*, "One's ambition is always in the inverse proportion of one's knowledge." He added, "Of the ambitious plan I had first conceived I have only executed fragments." These words might well have come from the pen of a more evolved Casaubon—one who has lived long enough to come to some degree of self-knowledge. In the light of the memoir it is difficult to disagree with Nuttall when he asserts that it would be strange "if this scholar, who clearly perceived himself as a failure, could have read all the way through *Middlemarch* without any uncomfortable twinges from the parts dealing with Mr. Casaubon."

I would be sceptical of *any* scholar who claims to read Casaubon's story without feeling uncomfortable twinges, so deadly accurate is Eliot in her characterization of the always-present threat of futility that looms over any scholarly endeavour—what V. S. Pritchett characterized as the scholar's "befogged and grandiose humiliations." And I can't help wondering whether Haight's own energetic and learned repudiation of the Pattison/Casaubon identification was at least partly motivated by an effort to deny what might be Casaubonish in himself. If I walk the streets Eliot walked, and read the diaries and letters she wrote—if I attempt, in some small measure, to enter sympathetically and imaginatively into her experience—it seems to me impossible to conceive that when, a few months after her visit to Oxford, she began writing a story about the marriage of a passionate young woman and a much older scholar, she did not have the Rector of Lincoln and his wife somewhere in mind.

One vivid image of George Eliot's stay in Oxford has endured. Mary Augusta Ward, who in subsequent decades became a popular novelist herself, was at the time a young woman living in Oxford, where she studied with Dr. Pattison. (No Oxford colleges admitted women in 1870; the first, Lady Margaret Hall, was not established until 1878.) In her memoirs Mrs. Ward recalled seeing Eliot in the quadrangle at Lincoln. "Suddenly, at one of the upper windows of the Rector's lodgings, which occupied the far right-hand corner of the quad, there appeared the head and shoulders of Mrs. Pattison, as she looked out and beckoned, smiling, to Mrs. Lewes," she wrote. "It was a brilliant apparition, as though a French portrait by Greuze or Perronneau had suddenly slipped into a vacant space in the old college wall. The pale, pretty head, *blond-cendrée,* the delicate, smiling features and white throat; a touch of black, a touch of blue; a white dress; a general eighteenth-century impression as though of powder and patches—Mrs. Lewes perceived it in a flash, and I saw her run eagerly to Mr. Lewes and draw his attention to the window and its occupant. She took his arm, while she looked and waved. If she had lived longer, some day, and somewhere in her books, that vision at the window and that flower-laden garden would have reappeared." Mrs. Ward thought she witnessed the novelist's imagination at work, absorbing material, storing it up for transformation.

Today, the Pattisons' drawing room is the study of a don: a young, female one who teaches history, which might have pleased Mrs. Pattison. What would have been the Pattisons' dining room is used as a reception room, and when I visited, sherry glasses were laid out on a table, ready for awkward students unaccustomed to aperitifs, emulating sophistication with the rector. But the rooms still bear the traces of their earlier incarnation, with gilded carvings of flowers and leaves around the fireplaces and doorways, a Persian rug underfoot, and a view on to quiet gardens and the Radcliffe Camera beyond.

As I walked around the rooms, I wondered what the rector and his wife must have thought when they read *Middlemarch*—as they both certainly did, although later, as Lady Dilke, Francis pretended she hadn't, doubtless to fend off the Dorothea question. I imagined Francis, frustrated in her marriage, recognizing her younger self in Dorothea's devout earnestness, as A. D. Nuttall suggests; and I pictured the rector comprehending Casaubon's miseries in the light of his own sense of intellectual underachievement.

But that simple sense of recognition would not be the only way in which each would have received the book. Mark Pattison relates in his memoir that he was extremely religious in his youth, and was at one point even tempted to convert to Catholicism, under the influence of Cardinal John Henry Newman, the leader of the Oxford Movement. Pattison spent time at Newman's retreat in Oxford, known as "the Monastery," where he fasted and prayed. ("Spent nearly two hours this morning in devotion and self-examination," he wrote in his diary.) As well as being religious, he was an intellectual seeker: he arrived at Oxford longing for wise guidance and like-minded company. "I thought that now at last I should be in the company of an ardent band of fellow-students, only desirous of rivalling each other in the initiation which the tutors were to lead into the mysteries of scholarship, of composition, of rhetoric, logic and all the arts of literature," he wrote. In the event, he was bitterly disappointed by the dullness of his peers and the uninspiring nature of his teachers.

Reading this, I wonder whether the gruff Rector of Lincoln might have recognized himself in the ardent, devout, hungry Dorothea, just as much as he saw himself in her scholar-husband.

Who is to say that a middle-aged man, given the free space for imaginative sympathy that a great work of literature provides, might not identify with a naïve young woman within its pages? That for all his apparent gravitas he might not feel that in certain orders of experience he is still young?

Francis, too, might not simply have seen herself in Dorothea. The former Emily Francis Strong also had ambitions for writing large, authoritative works—ambitions that eventually had to be scaled down to size, or remained unfulfilled. In her middle years, she began to realize that she might not achieve all she aspired to. "Sometimes I think even that the best use one could make of one's own life would be to devote oneself to knowing everything, to become a master—at least in the general meaning of the word—of all that the human mind has conquered in all fields," she once wrote. "But I am forty, and it is too late."

Too-lateness of this sort is Casaubon's condition, and if Francis revisited *Middlemarch* in middle age, surely she would have recognized aspects of herself in the sad, unproductive scholar. Like all readers of the novel after them, both the rector and his wife would have had their own internal version of *Middlemarch*, slightly different from anyone else's, informed by their own history and experience, shaped by the moods of their memories.

In the months after *Middlemarch* was published, Eliot received several letters from young women. Each wrote that she recognized herself in Dorothea—so much so that she believed Eliot must have modelled Dorothea upon *her*. Eliot was amused and, a friend reported, "asked each of these interesting ladies to send me her photograph. Alas, how little they resembled, at least in appearance, the heroine as I imagined her myself."

Such an approach to fiction—where do I see myself in here?—is not how a scholar reads, and it can be limiting in its solipsism. It's hardly an enlarging experience to read a novel as if it were a mirror of oneself. One of the useful functions of literary criticism and scholarship is to suggest alternative lenses through which a book might be read. (Or even, in the case of J. Hillis Miller, to tease out the uses to which the metaphors of mirror and lens are put in the text: "Seeing, then, is for Eliot not a neutral, objective, dispassionate or passive act. It is the creative projection of light from an egotistic center motivated by desire and need.")

Eliot was scornful of idle women readers who imagined themselves the heroines of French novels, and of self-regarding folk who saw themselves in the most admirable character in a novel, and she hoped for a more nuanced engagement from her own readers. Even so, all readers make books over in their own image, and according to their own experience. My *Middlemarch* is not the same as anyone else's *Middlemarch*; it is not even the same as my *Middlemarch* of twenty-five years ago. Sometimes, we find that a book we love has moved another person in the same ways as it has moved ourselves, and one definition of compatibility might be when two people have highlighted the same passages in their editions of a favourite novel. But we each have our own internal version of the book, with lines remembered and resonances felt.

"The secret of our emotions never lives in the bare object, but in its subtle relations to our own past," Eliot wrote in *Adam Bede*. The bare object of a book—of a story—might also have a subtle relation to our own past. Identification with character is one way in which most ordinary readers do engage with a book, even if it is not where a reader's engagement ends. It is where part of the pleasure, and the urgency, of reading lies. It is one of the ways that a novel speaks to a reader, and becomes integrated into the reader's own imaginative life. Even the most sophisticated readers read novels in the light of their own experience, and in such recognition, sympathy may begin.

Chapter 6

The Widow and the Wife

*"If youth is the season of hope, it is often so only
in the sense that our elders are hopeful
about us; for no age is so apt as youth to think
its emotions, partings, and resolves are the
last of their kind."*

—MIDDLEMARCH, CHAPTER 55

After her slow start, George Eliot wrote *Middlemarch* in a dauntingly short space of time. Books One and Two were completed by early summer 1871, and she wrote the rest of it—the total is more than twelve hundred manuscript pages—by September of the following year. This achievement is all the more impressive because she was suffering from various ailments throughout. She had inflammation of the gums, gastric complaints, attacks of migraine—the encroachment of age on the body. "Did you ever, in your young life, have a whole week of headache?" the fifty-two-year-old author wrote to one correspondent in the spring of 1872, when she was in the midst of writing Book Six.

She was working under professional as well as physiological pressure. Blackwood published the beginning of *Middlemarch* before she'd completed even half the novel, so there was no room for failure, or major revision. She tormented herself by rereading parts of *Felix Holt*, her most recent novel, and feeling sure she could never write as well again. As they often did at times of stress, she and Lewes moved to the countryside, this time to a rented house in Redhill, Surrey, better to concentrate on the three volumes of *Middlemarch* that remained to be written. There they were "shut out from the world amid fields," Lewes wrote to his son Charles. "Not a sound except hens cackling and dogs barking reaches us." Eliot was scrupulously disciplined. She didn't permit herself much letter writing, though sometimes late in the evening she would correspond with a few close friends. One was Barbara Bodichon, to whom she confessed, "I of course am still anxious, as I always am when any work is not safely finished."

Lewes wrote in her stead to less intimate correspondents, giving an account of her progress. "She improves visibly, almost day by day," he told one friend. "The colour has come back to her cheek and the oval also. I tell her she will 'put on flesh.' And she is writing—writing—writing!" Lewes went on to parody a line from a poem by Oliver Goldsmith, in which the author characterized the energies of David Garrick, the eighteenth-century man of the theatre. Lewes wrote, "I will say—'Why, Sir, *away* from the desk she is a perfect woman, but *at* the desk—oh!—my!!—God!!!'"

Lewes's conjuring of Eliot's animated creativity is appealing, not least because it provides a useful counterpoint to her own frequent characterization of herself as working slowly and laboriously, depressed by a sense of underachievement and hampered by infirmities. Her letters and diaries are filled with references to feeling unwell: upon reading Cross's biography Alice James, the sister of Henry James, remarked waspishly, "What an abject coward she seems to have been about physical pain, as if it weren't degrading enough to have head-aches, without jotting them down in a row to stare at one for all time." Eliot's headaches, like Proust's neurasthenia, seem an integral part of her creative identity, as if her extraordinarily intelligent brain could not work without overloading. Still, one wonders how different her life might have been if she'd had aspirin. She was, as the critic and novelist Elizabeth Hardwick wrote, "melancholy, head-achy, with a slow, disciplined, hard-won, aching genius that bore down upon her with a wondrous and exhausting force, like a great love affair in middle age."

Eliot's great love affair did come in middle age—with Lewes, that sprightly partner who was lively where she was lugubrious and sociable where she was retiring. Lewes's note about Eliot at her desk, racing to meet her deadline, describes her well, but it also brings Lewes himself vividly to life—in the midst of taking care of Eliot's epistolary needs while at the same time madly exceeding the rules of punctuation, overstepping the boundaries of what's proper to convey what's true. His writing style has the vivacity of the man himself, with an appealing ebullience and enthusiasm.

Some of Lewes's contemporaries found him altogether too ebullient. Charles Eliot Norton, who visited the Priory in 1869, wrote with disdain that Lewes "looks and moves like an old-fashioned French barber or dancing-master, very ugly, very vivacious, very entertaining. You expect to see him take up his fiddle and begin to play." Norton sounds like a snob and a prig, while Lewes strikes me as much more appealing: funny, charming, and above all, cheerful. I think I can understand how refreshing Lewes's sense of optimism must have been to Eliot, especially after her demoralizing, belittling experience with the complicated Herbert Spencer. At a certain age, what might once have seemed fascinating in a prospective partner—moodiness, indecision, all seeming to indicate emotional depth—becomes altogether less appealing. After an experience like that, to find a partner as accepting and generous as Lewes is a great and unexpected gift.

Lewes was indispensable to Eliot, and commentators agree that without his encouragement and ministrations she might never have had the confidence to attempt fiction, or enjoyed a working environment conducive to doing so. He acted as her agent, negotiating on her behalf with Blackwood, and he shielded her from reviews and criticism. By her own account, the novelist George Eliot would never have been born from the critic and editor Marian Evans were it not for the germinating spark that Lewes provided. He had encouraged her to try her hand at a novel early on, and then when she did not immediately act upon his urgings he arranged things practically so that she could not avoid the challenge any longer. After she'd written the first few pages of "The Sad Fortunes of the Reverend Amos Barton," the first of the stories that became *Scenes of Clerical Life*, Lewes was convinced that she was capable of writing entertaining dialogue, and left her alone one evening to write a death scene, to see if she could produce something persuasively sad. "I read it to G. when he came home," Eliot later wrote in a memorandum called "How I came to write Fiction." "We both cried over it, and then he came up to me and kissed me, saying 'I think your pathos is better than your fun.'"

How delightful that she included the kiss. It's a crucial detail, but I can imagine other writers skipping over it in an account of their creative origins—dismissing it as irrelevant or embarrassing, or forgetting it altogether. But they did kiss, and their kissing was essential. Lewes adored Eliot, whom he called by the pet name of Polly, with an intuitive kindness and a gratitude in which there was no trace of resentment. "To know her was to love her," he wrote in his diary in 1859, recalling their first acquaintance. "Since then my life has been a new birth. To her I owe all my prosperity & all my happiness. God bless her!" The sense of grateful, joyful indebtedness was mutual. The name under which she became famous was a tribute to him: she was George because he was George. An early biographer, Blanche Colton Williams, whose book was published in 1936, wrote that "Eliot" is a further, concealed honouring: "To L— I owe it."

Middlemarch mostly concerns itself with the problems of young love, the problems of young love being a natural subject of literature. But the book was nurtured by love that was arrived at late, and cherished all the more for its belatedness; and Lewes, George Eliot's own George, is its bustling, cheering, loving hero. Embedded in this story of young love is another love story, one about the unexpected possibilities presented by middle age.

THEY were introduced in a bookshop. Eliot had gone to Jeffs, a compact establishment in the Burlington Arcade, after taking a long walk through Hyde Park in the company of John Chapman. The elegant, glassed-in shopping arcade had been opened thirty years earlier by Lord Cavendish to prevent passers-by from throwing rubbish into the garden of Burlington House, his imposing residence on Piccadilly. (Oyster shells had been a particular problem.) By the 1850s the arcade was home to leather shops and shirtmakers and tobacconists; and, at number 15, Jeffs, which specialized in foreign-language books imported from the Continent. The shop was tiny: only nine feet deep and not much wider, with a spiral staircase leading to storerooms above. There would barely have been room to turn around, especially while wearing an ample Victorian gown, and Eliot and Lewes were thrown instantly into close proximity. Eliot mentioned meeting him there in a letter to Charles Bray, describing him as "a miniature Mirabeau."

Eliot's biographers agree that this is probably a reference to Thomas Carlyle's description of the French revolutionary's "shaggy beetle-brows and rough-hewn, seamed, carbuncled face," through which none the less shone a "burning fire of genius." Lewes, who was two years Eliot's senior, was "the ugliest man in London" according to one member of his literary circle. He was slight in stature, with a receding jaw, protruding teeth that were concealed by a bushy moustache, and dark, intense, intelligent eyes. Jane Carlyle unkindly called him "the Ape," though her husband gave testimony that Lewes was "ingenious, brilliant, entertaining, highly gifted and accomplished." He had contributed to the *Westminster Review*, had authored *A Biographical History of Philosophy* and two novels, and was currently serving as editor and columnist for the *Leader*, as well as contemplating a biography of Goethe.

Lewes's vivacity and informality impressed themselves upon others in even the briefest of encounters. In her biography of Lewes, Rosemary Ashton highlights a conversation between Thomas Carlyle and the much younger Lewes, as witnessed by a friend. During the interview, which took place on a hot July evening, Carlyle sat upright in a chair "with his deep stock and high waistcoat," while Lewes lounged in an easy chair, "his frock coat thrown open, and revealing the greater amplitude of shirt front from the fact that he had no waistcoat." He sounds like one of the Romantic poets he admired, conspicuously careless of social convention.

He was quick and clever. The novelist Eliza Lynn Linton, who was not fond of Lewes and thought him coarse and vulgar, none the less said that wherever he went there was "a patch of intellectual sunshine in the room." His air of confidence rubbed some acquaintances up the wrong way, among them Margaret Fuller, the American journalist, who described him as "a witty, French, flippant sort of man." Lewes wasn't French, but as a child he had lived in France and upon the Channel Island of Jersey, mastering the language fluently and without an accent; he retained an exotic aura amid his more stolid English brethren. In letters and in conversation he slipped easily from English into French, not for the sake of inserting a pretentious mot juste, but because he was equally lucid and at ease in both languages. (He also knew German, Italian, Spanish, Latin, and Greek.)

Lewes had grown up under unconventional circumstances, which added to his status as an outsider. His father and mother were never married. John Lee Lewes had fathered four children with his legal wife, whom he then abandoned in favour of Elizabeth Ashweek, Lewes's mother, who bore him three children before being abandoned herself when George Henry was just a baby. As a small boy Lewes acquired a hated stepfather, and was obliged to move frequently—from Gloucestershire to Nantes to Saint Helier and eventually to London, where he went to a school described by a contemporary as huge and unregenerate, where boys were bullied by each other and kept half-starved by the masters. He did not go to university, though he did think of attending medical school, but by his early twenties he was making a very modest living through his writing. In a novel called *Ranthorpe,* published four years before he first encountered Eliot, Lewes drew on his own experience to portray a young clerk with "a passion for books—no matter what editions, what bindings," who hungrily spends his last sixpence on a tattered edition of Shelley's poetry.

Lewes's bohemian manners and radical precepts were partly inspired by Shelley, of whom as a young man he had described himself as a worshipper, and whose biography he had tried to write when he was just twenty, a project that foundered because he could not get the approval of Mary Shelley, the poet's widow. Lewes's manners were also influenced by the customs of the theatre, with which he had close links as a critic, a playwright, a theatrical translator, and an actor. Rosemary Ashton notes that his sympathetic portrayal of Shylock, whom he played in a provincial production as a young man, was highly intelligent and unusual for its time. ("I say if Shylock be not represented as having the feelings of our kind, 'The Merchant of Venice' becomes a brutal melodrama," Lewes wrote.) One contemporary reported that Lewes had "a wonderful gift for dramatic representation, and could tell a story, reproducing the dialect and gestures of each actor in it, with lifelike effect." He was at home in the theatre in a way that made an impression on Eliot. A few weeks after their encounter in the Burlington Arcade, Lewes joined her, Chapman, and Herbert Spencer in their box at an inept production of *The Merry Wives of Windsor,* and made jokes all evening at the actors' expense. It could have been obnoxious, but Eliot found it amusing.

Their acquaintance grew at a trying time for both. Lewes had separated from Agnes, and later spoke of the year 1851 as "a very dreary wasted period of my life. I had given up all ambition whatever, lived from hand to mouth, and thought the evil of each day sufficient." Eliot, meanwhile, was being squired by Herbert Spencer—and then smarting from Spencer's rejection. In the wake of that experience, she was not inclined to fall in love with Lewes, or anyone. "If you insist on my writing about 'Emotions,' why I must get some up expressly for the purpose," she wrote to Charles Bray from her summer retreat at Broadstairs in July 1852. "But I must own I would rather not, for it is the grand wish and object of my life to get rid of them as far as possible, seeing they have already had more than their share of my nervous energy."

But Lewes's good nature impressed itself upon her, and in letters to Coventry over the next few months she dropped his name with an increasing note of arch fondness. On passing on some literary gossip, she wrote, "I am frightened to have told you this, for everything I say to any one at Rosehill gets around by some incomprehensible means to Lewes—Lewes can tell you the whole state of your domestic affairs, if you like, of course with additions, if not emendations, by the editor or editors." By the spring of 1853 the archness had dissipated, and her friends could not but have noticed his growing significance in her life. To Cara Bray she wrote, "Mr. Lewes especially is kind and attentive and has quite won my regard after having a good deal of my vituperation. Like a few other people in the world, he is much better than he seems—a man of heart and conscience wearing a mask of flippancy."

By the autumn of that year Eliot had moved out of Chapman's house to rented rooms in Cambridge Street. She and Lewes were discreet, but the degree of their intimacy would have been obvious to their more sophisticated friends. (A neighbour observed that Lewes called there every day; after his visits Eliot would be left in tears.) Discretion was dispensed with in July 1854, when Eliot boarded a steamer to Antwerp, destined for Weimar and what would turn out to be an eight-month tour through Belgium and Germany, the ostensible reason for which was Lewes's research on Goethe. In her anxiety Eliot had arrived early to the ship, and spent twenty anxious minutes waiting for Lewes. "But before long I saw his welcome face looking for me over the porter's shoulder, and all was well," she wrote in her diary. From the deck they watched the sunset, and the sunrise, too.

Landing in Antwerp they checked into the Hôtel du Rhein and strolled through streets and squares, visiting the cathedral and the museum to look at the works of Rubens; in Brussels they bought cheap French novels at the market and walked in the Galerie de la Reine, an arcade similar to the one in which they had been introduced. Unlike some celebrated diarists and letter writers Eliot rarely describes sensual experience, and the general absence of such accounts emphasizes her braininess, as if she were divorced from the lower instincts. But in Brussels she tells of drinking chocolate, of taking "rambles in the morning, lying melting on our beds through the middle of the day"—moments suggestive of the wondrous and exhausting pleasures of the honeymoon.

She wrote to Charles Bray from Weimar, which she and Lewes eventually reached in the first days of August. "I have had a month of exquisite enjoyment, and seem to have begun life afresh," her letter reads. "I am really strong and well and have recovered the power of learning in spite of age and grey hairs." Even her predict-able self-disparagement cannot obscure her radiant happiness.

"FEW women, I fear have had such reason as I have to think the long sad years of youth were worth living for the sake of middle age," Eliot wrote in her diary on the last day of 1857. She was thirty-eight, and even if today's thirty-eight-year-old might hope to fend off an acknowledgement of middle age for another couple of years, in the mid nineteenth century a woman was thought matronly at least by her early thirties. Eliot had long been taken for older than her years: as a thirteen-year-old student at the Miss Franklins' school in Coventry she had been mistaken by a visitor for one of the Misses Franklin, who were about twenty years older. George Combe, the phrenologist friend of Charles Bray, thought the first time he met her that she was forty; she was thirty-one.

The notion of middle age as a distinct stage of life was a rela-tively recent concept; its onset was earlier than would be reckoned today, and much more of middle life would fall within it. (An American commentator writing in 1828 placed its outer bound-aries at twenty-five and sixty, demarcating the interval during which one has achieved independence and acquired responsibili-ties.) Eliot did not regard twenty-five as middle-aged, but she did recognize that a shift from youth into something else happened not long thereafter. In her case, it was not an unwelcome progress. "One has to spend so many years in learning how to be happy," Eliot wrote to Sara Hennell, when she was twenty-four. Child-hood, she contended, is only glorious in retrospect—to the child it is full of deep, incomprehensible sorrows, and old age is even worse. "All this dear Sara, to prove that we are happier than when we were seven years old, and that we shall be happier when we are forty than we are now, which I call a comfortable doctrine and one worth trying to believe."

Eliot drew upon her intense recollection of the sorrows of childhood in *The Mill on the Floss*, and in that novel, too, she gave a defence of middle age, an argument for its virtues and usefulness. A man or woman in middle age, she said, could remember youth well enough to have sympathy with the troubles of the young, but had experience enough to know that those troubles would pass, however severe they might seem now. "The middle-aged, who have lived through their strongest emotions, but are yet in the time when memory is still half passionate and not merely contemplative, should surely be a sort of natural priesthood whom life has disciplined and consecrated to be the refuge and rescue of early stumblers and victims of self-despair," she wrote.

Ladislaw is one of those early stumblers when the reader meets him at the outset of *Middlemarch*. He does not have a middle-aged priest-figure offering him kindly advice—on the contrary, the middle-aged priest-figure in his life, the Reverend Edward Casaubon, is disapproving and judgemental. But it's not clear Ladislaw would listen to a more sympathetic authority figure even if one presented him- or herself. He is impetuous, mercurial, and very confident of his as yet unproven abilities. "He seems to me a kind of Shelley, you know," Mr. Brooke says. "I don't mean as to anything objectionable—laxities or atheism, or anything of that kind, you know . . . But he has the same sort of enthusiasm for liberty, freedom, emancipation."

Ladislaw cuts a striking and unusual figure in the town of

Middlemarch, with hair curling off his brow ("John Bull doesn't do much of that," one observer comments) and habits that make certain of the townsfolk compare him to a gypsy. He has a clouded, if not actually dishonourable, parentage. His grandmother was disinherited for marrying the man of her choice, an impoverished Polish musician, whom Mrs. Cadwallader disparages as "a rebellious Polish fiddler or dancing master." His mother voluntarily left her family, too, though Ladislaw knows less about his maternal ancestors, at least at the beginning of the novel. Mrs. Cadwallader, who gives voice to the conservative outlook of Tipton's gentry—and is, in fact, rarely very far off in her insights about character—calls Ladislaw himself "a dangerous young sprig . . . with his opera songs and his ready tongue. A sort of Byronic hero—an amorous conspirator, it strikes me."

Being viewed as an outsider, Ladislaw defiantly embraces the identity. In one particularly striking departure from convention he leads a group of ragged children on an expedition to gather nuts, providing a feast of gingerbread and performing a Punch and Judy show with homemade puppets, as if he were a benign Pied Piper. Later in the novel, there is a rumour among residents of Middlemarch that Ladislaw is of Jewish descent—the ultimate in outsider status for a provincial English town.

Some very eminent critics writing in the decades immediately after the novel's publication felt that Eliot failed to maintain sufficient critical distance in her depiction of Ladislaw—that she fell in love with her creation in a way that shows a lack of artistic control and is even unseemly, like a hoary movie director whose lens lingers too long on the young flesh of a favoured actress. Lord

David Cecil called Ladislaw "a schoolgirl's dream, and a vulgar dream at that," while Leslie Stephen complained, "Ladislaw is almost obtrusively a favourite with his creator," and deprecated him as "an amiable Bohemian." Another grand man of letters, Henry James, was similarly sceptical of Ladislaw. James found Dorothea entirely credible—"we believe in her as in a woman we might providentially meet some fine day when we should find ourselves doubting of the immortality of the soul," he wrote—but said that Ladislaw's characterization was a failure, "vague and impalpable to the end."

I find James's failure to grasp Ladislaw entirely incomprehensible. (But then I think James was fundamentally wrong in his appraisal of *Middlemarch*, which he admired as "a treasure-house of details" but called "an indifferent whole.") Ladislaw is very vividly drawn; what vagueness there is about him is a deliberate element of his characterization—an indication of his unformed future, as well as a suggestion of the persistent mobility one sometimes sees in the faces of the young before they have set into the contours of maturity. "Surely, his very features changed their form; his jaw looked sometimes large and sometimes small; and the little ripple in his nose was a preparation for metamorphosis," Eliot writes, and anyone who has watched a young man go through adolescence will recognize this phenomenon.

"When he turned his head quickly his hair seemed to shake out light, and some persons thought they saw decided genius in this coruscation," Eliot writes. Like Lewes, who shone a patch of intellectual sunshine wherever he went, Ladislaw is charismatic and magnetic. He is capable of conventional charm, as his thoughtless flirtation with Rosamond shows, and one can only imagine what a spell he has cast over female members of the bohemian demi-monde in which he has moved, beyond the pages of the novel, experimenting with opium and other interesting means of intoxication. But Ladislaw does not seek to charm Dorothea. Rather he adores her, and he does so long before it occurs to her to imagine that he might.

In depicting Ladislaw's devotion to Dorothea, Eliot shows what it is like to be fallen in love *with*—the delight of discovering oneself to be the object of love, not just its troubled subject. Ladislaw was not manly enough for Henry James, who used that term approvingly to describe Lydgate, whose characterization he admired as "powerful, ambitious, sagacious, with the maximum rather than the minimum of egotism, strenuous, generous, fallible, and altogether human." But Ladislaw's masculinity is of an order that Eliot knew from experience to be immensely powerful in its own way. It is that of a man who can make a woman feel beloved.

Those who think Eliot dotes too much on Ladislaw miss this, and they also seem to miss the undernote of affectionate scepticism with which he is portrayed. Ladislaw's youthful egoism and lightness of temperament are observed by the knowing eye of the novel's much older author: "Sometimes when he took off his hat, shaking his head backward, and showing his delicate throat as he sang, he looked like an incarnation of the spring whose spirit filled the air—a bright creature, abundant in uncertain promises." This is another of Eliot's deliciously subversive sentences, worth the close attention of any would-be writer: it seems to be heading in an extravagantly sentimental direction, but then punctures its own inflated rhetoric with the simple, devastating word "uncertain." No less than Fred Vincy, whose fecklessness is more categorically delineated, Ladislaw is a young man who remains unworthy of his projected prize, but is more than certain of his own worthiness.

The sixth volume of *Middlemarch*, "The Widow and the Wife," is bookended by two parallel chapters, both of which depict charged encounters between Ladislaw and Dorothea. When the first encounter takes place, Ladislaw is still in ignorance of the codicil to Casaubon's will that attempts to thwart a possible marriage between himself and Dorothea. He has come to say goodbye for what he says must be many years. But despite insisting that he must leave town, Ladislaw is not able to bring himself to do so for some weeks. He determines that he must see Dorothea once again before really departing—although, as he realizes, "a first farewell has pathos in it, but to come back for a second lends an opening to comedy." By the time of the second encounter he has learned about the codicil and has discovered more about his family origins; this time, he says, he must bid her farewell for ever.

Both scenes are masterpieces of misunderstanding, with Dorothea and Ladislaw speaking at entirely cross purposes. In the first, Ladislaw has told himself that he might become worthy of marrying Dorothea if he goes away first, and he is anguished by the apparent moderation of her emotion at the prospect of his departure. Dorothea—who has been longing to see Ladislaw, but has barely registered that what she feels for him is love—thinks, mistakenly, that he knows of the codicil, and she interprets his coming to her as demonstrating no more than friendly feeling. "Something was keeping their minds aloof, and each was left to conjecture what was in the other," Eliot writes.

In the second meeting, Ladislaw tries to makes it clear that he is beset by a forbidden love, but deliberately does not tell Dorothea that she is its object, leaving her to deduce what he thinks must be obvious. "It could not be fairly called wooing a woman to tell her that he would never woo her," Eliot writes. Dorothea has by now begun to realize that she is attached to Ladislaw; however, she misinterprets his words. She does not realize that he is in love with her, but instead imagines that the forbidden love of which he speaks is for Rosamond, with whom she has encountered him playing the piano.

Both scenes are charged with sublimated passion: one critic, David Trotter of the University of Cambridge, has made the striking observation that a moment in chapter 54, in which Ladislaw rises from his chair, face and neck flushed with frustrated anger, "may be the closest the Victorian novel ever came to describing an erection." And both scenes are powerful evocations of the intensity of first love: what one feels when one has no prior experience of either love's sad dwindling or its satisfying maturation, and feels only its consuming heat.

The chapters are also both deeply comic. When Ladislaw declares, "There are certain things which a man can only go through once in his life; and he must know some time or other that the best is over with him," or when he feels, wildly, that something must hinder their parting—"some miracle, clearly nothing in their own speech"—Eliot strikes a distinct note of humour, distancing her authorial self from the consciousness of her protagonists. But this humour is not necessarily something a young reader appreciates. I know I didn't. When I read these passages in my early twenties they seemed entirely fraught, and not at all funny. The way that Ladislaw feels is the way I felt during my first serious love affair, with a fellow student towards the end of my time at Oxford, when our impending parting was built into the drama of our days together. (He sent me poems not by Shelley but by Baudelaire, whom I am sure Ladislaw would have approved had their dates lined up.) There is a self-involved intensity to young love that cannot imagine the world without it, and it's one of the peculiarities of modern life that—unlike Dorothea and Ladislaw—young people go through that experience with a residual consciousness that this love affair will not be their last. Many of us do not end up marrying—or staying married to—the person we loved in school or college. But even with this awareness of young love's transience, it's hard at twenty-one or at twenty-three to imagine that love might strike us just as intensely later in life, too—even when we're middle-aged, and in spite of grey hairs, as Eliot put it.

In the fall of 1872, Eliot wrote to Harriet Beecher Stowe, with whom she had developed a rewarding epistolary relationship, to caution her against thinking that the Dorothea-Casaubon marriage was drawn from her own experience. "Impossible to conceive any creature less like Mr. Casaubon than my warm, enthusiastic husband, who cares much more for my doing than for his own, and is a miracle of freedom from all author's jealousy and all suspicion," Eliot went on. Sometimes in his own letters Lewes did compare himself comically to Casaubon, referring to his unfinished work, *Problems of Life and Mind*, as "the Key to All Psychologies." Eliot he cast as Dorothea, who, Lewes told Blackwood, "is more like her creator than anyone else and more so than any other of her creations."

But for all Lewes's comical affectation of seeing himself represented in the toiling scholar, it seems unlikely that he missed the tribute that Eliot made to him in the bright portrait of Ladislaw. Ladislaw is not entirely Lewes; he lacks Lewes's abundant generosity of spirit, and he does not share Lewes's miraculous deficit of egoism in the primary relation of his life. But there is enough of Lewes in Ladislaw—who is disparaged for lightness, frivolity, foreignness, and dilettantism—to suggest that Eliot meant him to be her beloved's vindication. No wonder Eliot loved the character she created. In Ladislaw, she reimagined the aging, unprepossessing Lewes as a young, handsome, passionate lover. Or perhaps in the loving eyes of Eliot Lewes simply was all those things, whatever he might have looked like to others.

Of course, they never married. Former friends and acquaintances were aghast at Eliot's departure for Weimar with Lewes, and cold upon her return. George Combe, the phrenologist who had previously examined Eliot's head and detected only low degrees of "amativeness," or sexual feeling, demanded to know whether there was any madness in her family. Cara Bray, Eliot's close friend, was a long time coming round. To Cara, Eliot wrote an eloquent defence, saying, "If there is any one action or relation of my life which is and always has been profoundly serious, it is my relation to Mr. Lewes." The tears shed in the rooms on Cambridge Street show the gravity with which Eliot regarded her choice. "Light and easily broken ties are what I neither desire theoretically nor could live for practically," she continued, with a touch of proud sarcasm. "Women who are satisfied with such ties do *not* act as I have done—they obtain what they desire and are still invited to dinner."

Being excluded from dinner parties turned out not to be such a bad thing. Their life together took its own course, free of the necessity to observe propriety. They read widely, wrote copiously, talked endlessly. They travelled often, sometimes to the English seaside, sometimes on tours through Italy. "How I worship his good humour, his good sense, his affectionate care for everyone who has claims on him!" Eliot wrote in her journal in 1865. An American visitor to the Priory, the writer Annie Fields, wrote of being taken by Lewes into the room in which he worked, where he drew back a curtain obscuring some shelves, upon which the bound manuscripts of Eliot's novels were arranged. "She was his chief topic of conversation, the pride and joy of his life, and it was quite evident that she returned his ardent devotion with a true love," Fields recalled.

My favourite image of Eliot and Lewes is provided by a neighbour who used to see them out walking Pug, and reported, Mrs. Cadwallader-like, "They were both very unattractive people to look upon, and they used to wander about the neighbourhood, the biggest pair of frights that ever was, followed by a shaggy little dog who could do tricks." The censorious glimpse from behind the net curtain is a peculiarly English phenomenon, and I derive delicious pleasure from the two Georges' carelessness about the judgement delivered by smaller minds and smaller hearts than their own.

To later generations untroubled by the notion of cohabitation, Eliot and Lewes provide a model of coupled contentment. The critic Phyllis Rose has written that "the Leweses managed to be as happy together for the twenty-four years they lived together as any two people I have heard of outside fantasy literature." Robert Lowell, in an unrhymed sonnet about George Eliot, called their union "Victorian England's one true marriage."

I'm inclined to join in this celebration of Eliot and Lewes's life together, and I cherish their late love all the more because it was not until I was thirty-five that I met the man who was to become my husband—a kind, optimistic man whose strengths include the gentle power of making me feel beloved. He is a writer, too, and on those days when we are working in different corners of our house, or travelling together for research, or reading one another's work before any other editor has seen it, I think I have a glimpse of what Eliot and Lewes's writerly companionability must have been like: "working, reading, correcting proofs, travelling, entertaining, receiving and writing letters, planning literary projects, worrying, doubting their powers, experiencing a delicious hypochondria," as Elizabeth Hardwick described it, with almost concupiscent precision. Hardwick was married to Robert Lowell when she wrote her essay on Eliot, and in her description of Victorian literary couples—"Before the bright fire at tea-time, we can see these high-strung men and women clinging together, their inky fingers touching"—there seems to be a touch of admiring identification, too. It would be hard to find a happier model for a writers' marriage than that of Eliot and Lewes.

They were unconventional, and unashamed to be so, but Eliot didn't remain unmarried as a feminist act, or as deliberate social defiance. It is difficult to appreciate today the boldness that it took to make her choice, which met with such widespread censure from close friends as well as from titillated onlookers. She became notorious in an age when notoriety could not be transformed by the alchemy of public relations into a tarnished badge of honour, and in later years she would write of herself ruefully as "the criminal usually known under the name of George Eliot."

Eliot was not at all opposed to the institution of marriage. She took very seriously its commitment—"its demand for self-suppression and tolerance," as she characterized it in *Middlemarch*. But she believed that there was a limit to the degree of self-suppression and tolerance that even marriage could demand. In *Middlemarch*, Eliot dramatizes the question of how much a woman should submit in marriage by showing Dorothea wrestling with a dilemma: should she agree to continue her husband's work on his behalf after his death? "She pictured to herself the days, and months, and years which she must spend in sorting what might be called shattered mummies, and fragments of a tradition which was itself a mosaic wrought from crushed ruins—sorting them as food for a theory which was already withered in the birth like an elfin child," Eliot writes. Dorothea is spared the necessity of promising Casaubon that she will submit: he dies before she is able to. Appalled by the discovery of his jealous codicil, she declines to look any more at his documents. "The living, suffering man was no longer before her to awaken her pity: there remained only the retrospect of painful subjection to a husband whose thoughts had been lower than she had believed."

Dorothea is saved by Casaubon's death, but Eliot also believed that a marriage could be dead while both partners were still living. In a critique of *Jane Eyre* she made when she was in her late twenties, she wrote, "All self-sacrifice is good—but one would like it to be in a somewhat nobler cause than that of a diabolical law which chains a man soul and body to a putrefying carcase." We might wish that the young Eliot had extended a little more sympathy to poor Bertha Mason, the unfortunate Mrs. Rochester, but her perspective upon matrimony—viewing it not as an eternal sacrament, but as a construct of sometimes erring law—anticipated the way she would later regard Lewes's obsolete union with Agnes. In 1855, a year after she and Lewes took off together to Weimar, Eliot wrote a review for the *Leader* of a biography of John Milton, by Thomas Keightley. In it, she addressed Milton's *Doctrine and Discipline of Divorce*, approvingly quoting Milton's wish "not that licence and levity and unconsented breach of faith should herein be countenanced, but that some conscionable and tender pity might be had of those who have unwarily, in a thing they never practised before, made themselves the bondmen of a luckless and helpless matrimony."

She regarded Lewes's union with Agnes as luckless and helpless, and thought of her own relation to him as a true marriage—as characterized by Feuerbach, whose words she had translated in 1854: "A marriage which is not spontaneously concluded, spontaneously willed, self-sufficing, is not a true marriage, and therefore not a truly moral marriage." The evident contentment with and commitment to each other of Eliot and Lewes struck some observers as unbearably smug, including Eliza Lynn Linton, who in her memoir of literary London wrote nastily of "the pretence of a sanctioned union" between them. Other early commentators did not quite know how to square Eliot's pseudomarriage with her clearly deserved reputation for moral seriousness. Some sought to argue, implausibly, that Lewes had been the ruin of her creativity, rather than the making of it. Writing a few years after her death, John G. Lord disapproved of Lewes's living "in open defiance of the seventh Commandment and the social customs of England," and called the union an "unfortunate connection, which saddened the whole subsequent life of Miss Evans, and tinged all her writings with the gall of her soul."

In Lord's view, the gall-tinged *Middlemarch* was more faulty than any of her earlier novels—"It has a miserable plot; it has many tedious chapters, and too many figures, and too much theorizing on social science," he complained. A reader need not agree with this questionable assessment to believe that the moral quandary Eliot faced in deciding to live with Lewes did inform her fictional preoccupations. The heroines of *The Mill on the Floss* and *Romola* and *Daniel Deronda* are all profoundly concerned with determining the limits of commitment, to a spouse or to one's own sense of self. In *Middlemarch*, the question of marital renunciation preoccupies not just Dorothea and Lydgate, but other characters, too. One of the book's most indelible episodes is that in which Harriet Bulstrode, the banker's wife, learns from her brother about her husband's proliferating deceptions and possible crimes. She withdraws to her room, where she removes her jewellery and her fancy, decorated cap and puts on a black gown, all in preparation for descending the stairs and embracing his shame and humiliation as her own— deliberately choosing to embody the fidelity that characterizes a true marriage, in spite of her husband's transgressions.

Eliot knew what renunciation was—she essentially gave up her ties to her family in order to be with Lewes. But there is no evidence to suggest that there was a knot of sadness and gall at the heart of her relation with Lewes. She was joyful in Weimar, and while her first pitch of happiness might not have been sustained among the mundane woes of headache and toothache, her joy in Lewes did not abate. "In my private lot I am unspeakably happy, loving and beloved," she wrote in her diary at the end of 1870, almost twenty years after their first meeting. Beyond youth when they met, Eliot and Lewes seem to have been one of those enviable pairs who appreciate each other only more as they grow older together, for reasons she hinted at in an essay she wrote about Madame de Sablé, the seventeenth-century *salonnière*. She wrote it while on her unconventional honeymoon in Weimar, discovering her power of learning renewed. "It is undeniable, that unions formed in the maturity of thought and feeling, and grounded only on inherent fitness and mutual attraction, tended to bring women into more intelligent sympathy with men," she wrote. She makes late love sound irresistibly romantic—different from young love, but no less appealing and considerably more satisfying.

Eliot uses a quotation from the apocryphal Book of Tobit to introduce a late chapter of *Middlemarch*: "Mercifully grant that we may grow aged together," she writes, and the line is worth remembering. I like to think of Eliot and Lewes growing together as they aged, remembering their beginnings. Sometimes, Eliot once told a friend, they would talk fondly of their early years together, when they were poor. (In fact, Lewes urged Eliot to write fiction not just as a matter of artistic fulfilment, but because he reckoned it would be a more effective means than journalism to pay the bills—which in those days it was.) Eliot told her friend that they laughed at all their troubles, with Lewes, in his theatrical way, exaggerating for comic effect the extent of the troubles that Eliot had endured. In *Middlemarch*, Lydgate has a belated inkling of what this kind of married life might be like: "He was beginning now to imagine how two creatures who loved each other, and had a stock of thoughts in common, might laugh over their shabby furniture, and their calculations how far they could afford butter and eggs."

The laughter—like Lewes's kiss for her first effort at fiction—is crucial. A compensation of getting older is an increasing ability to recognize the comedy of human relations, which can be obscured by the tempests of youthful emotion. Even stormy, passionate Ladislaw later comes to see the element of comedy in his desperate non-courtship of Dorothea—something Eliot shows the reader by offering a glimpse of him, mature and middle-aged, telling their love's origin story.

It happens during that charged meeting with which Book Six begins, at the moment when Dorothea tells Ladislaw that she expects him to be gone from Middlemarch a long while. "Will never quite knew how it was that he saved himself from falling down at her feet, when the 'long while' came forth with its gentle tremor," Eliot writes. That touch of melodrama is quietly modified by the next sentence, however: "He used to say that the horrible hue and surface of her crape dress was most likely the sufficient controlling force." Dorothea is wearing elaborate mourning clothes in the prevailing fashion—"her dress was an experiment in the utmost laying on of crape," Eliot writes—which reminds Ladislaw of how inappropriate it would be to woo her. But I hear in that sentence the note of ironical retrospection that can be achieved when one is not yet merely contemplative, but still half-passionate, and still capable of the power of learning.

Upon her death in 1880, Eliot bequeathed all but one of her manuscripts to the British Library. (The exception is *Scenes of Clerical Life*, which Blackwood kept for himself, and which ended up at the Morgan Library in New York.) One late summer's day I went to the manuscripts reading room at the British Library to view *Middlemarch*, which is kept there under high security.

A librarian handed me the first volume in its blue storage box, and I took it to a well-lit blond-wood carrel nearby. Opening the box, I gently lifted out the volume, which was bound in oxblood-coloured leather with gold lettering on its spine. I carefully settled it into a book rest that was equipped with a grey padded cushion, like something you might optimistically purchase at an airport store before an overnight flight, and turned the pages of the manuscript, reading the by now familiar words.

A wide margin had been left on the side of the page for corrections, which were few, but illuminating. I read Dorothea's letter to Casaubon accepting his marriage proposal. "I am very grateful to you for thinking me worthy to be your wife," Eliot had written, before amending the line with a poignant shift in register: "I am very grateful to you for loving me, and thinking me worthy to be your wife." In chapter 9, when Ladislaw makes his first appearance, strolling in the gardens at Lowick with a sketchbook, Eliot had initially described him as having "light curls"; she had afterwards inserted the word "brown," beginning to give colour to her creation, whose lightness had been established from the start.

And at the very beginning of the manuscript was a dedication, written in violet ink. "To my dear Husband George Henry Lewes, in this nineteenth year of our blessed union," it read, and was dated December 1872, the month in which the final volume of *Middlemarch* was published. As I read the inscription, I felt as Annie Fields did when Lewes drew back the curtain from the bookshelf at the Priory—privileged to come within the orbit of their endearing intimacy. After finishing her own novel Eliot moved on to other things, principally reading Lewes's manuscript. "It is a holiday to sit with one's feet at the fire reading one's husband's writing—at least when, like mine, he allows me to differ from him," she told Francis Pattison in a letter. "I flourish on this pasture very well, and he too is in tolerably good condition," she wrote. "I hope we are not the happiest people in the world, but we must be among the happiest."

Lewes died just six years later, in November 1878, at the age of sixty-one. Eliot was devastated. At first, she shut herself away, howling with grief, wishing that she, too, could die; she did not even attend his funeral, in Highgate Cemetery. Her diary for the period contains little but fragmentary quotations about loss from Shakespeare, Heine, Goethe. "Weary and heavy laden," she wrote. "Head miserable and heart bruised." When she felt able to work the only thing she wanted to do was to prepare for publication Lewes's unfinished *Problems of Life and Mind*—the act of devotion that Dorothea could not bring herself to perform for Casaubon. She sorted his papers. "Wrote memories, and lived with him all day," she wrote that January. "Read in his diary 1874—'Wrote verses to Polly—Wrote verses on Polly.'" Those verses have not survived: perhaps she packed them up with the letters he wrote to her, which were buried with her upon her own death.

But her extremity of grief abated, and after it did so, she did something that almost all observers have considered even more shocking than eloping to Weimar. Seventeen months after Lewes's death she married John Walter Cross, a family friend and their financial adviser, who was twenty years younger than she. They had first met in Rome in the spring of 1869, and later Cross recalled his impressions of her then: the low, earnest, musical voice, the abundant auburn-brown hair, the kindly grey-blue eyes, constantly changing in expression. A woman's hands can betray her age more than any other feature, but Cross remembered hers as remarkable: finely formed, and so thin as to seem translucent.

Cross, whom Lewes and Eliot had long addressed as "nephew," had been one of the few friends admitted during the first weeks of her widowhood. He, too, had recently been bereaved, his mother dying only ten days after Lewes. Within a few months, they began to read Dante together. She saw him often at Witley, in Surrey, where she and Lewes had bought a country house just two years earlier. In London they visited the National Gallery and the British Museum together. "This constant association engrossed me completely," Cross later wrote. "A bond of mutual dependence had been formed between us." The quality of Eliot's dependence is shown in a letter she sent Cross less than a year after Lewes's death. "Through everything else, dear tender one, there is the blessing of trusting in thy goodness," she wrote. "Thou dost not know anything of verbs in Hiphil and Hophal or the history of metaphysics or the position of Kepler in science, but thou knowest best things of another sort, such as belong to the manly heart—secrets of lovingness and rectitude."

She told almost no one of her impending marriage, only issuing a few vague warnings. "When I act in a way which is thoroughly unexpected there are reasons which justify my action, though the reasons may not be evident to you," she wrote to one friend. After the wedding, which took place on the sixth of May at St. George's, Hanover Square, she wrote brief notes to a few intimates, but offered no explanation of her actions. "I can only ask you and your husband to imagine and interpret according to your deep experience and loving kindness," she wrote to one friend. In *Middlemarch*, Celia asks Dorothea to explain how she fell in love with Ladislaw. "No, dear, you would have to feel with me, else you would never know," Dorothea replies. Eliot asked her friends to extend to her the imaginative sympathy with which her books were charged, and which they sought to nurture.

She knew, though, that anyone who could not feel with her might well judge her, both on grounds of infidelity to Lewes's memory, and because of the unusual age gap between herself and her new husband. The gossip came. One contemporary noted that Eliot had been buying new clothes for her wedding journey, unkindly remarking that everything possible had been done to make her look not too unsuitable a bride for a man of forty. Eliot had anticipated in literature the kind of censure she received in life. The citizens of Middlemarch criticize Dorothea's two marriages, observing that she had first wed a sickly clergyman old enough to be her father, then, less than a year after his death, renounced her estate to marry the clergyman's young, impecunious cousin: "She could not have been 'a nice woman', else she would not have married either the one or the other."

Isaac Evans, Eliot's provincially minded brother, saw events from a different if equally conservative perspective. Now that she was at last legally married, no matter to whom, he wrote to her to offer his congratulations. Eliot's biographers have scourged Isaac for his woefully conventional and unsympathetic stance towards his sister, and he certainly doesn't emerge from the story of her life looking good. But on my visit to the Nuneaton museum I was moved to discover that, after her death, he had labelled the case in which she had saved their father's eyeglasses: "My father's spectacles kept by George Eliot." At the end, he acknowledged who she really was.

The most gratifying response to the unexpected turn of events came from Barbara Bodichon. "Tell Johnny Cross I should have done exactly what he has done if you would have let me and I had been a man," Bodichon wrote. "You see I know all love is so different that I do not see it unnatural to love in new ways—not to be unfaithful to any memory." The marvellous Bodichon was the kind of friend we might all hope to have, or strive to be: warm and generous and intuitive. She added that, from all she knew of Lewes, she was sure he would be glad for Eliot.

Charles Lewes, Eliot's stepson, who gave her away at the wedding, said the same thing. He told Anne Thackeray Ritchie, the novelist's daughter, that his father had not a grain of jealousy in him, and would have wanted Eliot to be happy. To Ritchie, Charles also reported a comment of Eliot's, which stands as an unarguable justification for having done what seemed so implausible: if she hadn't been human with feelings and failings like other people, how could she have written her books?

THOSE who cared best for Eliot approved of Cross; literary posterity has been less generous. Scholars have been frustrated by his destruction of the early portions of her diary—the pages dating from 1849, her trip to Geneva, until 1854, when she and Lewes left for Weimar, have been excised—and for the sanitized version of Eliot which he presented in his selections from her letters and journals in his *Life*, a book which William Gladstone disparaged as "a reticence in three volumes." He wasn't her intellectual equal: his one literary production outside of the biography was a volume published in 1893 with the unprepossessing title *Impressions of Dante and of the New World, with a Few Words on Bimetallism.* (This book begins, winningly enough, with an apology: "I confess that it is difficult to find a valid excuse for republishing old magazine articles, and in my own case I cannot plead that any host of admiring friends has put pressure on me to collect mine.")

Perhaps, having become accustomed to veneration in the later years of her literary celebrity, Eliot liked having an adoring acolyte—although it doesn't seem that she made the Casaubon-like demand that he compile her biography after her death, the book being Cross's own enthusiastically embraced project. Or perhaps, as the scholar Rosemarie Bodenheimer has persuasively argued, Eliot knew she needed a caring and invested manager, particularly after seeing how complicated her affairs had become after Lewes's death, when she had distressing difficulty accessing the money she had earned because it was all in a bank account under Lewes's name. The marriage may have been surprising, even to its participants, but it made a certain kind of sense as well.

One lurid detail of Eliot and Cross's brief life together threatens to overwhelm their marital history, as the obituary of a politician will be dominated by the retelling of the embarrassing personal indiscretion that besmirched an otherwise distinguished reputation. While on their wedding trip, a month's meandering tour through France and northern Italy that brought them eventually to Venice, Cross jumped from a window into the Grand Canal. In his *Life* of Eliot he said that the poor air in Venice and the lack of exercise there were to blame. Contemporary gossips and later biographers have speculated that his illness was grounded in psychology, evidence that the scandalous marriage was indeed a dreadful mismatch of temperaments and desires.

Cross's plunge *is* perplexing, and to admirers of Eliot it remains embarrassing—an anomalous digression in what can otherwise be cast as a heroic life's journey. Many critics have been tempted to assume a position of post-Freudian superior knowledge, and to suggest that there must have been a compensatory element in Eliot and Cross's attraction for each other, a submerged desire that was elusive to the participants and that could not survive the ordeal of a bedroom scene. This approach seems to me to be both arrogant and inadequate, and not just because Cross and Eliot had survived bedrooms all across Europe before they got to Venice. Whatever hidden or repressed motives may have influenced Cross's wish to marry Eliot are obscure to us, given how little we know about him, but the suggestion that he sought in Eliot a mother-replacement—and was horrified to discover that his mother-replacement made sexual demands—seems a little too quick, and too pat. What we do know is that Eliot was the author of the most psychologically penetrating novels yet written in the English language, and while all of us are capable at any age of acting upon impulses we don't understand, it seems to me unlikely that Eliot would blunder into a marriage under such a tremendous psychological misapprehension, about her own motivations or about Cross's.

My own inclination is to step back from the bedroom—as a Victorian novelist would have been obliged to do—and to let the event stand in its singular, perplexing strangeness, one episode in Eliot's life, but not its defining one. I prefer, instead, to notice the strange consonance of Cross's leap into the canal with the deaths by water that recur in Eliot's novels: characters drown in *Adam Bede*, *Silas Marner*, and *Daniel Deronda*, and, of course, *The Mill on the Floss*. That novel famously ends when Maggie Tulliver, who has been shamed by an attempted and then aborted riverboat elopement, drowns in the floodwaters of the river powering the mill in which she grew up. Unlike her creator, Maggie cannot escape the provincialism of the world she has been born into.

I prefer to reflect upon something that occurred to me while visiting Eliot's childhood home, where a small pond has now been dug to suggest the one that inspired the Red Deeps in *The Mill on the Floss*—that for all the time Eliot spent living by ponds or canals and visiting seashores, it's unlikely that she ever learned to swim. She never experienced that sense of physical freedom, moving with and against the waves: the elemental awe, the exhilarating solitude that for me is a summertime commonplace. There are areas of experience we take for granted today that for Eliot and her contemporaries were unavailable or obscure. Whatever she and Cross discovered about themselves and each other in their marriage must surely be in some ways unavailable or obscure to us.

What is clear is that Eliot's letters from her wedding journey are those of a woman surprised by joy, and held by it. In Paris they went to La Sainte-Chapelle and to the Luxembourg museum, neither of which Cross had ever seen; they wandered the Champs-Élysées, "looking at our fellow mortals who seem, like ourselves, immensely improvable," and enjoying the late-spring blossoms everywhere. Near the city of Chambéry they gathered roses in the garden that had belonged to Rousseau. In Turin they stayed in a palatial apartment with blue satin draperies and marble baths. Her letters to Cross's family are barely short of blissful. "We seem to love each other better than we did when we set out, which seemed then hardly possible," she wrote to one of her new sisters-in-law.

Letters to Charles Lewes were similarly filled with enthusiasm for the sights she and Cross were seeing and the companionship they were sharing, though her reported happiness was not entirely without qualification. She had but one regret in seeing the beauty of the Alpine foothills, she said, and that was that Lewes had not seen it. "I would still give up my own life willingly if he could have the happiness instead of me," she wrote.

To Barbara Bodichon, the least prejudiced, most broad-minded auditor she knew, Eliot attempted to articulate what this marriage meant to her, coming when she thought that her life might as well have been over. "Deep down below there is a hidden river of sadness but this must always be with those who have lived long," she wrote. But in spite of that sadness, she said, she was able to enjoy her renewed life. She felt that she would be a better creature—less selfish, more open—than she could have been had she remained in solitude. "To be constantly lovingly grateful for the gift of a perfect love is the best illumination of one's mind to all the possible good there may be in store for man on this troublous little planet," she wrote. Her novelistic powers had taken root in the fertile soil of her domestic happiness with Lewes, and she had no faith in her ability to produce anything else without recreating, as best she could, that sense of connectedness and interdependency.

Eliot's sudden death from kidney failure in December 1880, seven months after the wedding, obviated the question of whether life with Cross could prove as generative as her union with Lewes. Cross was left, as he wrote to a friend of Eliot's immediately upon her death, "alone in this new House we meant to be so happy in." That house, in which they lived together for just three weeks, was 4 Cheyne Walk, on the Embankment in London—an impressive terraced structure behind a high locked gate, which today has swagged curtains visible through its graceful Georgian windows and artfully pruned shrubs in its front garden.

I walked there one rainy afternoon through the dauntingly elegant streets of Chelsea. I lived in this neighbourhood once, for a few months, working for a British newspaper when I was in my mid twenties. It was a period of professional turbulence: the job in London was better than the one I had in New York, but I had hated to wrench myself away from my New York life, and I returned within a year. It was also a period of personal confusion: romantically speaking, at least, I was tripping over myself with conflicting impulses towards commitment and towards freedom.

I hadn't yet discovered the two conditions need not be mutually exclusive, and that I might find freedom within commitment.

As I now walked through the wet streets with my head down and umbrella up, recalling that melancholy and lonely time, I pictured my husband on the other side of the Atlantic, imagining him reading on the couch in our living room, under an enormous mahogany bookcase that must have been installed more than a century ago. This bookcase was one of the reasons my husband and I wanted to buy this particular house—it was one of the things that made us think it could be a home to us, our first together, and we filled it with the books that we merged into one collection. A year later we celebrated our wedding in this room, with friends dancing to a band that my husband had recruited from a subway platform. I thought of him, and of Eliot's sober, moving characterization of the conditions of marriage, its demand for self-suppression and tolerance; and I remembered what it is sometimes easy to forget in the busy midst of marriage, that I had promised my husband the support and love that Eliot and Lewes found in each other, and that I was grateful for all the ways he granted me that, and more.

This was an area of London that was once home to all sorts of writers and artists, though judging by the property values it seems unlikely that many remained. Houses were marked with plaques for their illustrious former inhabitants. On Tite Street there was one for Oscar Wilde, who lived there with Constance, his wife, while eventually finding other interests elsewhere; and another for John Singer Sargent, who lived alone, very private about his private life. On Cheyne Walk, a few doors down from Eliot's address, is the house to which Dante Gabriel Rossetti moved after his wife, the painter Elizabeth Siddal, died of an overdose of laudanum. I thought about the often complicated personal lives of artists—about those who have needed to be free of personal encumbrances, or whose spouses have suffered neglect, humiliation, or worse. Perhaps the model of the artist who is willing to sacrifice all for his or her art—the artist who is not culpable for his or her domestic ruthlessness, because it is in the pursuit of something so much more significant—is the one to which the most romance is attached.

Domestic and familial ties are time consuming, and it's easy to imagine all the things that might be accomplished with fewer of them, particularly after breaking off mid paragraph to cook a child's dinner, or setting work aside to help a partner worry over his or hers. But I find Eliot and Lewes's model of a life of work embedded in a life of domestic commitment much more appealing. It gives me greater hope for my own life, with all its obligations. Having endless hours of free time in which to create is hardly useful if most of those hours are spent in a paralysing torpor of loneliness, overwhelmed by anxieties about that loneliness lasting for ever, as I am surely not alone in having discovered.

Eliot wrested for herself an alternative course. Her best work began in being beloved, while middle age granted her an expansion rather than a diminishment of possibility. I cannot exactly call this a comfortable doctrine: the physical and mental exigencies of growing older deny us the prospect of ease, as Eliot knew, too. But even so, I think, it is one worth trying to believe.

Chapter 7

Two Temptations

*"I had once meant to be better than that, and I
am come back to my old intention."*
—*MIDDLEMARCH*, CHAPTER 66

One day on my journey through *Middlemarch*, I found myself in Coventry with an hour or two to spare, and so I went to a bookshop in a pedestrian shopping centre to see if it stocked any volumes about the city's most celebrated author. I was looking for something local—something that I might have missed in my varied hunts through the holdings of secondhand booksellers and the shelves of academic bookshops.

The shop was part of a national chain, and had a chain store's usual priorities: plenty of cookbooks, and shelves filled with established bestsellers. There was, as I expected, a section dedicated to Eliot, though I was surprised at how small it was, and at the simple, hand-lettered sign on it, that read "George Eliot was born in Nuneaton and grew up in Coventry." I thought she deserved something professionally printed, at least.

But among her familiar novels there was one book I hadn't seen before: a volume with the dismaying title *"The Mill on the*

Floss": In Half the Time. It turned out to be one of a series of abridgements of Victorian heavyweights, designed for readers unwilling to countenance the five-hundred-page version of the novel. I flicked through it, trying to see what the editors had deemed dispensable. I could understand the impulse to make the novel more accessible—I want as many people as possible to read *The Mill on the Floss*, too—but, like paperback editions of classic novels issued with updated covers resembling those of *Twilight*, it seemed a pandering and misbegotten effort, as if no young reader today might possibly pick up a novel written 150 years ago unless the book were in sexy, neo-Gothic drag.

As I left the bookstore I wondered idly if I would be alone in welcoming a volume called *"Middlemarch": In Twice the Time.* "What's your favourite book?" is a question that is usually only asked by children and banking identity-verification services—and favourite isn't, anyway, the right word to describe the relationship a reader has with a particularly cherished book. Most serious readers can point to one book that has a place in their life like the one that *Middlemarch* has in mine. I chose *Middlemarch*—or *Middlemarch* chose me—and I cannot imagine life without it. My husband, the most avid reader I know, would choose *In Search of Lost Time* as his most treasured work. One friend insists on the primacy of *David Copperfield*, while another goes back to *The Portrait of a Lady*, and I know them better for knowing that about them.

I continued my walk through Coventry, and discovered a more enticing bookseller in the city's covered market. There, past the displays of halal meat, lemongrass, eddoes, and chow-chows—the foodstuffs of today's Midlands table—I found a stall selling secondhand volumes. Among the well-worn paperback and obsolete celebrity biographies was a prize: *Five Victorians*, by Lytton Strachey. This volume contains Strachey's most famous work, *Eminent Victorians*, a collection of scathing, satirical portraits of four nineteenth-century worthies—they are General Gordon, Florence Nightingale, Cardinal Manning, and Thomas Arnold—which was published in 1918, six months before the end of the Great War. *Five Victorians* also contains Strachey's short biography of Queen Victoria, which was first published as a separate volume in 1921.

If you describe people for a living, as I do, *Eminent Victorians* is an instructive volume as well as an entertaining one, illustrating how an individual can be characterized in a few pointed words or by a telling anecdote. Flicking through the book, I smiled with admiration as I read this passage, in which Strachey recounts the distress of Florence Nightingale's mother after Florence insisted upon becoming a nurse instead of a society wife. "At times, indeed, among her intimates, Mrs. Nightingale almost wept. 'We are ducks,' she said with tears in her eyes, 'who have hatched a wild swan.' But the poor lady was wrong; it was not a swan that they had hatched; it was an eagle."

Strachey didn't include Eliot—or any novelists—among the twelve candidates whom he originally considered to serve as representatives of the Victorian age. But she had moved easily among members of his long list. In her thirties, she had encountered Florence Nightingale; later, Charles Darwin was a visitor at the Priory. She went to the studio of George Watts, the portrait painter. She knew the philosopher Henry Sidgwick, a fellow at

Trinity College, Cambridge. Benjamin Jowett, the master of Balliol College, regarded her as "a kind of saint without a definite creed." She was an object of fascination to Thomas Carlyle (and to his wife, Jane), and she was editing the *Westminster Review* when John Stuart Mill appeared in its pages.

If anybody came to be regarded as an eminent Victorian by the Victorians themselves, it was George Eliot. The success that came in her later years displaced the scandal that had been attached to her name. No less an establishment figure than Victoria herself was an admirer: she sought out the novelist's autograph for her collection. (The queen's oldest son, later King Edward VII, was a devoted fan: by 1886, he had read *Middlemarch* fifteen times, or once a year since its publication.) Upon her death, in 1880, Eliot was acclaimed as a voice of the age. Lord Acton, the historian, compared her with Shakespeare, to Shakespeare's disadvantage. "In problems of life and thought, which baffled Shakespeare disgracefully, her touch was unfailing," Acton wrote in a letter a few days after she died. Five years later, in a review of Cross's *Life*, he wrote, "As the emblem of a generation distracted between the intense need of believing and the difficulty of belief, [her books] will live to the last syllable of recorded time."

Obituaries and recollections of Eliot dwelled upon her wisdom and her moral seriousness. Frederic W. H. Myers, who taught at Trinity College, Cambridge, gave memorable voice to the sentiment of veneration she inspired. "I remember how, at Cambridge, I walked with her once in the Fellows' Garden of Trinity, on an evening of rainy May," Myers wrote in the *Century*. "She, stirred somewhat beyond her wont, and taking as her text the three words which have been used so often as the inspiring trumpet-calls of men—the words *God, Immortality, Duty*—pronounced, with terrible earnestness, how inconceivable was the first, how unbelievable the second, and yet how peremptory and absolute the third." Myers continued in a similarly awestruck vein: "I listened, and night fell; her grave, majestic countenance turned towards me like a sibyl's in the gloom; it was as though she withdrew from my grasp, one by one, the two scrolls of promise, and left me the third scroll only, awful with inevitable fates. And when we stood at length and parted, amid that columnar circuit of the forest-trees, beneath the last twilight of starless skies, I seemed to be gazing, like Titus at Jerusalem, on vacant seats and empty halls—on a sanctuary with no Presence to hallow it, and heaven left lonely of a God."

Lytton Strachey was born only a few months before Eliot's death, and by the time he was a young man an anecdote like this one, told in such elevated language, would have been considered utterly risible. By then, Eliot's earnestness was considered not just terrible, but ludicrous. Eliot herself had become a byword for obsolescence: in a letter Strachey wrote in his twenties he dismissively summed up an older woman of his acquaintance by calling her "incredibly affected, queer, stupid and intelligent. She flowed with reflections on life, and reminiscences of George Eliot, and criticisms of obscure French poetesses who flourished in 1850."

A quirky coincidence links Strachey and Eliot: three days before Eliot died she attempted to write a letter to Jane Strachey, mother of the infant Lytton, with whom she was acquainted, but being ill, she left the letter unfinished in her writing case. "The pen which had delighted and comforted so many minds and hearts here made its last mark," Cross wrote in his *Life*, using language that would also have caused the grown-up Lytton to snigger. To Strachey, as well as to other intellectuals of the early part of the twentieth century, Eliot was part of a bygone era that was the better for being gone.

The falling-off of regard was precipitous. Almost immediately after Eliot's death critics vied with each other to demonstrate their own vitality by thinking up new ways to characterize her deadliness. "It is doubtful whether they are novels disguised as treatises, or treatises disguised as novels," one critic wrote of her works. Another delivered the verdict that her books "seem to have been dictated to a plain woman of genius by the ghost of David Hume." In 1895 George Saintsbury was able to note that while her novels might still be *read*, they were not admired by anyone whose opinion counted for anything. (Saintsbury was a well-known literary critic, whom no one now reads.)

Eliot's reputation was not helped by the publication of Cross's *Life* in 1886. In editing her letters and journals, Cross discarded the mundane or indiscreet and retained the oracular. This was an editorial choice that emphasized Eliot's own undeniable inclinations. Even in the unexpurgated editions of her private documents, published much later, she is sometimes unappealingly ponderous. The priggish, judgemental adolescent was not entirely displaced by the broad-minded, empathetic intellectual.

Some writers are as vividly engaging in their correspondence as they are in their published works—think of D. H. Lawrence. But if you were to read George Eliot's letters and journals to the exclusion of her novels, it would be easy to see her as pedantic, humourless—even unimaginative. Her observations about the places she visits are often surprisingly banal. "We walked through the Museum this morning and were struck with the beauty of the interior and the excellent arrangement of the works of art," she wrote while in Berlin; the museum had, she observed, "an interesting collection." She was sometimes snappishly misanthropic, as when she complained about the "disgustingly coarse Belgians with baboonish children" with whom she was obliged to share a railway carriage.

Everyone is entitled to resort to banality or misanthropy on occasion, especially in a private diary or correspondence, and noisy children on trains can be incredibly grating on the nerves, particularly when you are their mother. But, still, it is surprising and difficult to find Eliot so unappealing in moments like these. Her letters and journals are fascinating for the light they shed on her struggles and her achievements, and she is often admirable and almost always inspiring in them. But it is much harder to be in her company there, at length, than it is when reading her novels. Her humour, on the occasions when it is expressed, is often laboured. Once, after making note of the many comments she has received about *Adam Bede* and its "influence for good on individual minds," she added, "The merely egoistic satisfactions of fame are easily nullified by toothache, and *that* has made my chief consciousness for the last week." That's about as much fun as she gets.

Some who encountered her found her unbearable. Fellow novelist Eliza Lynn Linton wrote in her memoir of "the pretentious assumption of superior morality" that she detected in Eliot's self-presentation in her later years. "Not a line of spontaneity was left in her; not an impulse beyond the reach of self-conscious philosophy," Linton wrote. "She was always the goddess on her pedestal." Linton was jealous and her remarks were mean-spirited, but the characteristics she described were merely those that Myers admired, seen from a different angle.

By the time Eliot's centenary came around, in 1919, knocking the goddess from the pedestal was irresistible. When in that year the critic Edmund Gosse wrote an essay about Eliot he began it not with reference to her works but to her appearance, having once glimpsed her in a carriage on a London street, "a large, thick-set sybil, dreamy and immobile, whose massive features, some-what grim when seen in profile, were incongruously bordered by a hat, always in the height of the Paris fashion, which in those days commonly included an immense ostrich feather." Gosse added, "The contrast between the solemnity of the face and the frivolity of the headgear had something pathetic and provincial about it." She had become, as Virginia Woolf wrote in her own centennial reevaluation, "one of the butts for youth to laugh at"—an overly serious woman once taken overly seriously by a coterie of adoring, deluded admirers.

Woolf's essay was crucial in beginning the rehabilitation of Eliot, which culminated in her inclusion in *The Great Tradition*, by the critic F. R. Leavis, in 1948. But even Woolf could not resist a crack at Eliot's expense. She cited a scrap of Eliot's conversation that had been preserved in another person's reminiscence: "We know by our own experience how very much others affect our lives, and we must remember that we in turn must have the same effect on others," Eliot had said. About this remembered quotation, Woolf remarked: "Jealously treasured, committed to memory, one can imagine recalling the scene, repeating the words, thirty years later and suddenly, for the first time, bursting into laughter."

Is this still laughable? It seems to me that this reflex of embarrassment has diminished as our distance from Eliot has grown. In fact, turning Eliot's pronouncements—or what are taken to be Eliot's pronouncements—into inspirational mottoes has become a small industry, although when her words are used this way they inevitably seem more portentous or saccharine than in their original context. At the Nuneaton museum you can buy a pocket mirror on the reverse of which are words spoken by Mirah Lapidoth, a character in *Daniel Deronda*: "I think my life began with waking up and loving my mother's face." (This, from a novelist whose fictional mothers, almost without exception, are far from idealized.) A quotation attributed to Eliot, "It's never too late to be what you might have been," crops up endlessly on Twitter and on the websites of motivational consultants—although, after all my reading and all my questioning of scholars, I have yet to find it in her works. Its message, proposing the endless possibility of self-reinvention, seems precisely counter to what is implied by *Middlemarch*, which shows how it can grow altogether too late for lots of things.

Such quotations—even ones that Eliot actually wrote—are reductive, and not at all helpful to her contemporary reputation. Why read even *"The Mill on the Floss": In Half the Time* if you can get all the Eliot you need on a magnet? They eliminate the subtlety of her books and the pleasure they provide—including the pleasure of wondering whether there might be a simple, motto-like moral to her stories, as in a fable, and then discovering that there isn't. As a child Eliot had owned and adored an illustrated volume of Aesop's fables, but her novels were not intended to be didactic morality tales. Certainly some early readers thought her books alarmingly *immoral*, with their sympathetic depiction of alcoholics and child murderers and other supposedly lost souls.

Still, it's not difficult to see why Eliot's novels seem to invite this kind of excerpting. Eliot was absolutely convinced of her duty to instruct and enlighten. She thought a great deal about the moral effect of her works upon her readers, even if she rarely articulated her intentions in 140 characters or fewer. She said that the "inspiring principle" that gave her courage to write was that of "so presenting our human life as to help my readers in getting a clearer conception and a more active admiration of those vital elements which bind men together and give a higher worthiness to their existence." She took satisfaction in having produced work that would "gladden and chasten human hearts," an aspiration with a distinctly religious resonance.

To the extent that she had a faith, it was in what she called "meliorism"—the conviction that, through the small, beneficent actions and intentions of individuals, the world might gradually grow to be a better place. By the time that Woolf and Gosse were writing, in the terrible wake of the Great War, the world of Eliot's novels seemed far distant, as did the problem of wavering between faith and disbelief to which Lord Acton had alluded. "We happen to live, fortunately or unfortunately for ourselves, in a generation which is 'distracted' by quite other problems," Gosse observed. In 1919, with Europe ravaged and eight and a half million young men dead, a meliorist view of history would have been especially hard to sustain.

Even for Eliot, her slender, secular faith in the betterment of the world seems to have been willed—born of intellectual exertion, not received like a gift of grace. Critics called *Middlemarch* melancholy. She disputed that. "My book will not present my own feelings about human life if it produces on readers whose minds are really receptive the impression of blank melancholy and despair," she wrote to one correspondent. But her protest rings only partially true. *Middlemarch* is not a despairing book, but it *is* a melancholy one. Eliot is the great artist of disappointment. Her characters, even the good ones, stumble, fall, and fail—not into inexorable tragedy, for the most part, but into limited, mortal resignation.

Some among her admirers protested that her perspective was too bleak. Bessie Rayner Parkes, at one time Eliot's close friend, insisted in her own tribute that Eliot's Dorothea had set her ambitions too low, given the number of women of the time, including Queen Victoria and Florence Nightingale, who had made their mark. The example of the latter real-life heroine, born in 1820—about a decade after Eliot places the birth of Dorothea Brooke—might seem to belie Eliot's concluding observation that the world now cannot accommodate a new Saint Teresa because "the medium in which [her] ardent deeds took shape is for ever gone." Nightingale was no saint, as Strachey took delight in showing, but she was certainly more than the "foundress of nothing" Eliot put at the centre of her story.

But in *Middlemarch*, Eliot was not concerned with showing the effects of large, heroic acts, particularly those performed by extraordinary individuals. The gradual betterment with which she was concerned in this novel was not the good work of charity, or of grand, noble gestures of sacrifice. Eliot took it as a given that she should contribute to good causes, do good works, and help needier relations, however bizarre the relationship might be.

(It was mostly with her earnings that Lewes continued to provide for his estranged wife Agnes and her offspring with Thornton Hunt.) But she was more concerned with changing her reader's perspective than she was in encouraging that reader to contribute to soup kitchens. Her credo might be expressed this way: If I really care for you—if I try to think myself into your position and orientation—then the world is bettered by my effort at understanding and comprehension. If you respond to my effort by trying to extend the same sympathy and understanding to others in turn, then the betterment of the world has been minutely but significantly extended. "We want people to feel with us, more than to act for us," she once wrote to a friend.

In order to do as Eliot urges her readers—to feel with you, and care for you—I must take you seriously. And to do that, it follows that I must first take myself seriously. Eliot took herself very seriously, and in the backlash that followed her death that seriousness was sometimes taken to be sanctimony. It may be tempting to laugh at her remembered pronouncements, as even so sympathetic a reader as Virginia Woolf did. To Woolf's generation, Eliot's earnestness was an embarrassment. From the perspective of the youth of the immediate post-Victorian era, Eliot had committed the unforgivable offence of being old. A hundred years later, though, Eliot's melancholy, willed seriousness resonates. It suggests that we, her readers, should take ourselves as seriously as she took us.

"THERE is no general doctrine which is not capable of eating out our morality if unchecked by the deep-seated habit of direct fellow-feeling with individual fellow-men," Eliot writes in

Middlemarch. The object of this authorial observation is Nicholas Bulstrode, the wealthy, ostentatiously religious banker who has long adopted an attitude of pious subjection to God's will as "the mould into which he had constrained his immense need of being something important and predominating." By selectively lending and investing money, and contributing funds to pet causes, Bulstrode has exerted control over the worldly goings-on of Middlemarch, all the while professing to be thinking only of readying his soul for the world to come. Bulstrode is the closest thing *Middlemarch* has to a villain, but his villainy does not spring from pure malevolence. Rather it is the product of a moral deficit. In Bulstrode, Eliot presents a self-appointed man of God who fails to demonstrate compassion and sympathy—the ethical precepts that Eliot believed were worth salvaging from the Christianity she had rejected.

When Eliot rejected Christianity, she set herself the harder task of determining what her own guiding ethics would be. In the last essay she wrote for the *Westminster Review* Eliot gave as good an exposition of her moral code as she did anywhere. The essay is a scything indictment of Edward Young, the eighteenth-century poet-cleric whom she had adored in her youth. By 1858, when she wrote the essay, she had diagnosed a falsity in his theology and morality, which, she argued, contributed to a fundamental insincerity in his poetry.

Young, she wrote, adheres to abstractions—"Virtue sitting on a mount serene," "Religion coming down from the skies"—while paying no attention to "virtue or religion as it really exists." Virtue as it really exists, she went on to say, can be found "in courageous effort for unselfish ends, in the internal triumph of justice and pity over personal resentment, in all the sublime self-renunciation and sweet charities which are found in the details of ordinary life." Virtue is ethical practice, not theoretical doctrine.

Nicholas Bulstrode is not a clergyman, though as a young man he was active in a Calvinist dissenting church, and considered becoming a preacher or a missionary. At sixty, he is the oldest of the central characters in the novel, and not native to Middlemarch. He grew up in London, an orphan and a charity-school student, then became a subordinate to a pawnbroker—whose trade, it turned out, was in stolen goods. He rose in the business and was much admired for his acumen and his piety by the pawnbroker's wife, herself a devout woman who was unaware of the true contours of her husband's dealings. When the pawnbroker died, Bulstrode took over the business, and not long afterwards he also married the pawnbroker's widow. Within a few years the widow died, and Bulstrode's fortune was made.

By the time the reader meets him, Bulstrode is living comfortably in the town of Middlemarch, having for almost thirty years repressed, more or less successfully, one piece of knowledge from his past: the pawnbroker and his wife were survived by a daughter, who had run away from home upon discovering the criminal foundation of her father's business. This daughter was rightfully the heir of the fortune Bulstrode had appropriated. Now, a florid stranger named Raffles has arrived in Middlemarch, threatening to expose Bulstrode's past.

Raffles is no stranger to Bulstrode. Years earlier, Bulstrode engaged Raffles to track down the pawnbroker's daughter—and then, when she was found, having married the son of a Polish refugee, Bulstrode paid Raffles to keep quiet about her existence, so that he would not have to surrender his fortune to her. Eventually Raffles, shattered by drink and desperate for income, stumbles across the surviving son of the pawnbroker's daughter—none other than Will Ladislaw.

Raffles's discovery threatens to ruin Bulstrode, undermining his high social position and making a mockery of his professed piety. In Book Seven of *Middlemarch*, "Two Temptations," Bulstrode's mounting deceptions in the name of piety have a horrific consequence. He finds himself wishing for Raffles's death, and acting in a way that hastens it, claiming all the while the flimsy justification of Providence.

The Raffles subplot, with its piling up of extraordinary coincidences, looks in its outlines like something transposed from a very different kind of Victorian novel. Raffles's very name is Dickensian, and so are the twists that bring him into the path of Bulstrode and Ladislaw. Strange coincidences do occur in real life as well as in novels, but it is in the plot concerning Raffles and Bulstrode that a reader sees most clearly the machinery of the novelist at work. I find it the hardest part of the novel to hold in my head as I am reading, or to remember the details of afterwards. It is like being immersed in a new, complicated Victorian melodrama. The intrigue is crucial to the working out of the novel's plot, but it is far from being what *Middlemarch* is *about*.

What is most compelling about Bulstrode's story is not the outward unfolding of plot—though there is a satisfyingly lurid tension to it—but the depiction of his own inward, organic, psychological movement. Eliot accomplishes what D. H. Lawrence gave her credit for doing before any other novelist: "It was she who started putting all the action inside." The reader learns of Bulstrode's initial shrinking from involvement in the shady business of the pawnbroker—and then of his self-justification for taking the work on, since he would thereby be transforming illegally won gains into funds for doing God's work. Bulstrode, crucially, is not a coarse hypocrite. "He was simply a man whose desire had been stronger than his theoretic beliefs, and who had gradually explained the gratification of his desires into satisfactory agreement with those beliefs," Eliot writes. She adds, "If this be hypocrisy, it is a process which shows itself occasionally in us all, to whatever confession we belong."

Bulstrode holds to his faith as a set of rigid, abstract rules, not as a lived practice of compassion. In this, he differs entirely from Eliot's depiction of "virtue or religion as it really exists" in the person of the Reverend Camden Farebrother, the vicar of St. Botolph's church. A keen amateur entomologist, Farebrother has become a clergyman more out of familial obligation than a sense of vocation. He supports an elderly mother, an aunt, and an unmarried sister on an inadequate income of four hundred pounds a year. He delivers pithy sermons, which draw listeners from parishes other than his own, but his religion is shown in how he treats others, rather than how he preaches to them. "His position is not quite like that of the Apostles," Lydgate says of Farebrother. "He is only a parson among parishioners whose lives he has to try and make better." Farebrother, as his name suggests, is among the most appealing characters in the book: intelligent, caring, generous, and very far from perfect.

In Book Seven of *Middlemarch*, Farebrother faces his own temptation. He is in love with Mary Garth, and she admires and likes him. Fred Vincy, who hopes to marry Mary, has been playing billiards at the Green Dragon tavern, where participants often gamble on the outcome of games. Farebrother knows that if Fred is drawn back into a life of idleness and dissipation Mary might reconsider her commitment to marry him, and that she might then begin to look at the vicar in the light of a husband, instead. Farebrother is momentarily tempted to do nothing to hinder Fred's slide, but he quickly realizes that he could not bear to profit by Fred's moral devaluation. He speaks to Fred, reminding him of his commitment to be worthy of Mary, and in doing so Farebrother deprives himself of the possibility of finding his own happiness with Mary. It's an enormous sacrifice, given with a shake of the hand and the shrug of the shoulder that is the vicar's habitual gesture.

Farebrother never articulates his faith in *Middlemarch*—unlike Bulstrode, he feels no need to vaunt it. But in her essay on Young, Eliot gave voice to a man—or woman—who feels beholden to others out of felt sympathy, not because of abstract doctrine. "I am just and honest, not because I expect to live in another world, but because, having felt the pain of injustice and dishonesty towards myself, I have a fellow-feeling with other men, who would suffer the same pain if I were unjust or dishonest towards them," she wrote. "It is a pang to me to witness the suffering of a fellow-being, and I feel his suffering the more acutely because he is *mortal*—because his life is so short, and I would have it, if possible, filled with happiness and not misery."

This is not a doctrine the vicar of St. Boltoph's would be likely to preach from the pulpit, given that it relies upon humanist fellowship rather than Christian faith, but I can imagine him saying something like this to himself when he is alone in his study, turning over his insect specimens, irrevocably putting the happiness of others before his own.

In the summer of 1871, while working on *Middlemarch*, Eliot received a short letter from a young Scotsman called Alexander Main, who had a question: what was the correct pronunciation of *Romola*? Gratified by Main's admiration of the book, which had been published in 1863—he called its prologue "the sublimest piece of writing, thinking, and historical word-painting, all in one, that the pen of a human being has ever yet achieved in prose"—Eliot wrote back at some length, not only giving him the correct pronunciation (stress on the first *o*) but putting down some thoughts about Florentine literature and Sir Walter Scott. Main replied instantly with a longer letter, filled with impassioned praise. "You are doing a work in and upon this age such that future generations shall rejoice that you have lived," he said.

Eliot was notoriously diffident, and was susceptible to crippling self-doubt. She had as an author what Lewes called "a shy, shrinking, ambitious nature," and found it hard to hold on to any sense of her own accomplishment. She was well used to compliments, but even so, she may have been somewhat taken aback by this unusual outpouring from Main. She replied only briefly and with moderation, thanking him and telling him that she was "deeply affected" by his words, but taking pains to mention that she was too busy for much letter writing. Having been drawn in by Main's enthusiasm, she quickly sought to put a distance between herself and him.

There was, however, no chance of that. Main quickly went

on to write more letters further exalting Eliot and her works, particularly her long poem, *The Spanish Gypsy*—during the reading of which, he told her, "I have felt myself face to face with the Highest in Humanity." This was a statement that could not better have been calculated to please her, since Eliot was deeply invested in her poetry, which is almost never read today. She wrote back, telling Main that he had thoroughly understood her intention and had entered with perfect insight into the poem's significance. His letter had made her cry.

The letters from Scotland kept coming, arriving at a tremendous pace. (It's shocking to realize how much better the postal service was in the 1870s than it is today. If Eliot and her correspondents didn't quite have the instantaneous back-and-forth of e-mail, they had the advantage of multiple daily postal deliveries, and very swift physical transit of mail.) Emboldened, Main wrote back with a proposal. Her works, he said, contained "*essences* of high truth, heart-searching *Thoughts* which go to the very roots of our being—and all these expressed in single sentences and paragraphs." Would it not be doing her an act of justice, and the reading public a good turn, to collect such salient expressions of wisdom and compile them in a single volume?

Eliot—and Lewes, who always had an eye for the marketplace—agreed. Blackwood became Main's publisher, and Main went on to become the editor of a collection titled *Wise, Witty, and Tender Sayings, in Prose and Verse, Selected from the Works of George Eliot*. In a preface, Main declared that Eliot had "for ever sanctified the Novel by making it the vehicle of the grandest and most uncompromising moral truth." The book was dedicated to her, "in recognition of a genius as original as it is profound and a morality as pure as it is impassioned."

My copy of *Wise, Witty, and Tender Sayings*, which I bought a few years ago from a secondhand bookseller, is the tenth edition, from 1896, which gives Main an enviably long time on the backlist. It's bound in sage green, with delicate, ornamental gold lettering on the front, and inside it's inscribed with a dedication from someone called Mary to someone called Lillie, and a date, 1903.

When I thumb through its pages of quotations, some of them extending for more than a page, printed in a font size that has me reaching for reading glasses, I am overcome by a dreadful sense of depletion. I can think of no surer way to be put off the work of George Eliot than by trying to read the *Wise, Witty, and Tender Sayings*. On any given page is an out-of-context pronouncement—"iteration, like friction, is likely to generate heat instead of progress"—or a phrase so recondite that it requires several readings before it can be parsed. Consider this, from *Romola*: "A course of action which is in strictness a slowly prepared out-growth of the entire character, is yet almost always traceable to a single impression as its point of apparent origin." I know what it means—I even think I agree with it—but out of context, it is dead. Main's book is the nineteenth-century equivalent of the refrigerator magnet.

Blackwood dismissed Main as a sycophant, privately referring to him as "The Gusher" and "The Worshipper of Genius" even while making money from him, and most of Eliot's biographers have been similarly critical. Contemporary reviewers were not impressed by Main's effort, either. The *Westminster Review*, Eliot's old editorial home, wrote off the *Sayings* in its "Belles Lettres" section, saying that Main had done George Eliot a disservice. "He is one of those officious friends, who are always bringing you into trouble," the reviewer wrote. "As he does not know exactly what to worship, he worships anything, good, bad, or indifferent." Even more favourable reviewers acknowledged that Main had put Eliot's work to a challenging test by so sifting and reducing it. The *Nation* said that her assent to the book's publication "suggests that George Eliot thinks more of the duties of a teacher than of the reputation of a novelist."

Eliot had her own misgivings about the project, once it was finished at least. "Unless my readers are more moved towards the ends I seek by works as wholes than by an assemblage of extracts, my writings are a mistake," she wrote, when the second edition was being planned. She had thought about the reductive effect of extraction earlier in her career and been alarmed by the simplification that comes from quotation. In *The Mill on the Floss*, she warned against the "men of maxims," and wrote that all people of "broad, strong sense" are sceptical of such men, "because such people early discern that the mysterious complexity of our life is not to be embraced by maxims, and that to lace ourselves up in formulas of that sort is to repress all the divine promptings and inspirations that spring from growing insight and sympathy." Main found this thought so well expressed that he included it in his book of maxims.

So why did Eliot agree to the publication of *Wise, Witty, and Tender Sayings* in the first place? In part, certainly, she saw it as a marketing tool for her novels. And Main was not the first to suggest that Eliot's works be mined for moral wisdom: as Leah Price, a professor of English at Harvard, has demonstrated, quotations appeared during Eliot's lifetime in schoolbooks, parliamentary debates, an army officer's examination, and a calendar. But I suspect that Eliot's positive response to Main's proposal was not only a pragmatic decision. There was an emotional element to the choice, as well. He seems to have touched something in her, and she seems to have taken him seriously.

And so I wanted to take Main seriously, too. In order to read all his letters, not just the few that have been excerpted, often with belittling commentary, in books about Eliot, I went to Edinburgh, to the National Library of Scotland, where his side of the correspondence is kept. As the home of her publisher, Edinburgh was an important city to Eliot, though she only went there twice in her life. The first time was in 1845, when she was in her mid twenties, during a tour of the north of England and Scotland with the Brays. The physical drama of the city thrilled her, with twisting medieval lanes on one side of the castle mount, and, on the other, a harmonious street plan of handsome Georgian buildings.

She went back in 1852, and visited George Combe, the phrenologist. "I have a beautiful view from my room window—masses of wood, distant hills, the Firth, and four splendid buildings dotted far apart—not an ugly object to be seen," she wrote to the Brays. "When I look out in the morning it is as if I had waked up in Utopia or Icaria or one of [Robert] Owen's parallelograms." Blackwood invited Eliot to Edinburgh in the summer of 1871, to attend a centenary celebration for Sir Walter Scott, but she declined, in one of her letters that does show an appealing flash of wit. "I think that prudence advises me to abstain from the fatigue and excitement of a long railway journey with a great gathering at the end of it," she wrote. "If there is a chance that 'Middlemarch' will be good for anything, I don't want to break down and die without finishing it."

My first morning in the city, fortified with coffee, I went to a windowless room in the National Library and retrieved Main's letters, which are bound into a single volume. As I read, a picture of him began to emerge, enhancing somewhat jaundiced descriptions given by Blackwood, after their first encounter, of "a little fellow, dark with bright clear-looking eyes," who "used his knife in a dangerous manner at lunch."

Main was thirty years old when the correspondence began, and lived with his elderly widowed mother in Arbroath, a small town on the eastern coast of Scotland. In the letters he described no occupation beyond giving lectures on literary subjects to young men, whose moral growth he sought to mentor. He was not well off, and had to wait for Eliot's books to be published in cheap editions in order to own them. He was given to taking walks along the cliffs to the east of the town, finding a spot on the beach where he could sit and read aloud to himself from Eliot's works "without the awkward risk of being voted crazy," as he confessed in one letter.

As I read Main's copious correspondence I found myself alternately appalled and moved by the glimpses it offered into the life of this sad, shadowy man. There was something alarming, almost stalker-like, in his attentions. Over and over again he wrote Eliot long, effusive letters, then followed up with a demand for reassurance that his effusion had not given offence, then offered apologies for his neediness. On one occasion he told her, "I should like to see you in your home, but I think I should myself choose to be unseen the while—if that could be. I could not be disappointed in you, but you might easily be disappointed in me." I wondered how Eliot could not have recoiled from what started to feel to me like a creepy imposition.

For all the pages that he wrote—some of the letters cover a dozen sides of writing paper—Main gave very little of himself away. He devoted pots of ink to rhapsodic pronouncements of the beneficial effects Eliot's work had had on his life, but when Eliot asked him to tell her a little of "the general web" of that life—using a metaphor that figures prominently in *Middlemarch*—he darted out of sight. "I do not think that fuller knowledge would sink me in your estimation, but my life would look like a feature-less one indeed were I only to show you its outward aspect, with no thorough disclosure of the inner mechanism," he told her. He professed that he was not strong enough to offer that degree of disclosure, at least not yet. There was something he wasn't telling her—or there was something he was pretending not to tell her, so that she would be drawn further into an engagement with him.

Sometimes Lewes wrote to Main instead of Eliot, when she was too busy to respond, and then Main made a correspondent of Lewes, too. To him, Main confessed that he was still unmar-ried. "Perhaps I have hitherto *idealized* too much, and who, dear Sir, can find a *realized ideal* as you have done?" he wrote. He re-quested Eliot's photograph—a request that smacks today of fan-dom, though it was also borne of a simple desire to know what Eliot looked like, so few images of her were there in circulation. She said she didn't have one. When Eliot and Lewes asked him to send them his photograph so that they could picture him, he said he didn't have one, either. He had once had his portrait taken, he acknowledged. In it he looked like a Member of Parliament, according to a gentleman he knew, while a lady of his acquaintance observed that he looked painfully sad and world-weary. "I couldn't then, I cannot now, reconcile the two observations; but I feel at times that the *lady* must have caught some glimpse of the truth," he wrote.

In the letters he did sound world-weary for his years, prematurely despondent over the state of civilization. His book of quotations, he told Eliot, "will be one of the richest and rarest in the English language—almost too good to bestow upon a faithless and perverse generation like the present." Having once thought of entering the ministry—he told Blackwood he spent three years at Glasgow University for that purpose—he had become dismissive of clerical teaching. Instead, he chose to worship Eliot, describing her work, to her, as "a mighty protest against all emasculated forms of the religious feeling." He referred to his copy of a book of her poems as his "breviary." He was rapturous at Eliot's suggestion to him that she had been nourished by his appreciation of her. "To the benign influence which your works have shed over me for many years has now been added the closer and still more tender and potent influence of a strong personal regard," he wrote. "Every time I think of you (and, for the last five months especially, when have I *not* thought of you?) I feel and am better—more like what I ought to be."

The letters took me two long days to read, my eyes dry and strained by evening, much too fatigued to appreciate the inspired parallelograms of Edinburgh after the library shut its doors. But as I sat at my desk and went through them, I found myself drawn into Main's consciousness. He was in some ways repellent—fawning and pretentious and overly familiar. But he was intriguing, too, with his secret concealments and his mysterious involvements. Reading his letters was as suggestive as reading preliminary notes for a novel, in which a character and his motives are sketched out. There was a whole story submerged beneath.

And as I read, I thought I understood better why Eliot had responded to Main as she did. Obviously, she was gratified by his appreciation for her poetry and the novel *Romola*—which had not sold as well as expected, although Eliot was paid an enormous advance for it from George Smith, the publisher of *Cornhill Magazine*, the one occasion on which she strayed from Blackwood. (She received ten thousand pounds, "the most magnificent offer ever yet made for a novel," as Lewes trumpeted at the time.)

But Eliot must also have been moved by Main's frequent assurances that her work was achieving the elevated moral effect she had intended. In one of the few personal anecdotes he permitted himself, Main told her that he had been watching at the bedside of a twenty-three-year-old nephew, who had just died of an unspecified condition brought on by what Main characterized as a reckless indulgence in vice. "There I realized, as I had never done before, *the need for you* in a world where such things are: and I blessed you in the silence of that death chamber," Main wrote. "It is the supreme glory of your works that they both encourage the hearts of those who are manfully struggling to rise, and tend to stagger and sober the many who are falling away."

This goes beyond the usual compliments that an author like Eliot would be accustomed to receiving, and it would have appealed to her core. In Main's correspondence, Eliot received testimony that she was, as she hoped, doing something good for the world with her novels. At the same time, his praise would have answered her shy, shrinking ambition, her tremulous egoism—until, perhaps, she could not quite tell the two effects apart. And this may explain why she consented to the problematic project of the *Wise, Witty, and Tender Sayings*. In seeking to hold on to the principles of Farebrother, Eliot was tempted into the vanities of Bulstrode. Main encouraged her to bring the gratification of her desires into alignment with the satisfaction of her beliefs.

In her 1858 essay on Edward Young, Eliot criticized the poet's "unintermitting habit of pedagogic moralizing." Young, she says, views God as a didactic author, a "Divine Instructor," whose heavens are "forever *scolding* as they shine." This, she argues, is an indication of a moral deficit on the part of Young—at least when morality is defined, as Eliot defines it, as sympathetic emotion. It is also an artistic deficit. "In proportion as morality is emotional, i.e., has affinity with Art, it will exhibit itself in direct sympathetic feeling and action, and not as the recognition of a rule," she writes. "Love does not say 'I ought to love'—it loves. Pity does not say, 'It is right to be pitiful'—it pities. Justice does not say, 'I am bound to be just'—it feels justly."

She goes on to say that dependency upon a rule or theory only is necessary when moral emotion is weak. "We think experience, both in literature and in life, has shown that the minds which are pre-eminently didactic—which insist on a lesson and despise everything that will not convey a moral, are deficient in sympathetic emotion," she writes. "A man who is perpetually thinking in apothegms, who has an unintermittent flux of admonition, can have little energy left for simple emotion."

In her novels, Eliot sought to elicit simple emotion through complex means. She certainly wanted her readers to respond to her novels as more than compelling stories. She wanted to edify, but she wanted to do so without lecturing or hectoring. Alexander Main, her dangerous acolyte, sought to dispel the nebulous complexity of her work by deliberately reducing her to bright apophthegms that eliminated her subtler shading. This was something that even he seems to have recognized, however dimly, was an act of violence. Blackwood sent him an edition of her works from which he could physically cull his quotations. "Had anybody told me a few weeks ago that I should live to *cut up* George Eliot's works, and not only so, but to take pleasure in the operation, I fear I should have knocked him down," Main wrote to Eliot. "But here I am clipping and slashing great gashes out of writings every line of which I hold sacred, and finding a *delight* almost fiendish in the work of destruction." I am reminded of him wielding the knife dangerously at the publisher's dining table. This is a letter that must have made Eliot quietly glad her great admirer was several hundred miles away.

Wise, Witty, and Tender Sayings was published in January 1872, a month after the first volume of *Middlemarch* appeared. "Had your new and great work been to see the light just three or four weeks later than its proposed appearance—why, you and I might have made a *bona fide* exchange!" Main wrote to Eliot in the weeks before publication, with delusions of parity. He seems to have seen his work not only as an honouring of Eliot but also as an expression of his own creativity, claiming a kind of joint authorship with her, his idol. He pointed out to her, after receiving his copy of the first installment of *Middlemarch*, that his book had been advertised on its back page, and relished that their names would "go down the stream of time together, in loving fellowship, the one behind, the other before, as travellers on horseback used sometimes to journey when the world was not so nice as it now has become."

Over the next year, as *Middlemarch* was published, his letters multiplied. He catalogued his evolving responses to the work as he consumed each volume, which he seems to have read with his second edition very much in mind, always looking for passages to excise. He had firm ideas about plot and character, which he conveyed with an air of intimate confidentiality. "My dear Mrs. Lewes, you really must get that Casaubon quietly, decently, and gravely of course, *out of the way*," he wrote, after receiving a presentation copy of Book One. After reading Book Two, he wondered worriedly what would become of Dorothea. "I keep asking myself what I think she will *do*, when her sorrows become too great for passive endurance," Main wrote. "Will she *write*, I wonder?" Book Three prompted an extravagant fourteen-page letter in which Main exalted Dorothea's sacrifice in her marriage to Casaubon. "Less trial would mean less victory; less sorrow would mean less joy; less struggle would mean a smaller nature," he wrote. "She may indeed leave the world at least 'foundress of nothing'—but only in one sense; in another, foundress of a great moral empire, a kingdom within her own soul."

Upon receiving this last letter, Eliot sent a kindly warning. "Try to keep from forecast of Dorothea's lot, and that sort of construction beforehand which makes everything that actually happens a disappointment," she wrote, with impressive restraint. Main didn't take her admonition to heart. In yet another disquisition, he wrote in impassioned detail of what he saw clearly: that Dorothea and Ladislaw must be morally impelled to renounce each other, in spite of their mutual love. "She faithful and he faithful, they will keep their souls, like consecrated vessels pure and spotless, for each other's use, *some*where or *some*where, in some other corner of this mysterious Universe, in some other section of this mysterious Time," Main wrote, in a prediction that turned out to be as erroneous as it was overblown.

Reading these letters about *Middlemarch* was a disquieting experience. Main's assumption of intimacy with Eliot made me cringe, and yet I recognized in his enthusiasm for her works enough of my own admiration for her to feel an awkward fellowship with him. Main is the naive reader writ large—the kind of reader who approaches a book not with an academic's theoretical apparatus or the scope of a professional critic, but who reads with commitment and intelligence, and with a conviction that there is something worth learning from a book.

In his excessive, grandiose, desperately lonely letters, Main does something that most of us who love books do, to some extent or another. He talks about the characters as if they were real people—as vivid, or more so, than people in his own life. He makes demands and asks questions of an author that for most of us remain imaginary but which he transformed, by force of will and need, into an intense epistolary relationship. He turned his worship and admiration of George Eliot into a one-sided love affair of sorts, by which he seems to have felt sustained even as he felt still hungrier for engagement. He claimed Eliot as his.

ELIOT and Main never met, though he urged her and Lewes several times to visit him, promising to show them the sights of his part of Scotland, with its peculiar enticements. "Nineteenth century refinement has had very little do with Auchmithie. It is a bit of savage-land three miles from a civilized town," he wrote. He wanted to take her for a fish supper at an inn where Sir Walter Scott had stayed.

At one point in 1874, when Eliot was beginning to sketch her ideas for *Daniel Deronda*, Main floated the idea that he might make a trip to London, and asked if he might visit her and Lewes there. Might he have "one quiet meeting with you two alone: not a party, but one delicious evening by our three selves?" he petitioned. "The sight of you, dear friends, would constitute one glorious memory in a life not like to have many such."

The proposed trip evaporated, and the following year, Main was still writing to Eliot in a dreamy way about the possibility of an encounter. He told her that if he did not disclose more about himself when writing it was not for lack of trust in her, nor for a deficit of devotedness, but because it seemed impossible to do so in a letter. "But perhaps I shall visit you some day, and then your sweet look of willing helpfulness will draw it all out in the most natural way imaginable," he wrote.

He didn't ever experience her sweet look of willing helpfulness. Getting to London may have been beyond Main's capacities or budget, but it also seems likely that he preferred to keep Eliot as a deferred ideal to whom he could speak at length in a letter without the emotional demands that would be placed upon him were he actually to find himself face-to-face with her. Though in the surviving recollections of those who made Eliot's acquaintance there are few testimonials of specific pieces of advice or personal insight that she delivered, she seems to have engaged even passing strangers in conversations that showed the same degree of psychological acuity and sympathy that characterizes the depiction of the inner lives of her characters. William Hale White, her co-lodger at 142 Strand, remarked that when she was talking with any sincerely engaged person, "she strove to elicit his best, and generally disclosed to him something in himself of which he was not aware." In a pretherapeutic age, she instinctively initiated the kind of conversation that went below the surface of things. She wanted to know how people worked—not to expose them or embarrass them, but to move them towards a greater self-understanding, and to achieve with them a greater intimacy, however fleeting. "I have never seen anybody whose search for the meaning and worth of persons and things was so unresting as hers," White wrote. She would have made a great interviewer; and if I could spend an hour in her company, I think that, instead of hearing her answer questions about her own life, I would almost rather listen to her putting questions to a stranger about his or hers.

And so, perhaps, Main's evasion of her questions—a characteristic that at first seemed to me so off-putting—actually helps to further illuminate Eliot's sympathetic response to his attentions and her approval of the *Sayings*. There may have been something about the glimpses he offered into his circumscribed, lonely life that resonated in her novelistic imagination. Slight, opaque Mr. Main—the onetime would-be minister with the secret inner life of which he cannot bring himself to speak—is kin to that family of frail, flawed clergymen who appear throughout her fiction.

They appear in her very first book, *Scenes of Clerical Life*, where stories revolve around the Reverend Amos Barton, who is defeated by the disapproval of others, and the Reverend Maynard Gilfil, whose young disappointment in love has left him inwardly maimed. "It is with men as with trees: if you lop off their finest branches, into which they were pouring their young life-juice, the wounds will be healed over with some rough boss, some odd excrescence; and what might have been a grand tree expanding into liberal shade, is but a whimsical misshapen trunk," Eliot wrote in "Mr. Gilfil's Love Story." "The trivial erring life which we visit with our harsh blame, may but be as the unsteady motion of a man whose best limb is withered."

Main has been dismissed as trivial and erring by Eliot's biographers, but his letters suggest that he, too, felt his young life to be maimed—that he feared that his life-juice was being wasted. In this respect, he was Eliot's perfect reader, in whom some of her most preoccupying novelistic themes were embodied. As I spent long hours in the library in Edinburgh with Main, reading letters Eliot would have devoted long hours to reading, I saw how little deserving he is of harsh blame. And I came to wonder if he affected Eliot not because of his glowing words about her work, after all, but because of what he quietly suggested to her—in all that he left unsaid—about mortal limitation, disappointment, and loss. Perhaps Eliot took him seriously because she recognized that even if he misread *Middlemarch*, *Middlemarch* had not misread him.

Chapter 8

Sunset and Sunrise

"I don't think either of us could spare the other, or like any one else better, however much we might admire them. It would make too great a difference to us—like seeing all the old places altered, and changing the name for everything."

—*MIDDLEMARCH*, CHAPTER 86

The Priory, with its walled garden and its books and its red-and-green study, is long gone. It was torn down at the very end of the nineteenth century to make way for the Great Central Main Line railway, which ran from Marylebone Station over Regent's Canal and up through the Midlands to Sheffield in the north of England. At one point on its route, the railway passed within fifteen miles of Coventry. "Now, my lads, you can't hinder the railroad: it will be made whether you like it or not," Caleb Garth warns a group of truculent farm labourers, who seek to interrupt the work of surveyors who are measuring the land around the town. "It may do a bit of harm here and there, to this and to that; and so does the sun in heaven. But the railway's a good thing."

One day in late summer, I descended a stairway down to the

north bank of Regent's Canal, passed under the railway tracks that ran overhead, and emerged on to a sunny towpath. George Eliot's garden would have been close by this path, but there was nothing to be seen of it now: just a high wall beyond which was a block of flats. Houseboats were moored all along the canal's bank, and some of the occupants of the boats had built small gardens along the path. There were plots with runner beans climbing up bamboo canes, and tomato plants laden with ripening fruit, and stalky sunflowers turning their open faces to the sun, simple and beaming, like a child's drawing of a flower. It was peaceful on the bank, with few people to be seen—only one or two slightly bedraggled dogs slumbering on the roofs of houseboats. A barge slid by, and I noticed its name, *Mr. Pip*—a passing tribute to Eliot's literary peer, glimpsed in an environment changed beyond recognition.

I went back up to the street, where, around a corner, a short stub remained of the road Eliot and Lewes lived in. It terminated suddenly at the entrance to an electrical substation that lay behind a high brick wall that was topped with a wire fence. Yellow and black hazard signs were posted along the wall's length. "Danger of Death," they read, and in that melancholy moment, as I discovered Eliot's home not only gone but her street erased, the sign took on the aspect of a grimly humorous memento mori.

But I hadn't really expected to find any trace of George Eliot on North Bank, and perhaps this was no place to look, anyway. Eliot lived in London for most of her adult life, from her early days as a striving young editor at 142 Strand to her late years surveying the streets from a carriage as she was driven through town, wearing a fashionable hat. But she always insisted that she preferred to be in the countryside, which had the power to remind her, however obliquely, of the unexceptional terrain of her youth, with its primrose-filled hedgerows and its useful pastures and its creeping waterways. Like Wordsworth, whom she revered in adolescence and reread throughout her life, Eliot found regenerative inspiration in the remembrance of the landscape of her childhood. Her love for the deep green England of Warwickshire was the foundation of her belief that the love we have for the landscape in which we have grown up has a quality that can never be matched by our admiration of any environment discovered later, no matter how beautiful.

This love of a childhood landscape is exquisitely evoked in *The Mill on the Floss*. In one of that novel's most celebrated, and most Wordsworthian, passages, the narrator describes in an authorial aside a walk she has taken "on this mild May day, with the young yellow-brown foliage of the oaks between me and the blue sky." She details the plants she sees on her walk: the star-flowers and speedwell and ground ivy. "What grove of tropic palms, what strange ferns or splendid broad-petalled blossoms, could ever thrill such deep and delicate fibres within me as this home-scene?" she asks. "These familiar flowers, these well-remembered bird notes, this sky with its fitful brightness, these furrowed and grassy fields, each with a sort of personality given to it by the capricious hedgerows—such things as these are the mother tongue of our imagination, the language that is laden with all the subtle inextricable associations the fleeting hours of our childhood left behind them."

The description is so sensually precise that the reader is tempted to believe that Eliot did actually spend that morning walking through the woodlands of her youth. But, of course, she didn't. She had been living in London for almost a decade when she wrote *The Mill on the Floss*, and had to settle for walks on the heaths or commons of the city to satisfy her cravings for countryside.

And crave it she did. "If I allowed myself to have any longings beyond what is given, they would be for a nook quite in the country, far away from Palaces crystal or otherwise, with an orchard behind me full of old trees and rough grass, and hedgerow paths among the endless fields where you meet nobody," she wrote to a friend in February 1859, just as she was beginning to conceive of a new novel featuring a mill and an inundation. The landscape she would evoke so vividly in *The Mill on the Floss* is a lost landscape remembered, not one currently inhabited, and it seems all the more vivid and quivering because its earth and air and sky have been transmuted by imagination into inspiration. "At present my mind works with the most freedom and the keenest sense of poetry in my remotest past," she told Barbara Bodichon that spring.

By the summer of 1859, Eliot's projected novel about a mill was at its earliest, tender stage. "My stories grow in me like plants, and this is only in the leaf-bud," Eliot wrote to Blackwood. "I have faith that the flower will come." Towards the end of the summer, she decided that this plant might be nurtured by an escape from the limits of London; she and Lewes were both in ill health and sought fresher air and more open skies. First they went to Penmaenmawr, on the north coast of Wales, but they could not find lodgings, and the weather was bad, so before long they decided to repair to the south coast of England instead.

"Here we are at the other pole!" Eliot wrote to a friend from the seaside town of Weymouth on the fourth of September. They lodged at 39 East Street, with some "good Weslyans, honest and kind," Eliot wrote in her diary. Weymouth, made popular as a resort town by George III, was not exactly what they wanted—it was still the summer season, and the town did not provide the sense of contented isolation they hankered for. Within days of arriving, however, they took a walk up the river Wey to a village named Radipole, where they made a delightful discovery. "G.E. is in high spirits, having found a Mill and Millstream to his heart's content," Lewes wrote to Blackwood.

Radipole Mill, the first of five mills strung along the length of the Wey, was close to a stone bridge around which clustered the rest of the village. There was a manor house, a few cottages, and a very old church, dating to the thirteenth century. In Radipole, Eliot found the possibility of inspiration—the possibility of recovering in imagination the landscape of her youth, and transforming it in literature to become the landscape of Maggie Tulliver's childhood. "We are going to hire a labourer's cottage for a day or two, and live a poetical primitive life, the results of which will appear in Maggie," Lewes told Blackwood.

They returned to Radipole the next day but were disappointed to discover that the labourer's wife objected to the letting of the cottage. Efforts to find another rustic retreat failed, but in the end Weymouth itself proved tolerable, and they stayed there for two weeks. Most mornings Eliot worked on her novel while Lewes examined specimens under his microscope, and after lunch they went out and explored. They rambled on the sands and the cliffs around the wide crescent of Weymouth Bay, and took a steamer across Portland Harbour to the rocky peninsula of the Isle of Portland, which had supplied the stone for Sir Christopher Wren's London churches. They shopped for hare and partridge in the market, listened to a band playing on the Esplanade, and went to the town's small theatre, where they saw *The Hunchback*, a play by James Sheridan Knowles, "performed in true provincial style," as Lewes wrote in his diary.

I can picture them standing on the stone steps of the brick house on East Street, deciding which way to go. Turning left, they would have arrived at St. Alban Street, a narrow thorough-fare barely wide enough for the passage of a horse and cart, lined by narrow, bow-fronted shops and a stone house that had stood there since Elizabethan times. Heading towards the seafront, they would have found a grand Georgian mansion that had been built for George III's third son, the Duke of Clarence, which over-looked the bay that curved from distant white cliffs in the east to the harbour mouth in the west. Turning right, they would quickly have come to the harbour, edged by massive brick warehouses, two-hundred-year-old inns, and the handsome fish market, newly built of Portland stone. The tang of brine would have been in the air, and so would the pungent smell of hops and yeast from the brewery on Hope Square, across a harbour crowded with fishing boats plied by tanned mariners with soft Wessex accents. If they turned from the quay on to a side street and glanced up, they might have seen a cannonball fired during the English Civil War, embedded in the stone gable of a house that had stood there since the seventeenth century.

I can see them there, because this is my home-scene. This is the town I grew up in. As a small child I played in a brisk breeze on the beach, where a Punch and Judy show has been performed since Victorian times. At the harbour's edge, I navigated seaweed-twined lobster pots stacked along the dock, and watched shrieking seagulls swooping to the water to snatch whatever the fishermen had discarded. When I was the age of young Maggie Tulliver I went to school in Radipole—by then no longer a village separate from the larger town, but distinct none the less, with its low stone cottages along the banks of a river that is brushed by trailing leaves of weeping willow. Cows grazed what we knew as the Humpty Dumpty field, so named because it was rumpled with unusual hillocks, the remains of the medieval village that had once stood there. In the graveyard of the ancient church were the remains of sailors from the wreck of the ship *The Earl of Abergavenny*, a vessel of the East India Company captained by John Wordsworth, the poet's older brother, that foundered off Portland in 1805.

My own older brother and I would sometimes walk home from school along Mount Pleasant Avenue, at that time still an unpaved road edged by a field as pleasant as its name, though a new bypass has been ploughed through since then. Our route took us under chestnut trees that supplied conkers in autumn, and sycamore trees that scattered their helicopter seedpods, and shady elm trees, until the elm trees died. This is the landscape of my childhood, with its torn clouds scattered across unpredictable skies, its stony strand tossed with driftwood and bladderwrack, its backwater footpaths lined with crab apple trees and blackberry bushes.

"We could never have loved the earth so well if we had had no childhood in it," Eliot wrote in *The Mill on the Floss*. We delight in the landscape of our youth because it is imbued with the deepest of memories, she says, and those memories colour our experience of every landscape we enter into thereafter: "Our delight in the sunshine on the deep bladed grass today, might be no more than the faint perception of wearied souls, if it were not for the sunshine and the grass in the far-off years, which still live in us and transform our perception into love."

It would be easy at first glance to mistake this for sentimentality, just as it is easy to feel sentimental about the more poetical aspects of one's own childhood. (I am sure those backwater footpaths were often muddy under leaden skies, though that is not how I best remember them.) But while Eliot's evocation of the landscape of childhood is alluringly beautiful—it is intensely moving—her use of it is not at all sentimental, if sentimentality is defined as the cheap reliance upon the effectiveness of an appeal to emotion, a reliance that overrules or circumvents the application of critical thought.

Eliot's use of childhood landscape is much more complex than that. It is more rigorous, and more profound. She is not expressing a simple conservative longing for the good old days, when "the world was not so nice as it now has become," as Alexander Main remarked. The point she is making is that our earliest experiences provide the ground upon which our characters are built, and that some part of our character grows from the brilliant, scintillating, intense capacity for emotion that a child experiences. There is nothing particularly special about the landscape of our youth, she says, except for the important fact that it is where we learned to be human. "There is no better reason for preferring this elderberry bush than that it stirs an early memory—that it is no novelty in my life speaking to me merely through my present sensibilities to form and colour, but the long companion of my existence that wove itself into my joys when my joys were vivid," she writes in *The Mill on the Floss*. Loving something of where one comes from—and having emotional access to that love—is a moral imperative for Eliot. It is to be in touch with the kernel of one's character, one's most receptive self. For Eliot, being sensitive to one's memories of childhood is a sign of moral maturity.

Being reminded of this is one of the things her books do for me, by connecting me with the child I was before I had ever heard of a writer called George Eliot. In the green fields and shady by-ways of my youth, Eliot glimpsed the site of her own youth, in imagination, and when I read her books I am restored anew to that place of childhood. She shows me that the remembrance of a childhood landscape is not mere nostalgia for what is lost and beyond my reach. It does not consist of longing to be back there, in the present; or of longing to be a child once more; or of wishing the world would not change. Rather it is an opportunity to be in touch again with the intensity and imagination of beginnings. It is a discovery, later in life, of what remains with me.

OF the triad of young couples in *Middlemarch*, two move away from the town at the novel's end. Dorothea and Ladislaw, who marry in spite of the codicil to Casaubon's will, go to London, where Ladislaw enters Parliament. Lydgate and Rosamond move there, too, so that Lydgate can pursue a more lucrative, less idealistic medical practice. Only Fred Vincy and Mary Garth remain in Middlemarch, rooted there, as their parents were before them.

Through Dorothea and Ladislaw, Lydgate and Rosamond, Eliot gives different perspectives on the experience of yearning, and ambition, and aspiration for an unknown beyond. In them, the reader learns of hopefulness, and of falling short. But in Fred and Mary, who have loved each other for as long as they can remember, Eliot shows the virtues of rootedness, the value of the home-scene.

Mary is the wisest character in *Middlemarch*. She surpasses even her admirable father, Caleb Garth, who occasionally indulges in the foolishness of thinking well of those who don't deserve it. She also surpasses her mother, Susan Garth, a sharp, intelligent, competent woman who makes the mistake of underestimating her girl children in favour of her sons. Mary's wisdom lies in having an almost preternatural knowledge of what course in life will be good for her, wanting to follow that course, and having no doubts about its rectitude. She has none of the inclination towards self-sabotage that bedevils Dorothea or Lydgate. She is utterly ethical, just, and good-natured; but since she is also quick-tongued and sardonic, the mature reader at least is not tempted to dismiss her as too good by half. Mary is the character who grows the least during the course of *Middlemarch*, because she is already full grown. She already has the wisdom that it takes most of us at least until middle age to begin to acquire.

One of the things that Mary knows is that she does not want to leave home—home for her being Middlemarch, proximity to her family, and the countryside she loves. At one point in the novel, Mary is on the verge of going away to become a governess in another region. A change in her father's fortunes means she does not have to go, and in her customary ironical manner, she expresses her happiness in terms of a loss—the loss of anticipated nostalgia. "I thought it would always be part of my life to long for home, and losing that grievance makes me feel rather empty," she says. "I suppose it served instead of sense to fill up my mind."

In the final chapter of Book Eight of *Middlemarch*, "Sunset and Sunrise," Mary is seen again in her childhood home, glimpsed in a grassy corner of the garden. She is pushing Letty, her little sister, on a swing hung between two pear trees, "a pink kerchief tied over her head, making a little poke to shade her eyes from the level sunbeams." Her father comes to walk with her among the nut trees, to talk about the prospect of her marrying Fred at last. "I don't love him because he is a fine match," Mary tells Caleb, with a sceptical laugh. Her sober father asks her why then she is marrying him. "Oh, dear, because I have always loved him," Mary replies. "I should never like scolding anyone else so well; and that is a point to be thought of in a husband." Fred is not a romantic figure—an Orlando—to Mary. He is already an intimate. He is already family—which is what, in a marriage that works, all spouses end up becoming, even those spouses who started out as idealized objects of infatuation or desire.

Some readers have found Mary Garth to be the true heroine of *Middlemarch*, including Gordon Haight, who once argued her case in an essay with that title. And in fact an attempt was once made to cast Mary Garth as the heroine of her own book. In 1953 Oxford University Press published a curious volume called *Mary Garth: A Romance from "Middlemarch,"* in which an editor, Frederick Page, detached the love story of Fred and Mary from the web of the novel proper. The result was a slim, 170-page volume, built from George Eliot's own sentences—but largely stripped of her authorial asides—that charts the progress of the pair from being the best of childhood companions to being nearly-weds.

Mary Garth is a very peculiar piece of work, bearing the same relation to *Middlemarch* as does a melody played on a mouth organ to a symphony performed by an orchestra. Dorothea and Casaubon are eliminated: he's dead, and she is mentioned only once in passing. Lydgate is relevant only insofar as he is Fred's brother-in-law, and Rosamond matters only as a fleeting foil to Mary. Bulstrode's entanglement with Raffles is alluded to but quickly brushed aside as "part of another story." Ladislaw isn't even mentioned.

In *The Great Tradition*, F. R. Leavis notoriously suggested that Eliot's last great work, *Daniel Deronda*, would be much improved if half of it were discarded. (He wanted to keep the glittering, high-society half that pertained to Gwendolen Harleth, the novel's troubled heroine, and to discard the half that was concerned with Jewish life and history, which he saw as flawed and uninteresting.) Unlike Leavis's provocative proposal, the mutilation of *Middlemarch* that produced *Mary Garth* grew from a pedagogical impulse rather than from a judgement of literary worth. As the book's adapter explained in a preface, the intended purpose of *Mary Garth* was to introduce young readers to George Eliot. After *Mary Garth*, Page recommended, readers could go on to *Adam Bede*, *The Mill on the Floss*, *Silas Marner*, and *Scenes of Clerical Life*, before approaching the monumental *Middlemarch* itself. "They will thus be growing up with George Eliot, their minds enlarging as hers enlarged," he wrote.

I can't be sure what I would have made of *Mary Garth* when I was twelve or fourteen, the age for which it seems to have been intended. Perhaps I would have welcomed it; those years were tricky ones in which to find the right books, with the satisfactions of Frances Hodgson Burnett outgrown but the subtleties of Jane Austen still inaccessible. As a Radipole schoolgirl I might have been enchanted by the warmth of the worthy Miss Garth and amused by her good-hearted suitor. But by the time that I did first read *Middlemarch*, several years later, the characters that were of absolutely the least interest to me in the whole novel were Fred and Mary.

They were utterly lacking in glamour. Feckless, harmless Fred was just the sort of raw, fair English boy who left me cold: so unintellectual, so outdoorsy, so buoyantly optimistic, so resiliently uncomplicated. Mary, that clever brown patch, I should have had a greater interest in, but I was too busy identifying with the passionate, aspiring Miss Brooke to recognize my kinship with the shrewd, satirical Miss Garth. I found her brand of goodness boring. I did not share her sense of duty, or feel as she did the intense importance of family ties. "I consider my mother and father the best part of myself," Mary says. Like many children of my generation, I suspect, I rather fancied that *I* was the best part of *them*.

Most of all, I could not conceive of falling in love with a boy I'd grown up alongside and had known all my life. I had only vague notions of what I wanted from romantic love, but I felt sure that it involved passionate struggle on exotic frontiers. There was nothing I could imagine wanting less than the predictable domesticity of marrying a childhood sweetheart.

That was what my parents had done. They met in 1944, the year my mother turned thirteen and my father fourteen. My mother, a slender, pragmatic girl with fine brown hair and a broad smile, attended the girls' grammar school, to which she was permitted to ride her bike so long as she rode with an older cousin, who attended the boys' grammar school nearby. My father, a quiet, cricket-obsessed boy with black curly hair and olive skin, rode with them every morning, too. That was their beginning, and they married in the summer that he turned twenty-two and she twenty-one.

In their wedding picture, taken at the gate of the local church, my mother isn't wearing a bridal gown, but a belted dress—it was heavy, pale blue silk—with three-quarter-length sleeves and a knee-length skirt. Slim and elegant, she wears a pillbox hat with a chic fringe of veil. The dress comes from Harrods department store, in the advertising department of which she works, having left school at fifteen to become a messenger girl. From her work she has learned how to stand for the photographer, with one foot in front of the other, her firm chin slightly cocked.

My father stands square, hair gleaming, his new, imposingly formal grey suit hanging off his slender frame, smiling, looking vulnerable. He is already a civil servant, having left school at sixteen. His exam results were good enough that he could have continued his education into the sixth form, and then into college, but in his family that wasn't even a consideration: no one ever had. In his teens he had ambitions to become a sports writer—he went to evening classes to learn shorthand and typing—but his own father had died, and a relative advised him to enter a more secure line of work. He did, and stayed a civil servant for more than forty years, never letting my brother or me suspect that any sacrifice had been involved in our family's foundation.

The wedding photograph was tucked away in an old album, which was rarely brought out. My parents were not the type to have their wedding pictures on display, or to make a display of their marriage. They were undemonstrative in their affections to each other, but I never saw them arguing. They lived together in what looked like functional, contented complicity. If as a teenager I had stopped to think about it, I would have said they were happy together, but I rarely stopped to think about it. They provided the steadying, untroubled background to my own inward drama of growing up—giving me, in their understated English way, the opportunity to aspire to a life very different from theirs. It did not occur to me to think much about what their own dramas were, or might have been.

"MARRIAGE, which has been the bourne of so many narratives, is still a great beginning," Eliot writes in the conclusion to *Middlemarch*. The novel that ends with a wedding was conventional in Eliot's time, and has become only more conventional since. *Middlemarch*, though, is punctuated with weddings: it begins with one, features one in its middle, and ends with two more. None of them functions as an ending. Each suggests, instead, the start of a story, not its conclusion. With her quiet, majestic turn of phrase, Eliot writes that marriage is "the beginning of the home epic." It is "the gradual conquest or irremediable loss of that complete union which makes the advancing years a climax, and age the harvest of sweet memories in common." Every marriage—which we can take from Eliot's example to include every committed relationship, not only those sanctioned by church or state—amounts to an epic journey, an adventure of discovery.

From this perspective, the course upon which Fred and Mary are about to embark in the last chapter of *Middlemarch* is no less grand, in its way, than Dorothea's early aspirations for a life of significance, or than Lydgate's ambitions to make scientific discoveries. Throughout *Middlemarch*, Eliot has shown from different angles the demands that marriage makes. She has argued, in effect, that a good marriage is the expression of sympathy in its smallest unit. "Marriage is so unlike everything else," Dorothea says towards the end of the novel. "There is something even awful in the nearness it brings." The chosen adjective is deliberately ambiguous, connoting at once a sublime state and also one conducive to dread.

Of all the marriages that are made in *Middlemarch*, the one over which Eliot casts the most golden, glowing light is that of Fred and Mary. Eliot—who did not marry her young love, nor stay in her childhood home—gives Fred and Mary what many readers have felt is the one truly romantic love story in *Middlemarch*, a story that is free of regret or disappointment. (We might have wished for Mr. Farebrother's sake that Mary had chosen him, but it is hard to begrudge Fred.) They produce three sons, the same number that Eliot helped Lewes raise, and both Fred and Mary, surely not coincidentally, become authors—she of a book of tales for children taken from Plutarch, he of a work called the *Cultivation of Green Crops and the Economy of Cattle-Feeding*. (The residents of Middlemarch are convinced that each of them wrote the other's book. "There was no need to praise anybody for writing a book, since it was always done by somebody else," Eliot writes, in a private joke about her own peculiar history of pseudonymous authorship.)

Fred becomes the picture of uxorious devotion, the kind of man it is easier to see the attractions of at forty-five than it is at twenty. Having failed to inherit Stone Court, the house he hoped Mr. Featherstone, his rich, grumpy uncle, would bequeath him, he has an opportunity to gain the house anyway, through his own hard work and application. He maintains his love of hunting but risks the derision of his companions by refraining from jumping the highest fences, "seeming to see Mary and the boys sitting on the five-barred gate, or showing their curly heads between hedge and ditch." As a young reader, I skipped past this line without pausing, but now when I read it a lump always comes to my throat, so acute a description is it of familial fidelity.

Strikingly, Fred and Mary are the only characters in *Middlemarch* to whom Eliot refers in the present tense in the book's conclusion—as if, after all, they were real people a reader could go and track down, not characters formed by her imagination. Anyone who seeks to enquire, she writes, might find that Fred and Mary are still living at Stone Court, where "the creeping plants still cast the foam of their blossoms over the fine stone-walls into the field where the walnut-trees stand in stately row." For the first readers of *Middlemarch*, which was published some forty years after the period it describes, Fred and Mary, living beyond the pages of the novel, would have been in their mid sixties. For the rest of us, Eliot's belated readers, Fred and Mary are the representatives of our unassuming elders—watching over us, making no explicit imposition upon us, knowing and feeling far more than the young can ever imagine them capable of. They are as solid as those fine stone walls, and as connected to the land as the walnut trees in the fields. Fred and Mary dwell in the landscape of childhood, and they are the landscape of childhood, too.

"On sunny days the two lovers who were first engaged with the umbrella-ring may be seen in white-haired placidity at the open window from which Mary Garth, in the days of old Peter Featherstone, had often been ordered to look out for Mr. Lydgate," Eliot writes. This passage had no particular resonance for me when I was young, but now it thrills with depth and suggestion. Now I can see what I could not see as a teenager—the romance, and the epic dimension, of long-lasting marriage. It begins at the church gate, a bold embarkation in formal clothes and self-conscious smiles, and it ends with the fastening of buttons on the shirt of a spouse whose trembling, liver-spotted hands can no longer manage the task. What would it be for love to be rooted in a single place, for a life's length? This, of all experiences in love, is one I will never have, even if it is mercifully granted that I grow old together with the husband I met on the brink of middle age.

From where I stand in the middle of my own home epic— my own mundane, grand domestic adventure, in which I attempt to live in sympathy with the family I have made—I now look upon the accomplishment of early-dawning, long-lasting love with something like awe. When I turn the last pages of *Middlemarch* and read about Fred and Mary, I think of my parents, who met when they were barely past childhood, and who grew white haired together; until in the hours before dawn one winter morning, nearly sixty years after their wedding day, my father died with my mother at his side, holding his hand and speaking softly to him of sweet memories in common. *Middlemarch* gives my parents back to me. In the pages of my imagination they are still together, watching me and watching over me from the window of their lives, under the pale sunlight of the place I came from and still call home.

IN the end, more romance is attached in *Middlemarch* to the accomplishment of enduring love than to the trials of young love, the follies of which are so ably dissected. In Fred and Mary, Eliot gives a glimpse of what a contented old age might be like. The final chapter of Book Eight, by which time their marriage is decided, is prefaced by an epigraph in French, from Victor Hugo. The epigraph is not about the excitement of new love, but the gratifications provided by love in old age. "The heart is saturated with love as with a divine wit which preserves it; hence the undying attachment of those who have loved each other from the dawn of life, and the freshness of old loves which still endure," it reads. "This, then, is old age: a resemblance of evening with the dawn."

By the time Eliot was finishing *Middlemarch* she thought of herself as incipiently elderly, and within less than a decade she would join Lewes in Highgate Cemetery, where a bed of wildflowers now covers her tomb. Her diaries from her later years show that she entered what she regarded as old age with less than the complete equanimity that is recommended by the passage from Victor Hugo. In real life, her sunset years were filled with bodily aches and pains, as well as anxieties about work that she feared she would inevitably leave undone.

"As the years advance there is a new rational ground for the expectation that my life may become less fruitful," she wrote in her diary, on the last day of 1877. "Many conceptions of works to be carried out present themselves, but confidence in my own fitness to complete them worthily is all the more wanting because it is reasonable to argue that I must already have done my best." Still, in her old age, she felt the familiar spur of inspiration. "In fact, my mind is embarrassed by the number and wide variety of subjects that attract me, and the enlarging vista that each brings with it," she wrote.

She had come so far from her girlhood and youth, in geographical distance and in mental and moral capacity, with her mind surveying an ever-widening horizon. But thirty years earlier—still in the Midlands, still uncertain as to what would become of her—Eliot had characterized herself by an image precisely opposite to this one, in a letter to a friend. "It seems to me as if I were shrinking into that mathematical abstraction, a point—so entirely am I destitute of contact that I am unconscious of length or breadth," she wrote then.

At the time of that letter her father was weeks away from death, and her mood was sombre. She wrote of herself as a moon, a "cold dark orb," solitary and demoralized. "Alas for the fate of poor mortals which condemns them to wake up some fine morning and find all the poetry in which their world was bathed only the evening before utterly gone—the hard angular world of chairs and tables and looking-glasses staring at them in all its naked prose," she wrote. "It is so in all the stages of life—the poetry of girlhood goes—the poetry of love and marriage—the poetry of maternity—and at last the very poetry of duty forsakes us for a season and we see ourselves and all about us as nothing more than miserable agglomerations of atoms—poor tentative efforts of the Natur Princip to mould a personality."

This litany of life stages passing away is staggeringly expressed, and wrenchingly sad, but what Eliot did with the years that followed was redemptive. *Middlemarch* itself might be seen as capturing the poetry of girlhood, the poetry of love and marriage, the poetry of maternity, or motherhood, and the poetry of duty. In the novel she comes to terms with the hard, angular world of tables and chairs and looking glasses, and finds a struggling person's place within it. By the time Eliot was writing *Middlemarch* she had found a way to think of herself, and of everyone around her, as something more than a miserable agglomeration of atoms. In 1870 she wrote a letter of condolence to a friend and in it, not for the only time, she drew upon an image of death that recalled the grace-giving sunlight of childhood. "I try to delight in the sunshine that will be when I shall never see it any more," she wrote. "And I think it is possible for this sort of impersonal life to attain great intensity,—possible for us to gain much more independence, than is usually believed, of the small bundle of facts that make our own personality." Her aspiration was not for literary immortality—though she got that—but for a kind of encompassing empathy that would make the punishing experience of egoism shrink and dwindle. She believed that growth depends upon complex connections and openness to others, and does not derive from a solitary swelling of the self. She became great because she recognized that she was small.

"We cannot give the young our experience," a visitor to the

Priory once recalled Eliot as saying. "They will not take it. There must be the actual friction of life, the individual contact with sorrow, to discipline the character." She was right, of course, though as we grow older it can be hard to resist the temptation to tell younger people how to live—to believe that we have acquired some wisdom fit to impart to the benighted young. Only an occasional fictional character, like Mary Garth, is wise enough to know for sure at the beginning of her life what she will want in life's middle, or at life's end; and if more fictional characters were as certain as that, fiction wouldn't be worth reading. For most characters, and for most readers, the course is less clear.

Middlemarch has not given me George Eliot's experience, not on my first reading of it, or my latest. But in reading her works and her letters, and learning about her life and the lives of those near to her, it becomes clear to me that she could not have written this novel without her individual contact with sorrow. And as I continue to read and think and reflect, I also realize that she has given me something else: a profound experience with a book, over time, that amounts to one of the frictions of my life. I have grown up with George Eliot. I think *Middlemarch* has disciplined my character. I know it has become part of my own experience and my own endurance. *Middlemarch* inspired me when I was young, and chafing to leave home; and now, in middle life, it suggests to me what else home might mean, beyond a place to grow up and grow out of.

On this mild May day I sit in my Brooklyn backyard, reading and thinking. Between me and the sky grows a broad-limbed elm tree that must have been a sapling when my parents were young. Squirrels skitter through it, while sparrows flit from its branches to those of the copper birch beyond. This is a peaceful city garden, surrounded by high, ivy-covered brick walls that bring to my mind the walls around the very first garden I knew, as a small child under a London sky, before my parents moved to the coast.

This garden is my young son's home-scene, weaving itself into his joys now, while his joys are vivid. So is the less restful world in which he is being raised, discernible even from this retreat: the traffic passing on the busy street beyond; the subterranean rumble of the crowded subway train that we take to his school every morning, after waiting on a platform decked with posters for mayhem-filled movies; the ebullient calls of teenagers peacocking down the block to the hilly park on the corner. During the Revolutionary War this park was the site of a fort that was named for a maternal ancestor of my husband, a general who led American troops against the forces of George III. Later, Walt Whitman, the poet and editor of the *Brooklyn Eagle*, who lived in this neighbourhood, championed the construction of a park on the fort's site. When Whitman published *Leaves of Grass* in 1855 George Eliot was among the first reviewers to notice it, in the *Westminster Review*. She alluded to "the very bold expressions by which the author indicates his contempt for the 'prejudices' of decency"—a remark that sounds a little prudish until one remembers that Eliot herself was, by then, thought to have held decency in contempt. Whitman achieved his park, and in the 1860s Frederick Law Olmsted, the great nineteenth-century landscape designer, created a small acreage of imagined countryside, where now my son climbs among clusters of old-growth trees whose placement was conceived when *Middlemarch* was no more than jottings in a notebook and ideas in George Eliot's mind.

The mother tongue of my son's imagination has a very different accent to mine, and all this will be his inheritance, if he chooses to claim it. I cannot give him my experience. But as I sit in our garden I hope that here, at least, our languages will overlap, among these old-fashioned plants that remind me of England—mature hydrangea bushes with blue flowers that darken to purple as the season progresses, glossy-leafed euonymus that clambers up the wall, and clusters of hellebores bearing subtle green flowers, like those that grow on George Eliot's grave.

Finale

"Every limit is a beginning as well as an ending."
—*MIDDLEMARCH*, FINALE

The final sentence of *Middlemarch* is one of the most admired in literature, and with good reason—it is "quietly thrilling," as Stanley Fish, the literary critic, has written. The book ends, as it began, with Dorothea, and it discovers what may be redeemed from disappointment. Dorothea's fate is not to be another Saint Teresa, but to be a heroine of the ordinary—the embodiment of George Eliot's grave, demanding, meliorist faith. It reads, "But the effect of her being on those around her was incalculably diffusive: for the growing good of the world is partly dependent on unhistoric acts; and that things are not so ill with you and me as they might have been, is half owing to the number who lived faithfully a hidden life, and rest in unvisited tombs."

A vein of melancholy runs through the sentence. Dorothea's impact upon the people around her is diffusive, like vapour vanishing into the air. Things are not so ill with you and me as they might have been—but ill they still are, to some degree, and are not likely to be otherwise. Acts are unhistoric; lives are hidden; tombs are unvisited—all is unmarked and unnoticed. With its series of long clauses and then its short final phrase, the sentence concludes with a perfect dying fall. I cannot imagine reading these words and not sighing at the end of them.

But this isn't quite the sentence as Eliot originally wrote it. In this, the first published edition, she made several small but significant revisions from her original draft, which can be found in the manuscript in the British Library. The manuscript version reads as follows: "But the effect of her being on those around her was incalculably diffusive; for the growing life of the world is after all chiefly dependent on unhistoric acts, and that things are not so ill with you and me as they might have been is owing to many of those who sleep in unvisited tombs, having lived a hidden life nobly."

When I first came across this passage, in the library, I felt an acute sense of disorientation. There, in violet-coloured ink, was an only partly successful first stab at sublimity. It was like discovering that Leonardo had first tried painting a snub nose on the Mona Lisa, or learning that the question Hamlet originally asked was, "Not to be, or to be?" The music of the line was altered entirely, and so was its import. Instead of the "growing good of the world"—Eliot's meliorist vision, captured in a phrase—there was the "growing life of the world," an expression so much less specific, and so much less moving. There was the phrase "after all"—a rhetorical gesture of persuasion that undermined the solemn authority of the passage, absent in the first publication. There was "chiefly dependent" rather than "partly dependent," and "owing" rather than "half owing"—changes which give the sentence a much more optimistic tone than characterizes the revised, published version, with its irresistible melancholic grandeur.

Still more significant are the revisions to the word order after the final comma, which, in the final published version, is far more resonant. Those tombs may be unvisited, but in reading the sentence—in arriving at them, our ultimate destination, on the page—we are able to pay homage to the hidden lives they commemorate. Those hidden lives are, in the earlier, manuscript version, lived "nobly"—which, like its close synonym "admirably," is suggestive of moral qualities that are outwardly recognized by others. (The goodness of Miss Henrietta Noble, the Reverend Farebrother's elderly aunt, who filches sugar lumps from the table to distribute to the poor, is revealed to all by her name.) By replacing "nobly" with "faithfully," Eliot shifts the emphasis away from the implied judgement of an external observer—a dissonant suggestion when one is talking of "hidden lives." Instead, she places her emphasis upon a validation that comes from inward conviction.

Faithfulness is "solely the good in us," as Eliot characterizes Bunyan's Faithful, the allegorical figure at the centre of *The Pilgrim's Progress* whom she invokes in the penultimate chapter of the novel. By substituting faith for nobility, Eliot has made those hidden lives of which she writes more humble. But she has made them richer, too, as the fertile soil from which the good might grow.

By the end of the book, Dorothea has made her own progress, even if she has not had a chance to stray far beyond the boundaries of her provincial life. Having aspired at the novel's outset to do good for others in some grand but abstract way, she discovers that the good she is able to do is in relation to the lives that touch her own more closely, even if doing so may be inconvenient or painful for her. And there is a passage in chapter 80, only a few short pages before the end of this very long book, in which this is crystallized for Dorothea. It is here that she makes her own discovery of what *Middlemarch* is about.

It is early in the morning, and she is in her boudoir at Lowick Manor. By now she is a widow, Casaubon having died. Although she is convinced that she and Ladislaw must always be separated because of the codicil in Casaubon's will, she has, until now, clung to the knowledge that he loves her, and treasured him for the brightness he brought to the gloomy days of her marriage. But her confidence in him has been shaken: the day before, in an effort to help save Lydgate's reputation, she has visited the doctor's house—and there stumbled across Rosamond and Ladislaw in what she has mistakenly taken for a love scene. Shocked and disillusioned, she has spent an anguished night on the hard floor of her room, regretting the loss of her cherished ideal of Ladislaw's worthiness, and admitting to herself that she had loved him. By morning, though, she has forced herself to think beyond herself, and to consider how she still might act on behalf of Lydgate and even Rosamond, whose troubles she might yet help to remedy even though she feels her own hopes are shattered.

"She opened her curtains, and looked out towards the bit of road that lay in view, with fields beyond, outside the entrance-gates," Eliot writes. "On the road there was a man with a bundle on his back and a woman carrying her baby; in the field she could see figures moving—perhaps the shepherd with his dog. Far off in the bending sky was the pearly light; and she felt the largeness of the world and the manifold wakings of men to labour and endurance. She was a part of that involuntary, palpitating life, and could

neither look out on it from her luxurious shelter as a mere spectator, nor hide her eyes in selfish complaining."

There's a biblical gravitas to the image of husband and wife
as they walk through the landscape on the road to Middlemarch,
representing the hidden lives of all those people Dorothea now
realizes her own life is bound up with, and who must also be
recognized. In looking out upon them, small figures in an enlarging vista, Dorothea comprehends the next step she must take
on her own journey. We are called to express our generosity and
sympathy in ways we might not have chosen for ourselves. Heed-
ing that call, we might become better. Setting aside our own
cares, we might find ourselves on the path that can lead us out
of resignation.

In the late spring of 1871, just as *Middlemarch* was beginning to
fall into place imaginatively for Eliot, she and Lewes moved to
the countryside for several months, to Shottermill, in Surrey, a
village which in the nineteenth century was a centre for broom
making, and which was just being discovered by artists and intellectuals, including Lord Tennyson, who had built a house nearby.
They rented a house, Brookbank, the home of Anne Gilchrist,
whose late husband, Alexander Gilchrist, had been the biographer
of William Blake. It was "a queer little cottage," Eliot wrote to
Francis Pattison before her departure, telling her Oxford friend
that it "stands in the midst of a lovely country, where there are hill
tops from which we shall look down on a round horizon."

They went in the first week of May, anticipating a stay of four months while renovations were under way at the Priory. (A new bath was being installed, among other improvements.) At first, Eliot was slightly dismayed at her new circumstances. A blind was not working in the bedroom; a set of keys was unforthcoming; the housekeeper was painfully slow in her work. The local tradespeople were unhelpful: the butcher did not bring the meat, nobody seemed to want to sell them fresh milk, and eggs were scarce. "An expedition we made yesterday in search of fowls showed us nothing more hopeful than some chickens six weeks old which the good woman observed were sometimes 'eaten by the gentry with asparagus,'" she wrote with arch amusement to Mrs. Gilchrist.

But apart from these minor domestic frustrations there was much to be grateful for. "There is an exquisite stillness in the sunshine, and a sense of distance from London hurry, which encourages the growth of patience," Eliot wrote. Her letters from Shottermill became increasingly contented. She wrote in the mornings and in the early evenings walked with Lewes under a broad sky across the common, and the book began to fall into place at last.

The countryside "could hardly be surpassed in its particular kind of beauty," she wrote, remarking on the "perpetual undulation of heath and copse and clear veins of hurrying water, with here and there a grand pine wood, steep wood-clothed promontories, and gleaming pools." Having once been a girl on a farm, she was able knowledgeably to discuss fruit growth and butter manufacture with the wife of the local farmer, surprising the latter enormously. She came to love the quaint house, with its oddly shaped rooms, its prints of Reynolds and Romney on the mantelpiece, and the effect of afternoon sunshine in the parlour, where, she wrote to Charles Lewes, "The sun is sending yellow and blue patches through our painted glass onto my paper."

The village of Shottermill doesn't exist any more; in 1933 it was officially incorporated into the neighbouring town of Haslemere. I went to Haslemere one day in late summer, arriving at the train station that opened in 1859. The railway hastened the gentrification of the area; after the artists and writers came wealthy Londoners, entranced by the area's rural charms. Those charms were swiftly eroded by the construction of housing to accommodate the employees—gardeners, housekeepers—whose services the wealthy new residents required. These terraced houses look pleasant enough now, with more than a hundred years of accrued attractiveness, but they and the growth they were part of left the old village, with its mills and its taverns and its tannery on the river, utterly transformed.

Brookbank, a pretty house with a shingled facade and leaded windows, is close to the old tannery, up the hill from the river, past the railway bridge. A few years ago, a civic group put a sign up over the door. "George Eliot Author 1819–1880 Wrote Middlemarch while living here in 1871," it reads, with a perhaps understandable degree of overstatement. Brookbank's current occupants have lived there since the late nineties, and when I visited they served me tea and cream cakes in what was once Mrs. Gilchrist's parlour. It was a delightful room, with pale yellow walls and two large bay windows overlooking the garden, where shadow was cast by a thick-trunked yew tree that was already four or five hundred years old when Eliot was there. The glass of the windows was decorated with diamond shapes painted blue and yellow, through which the sun cast patches of coloured light.

Eliot and Lewes were obliged to leave Brookbank at the end of July, Mrs. Gilchrist having let it to another tenant. But because the Priory was not yet finished, and because they had been so contented in this quiet corner of the world, they rented another house, Cherrimans, which lay directly opposite, across the lane. This was a more substantial residence that belonged to a local landowner named James Simmons. There was an old half-timbered section, but much of it had been built in the eighteenth century.

The house had a large garden in which Eliot liked to sit and write when the weather permitted, her head shaded by a large deodara tree. One day Mr. Simmons found her there and reproached her for the exposure to the sun. "Oh, I like it!" she said. "Today is the first time I have felt warm this summer." Most of the time she sat and worked in the parlour, the deep country silence broken only by the rush of an occasional train. "Imagine me seated near a window, opening under a verandah, with flower-beds and lawn and pretty hills in sight, my feet on a warm water-bottle, and my writing on my knees. In that attitude my mornings are passed," she wrote in a letter. This must be the most vivid picture Eliot ever gave of herself in the act of creativity, and the least anguished. She sounds contented, comfortable, and self-aware. One evening she read aloud to Lewes the pages she had been working on—Book Three of *Middlemarch*—and he declared it splendid.

The house's current residents have recently restored the verandah according to its appearance in a photograph from the Victorian era, as they showed me when I visited, pointing out the grapevine that had begun to wreath its way around the wooden supports. The verandah borders an elegant living room, from which three French windows face the garden. Two of the windows look over the garden towards the lane, while one faces a lawn, with countryside beyond.

The house's owners left me alone in the living room, from which I could hear the banging of further renovations under way in the kitchen, where windows installed in the 1950s were being replaced by new ones with decorative cast-iron frames, painstakingly reproduced from a Victorian original. I looked around at the living-room windows, under the verandah. The third one, facing away from the lane, must have been the one before which Eliot sat as she wrote the letter. There was an armchair by the window, and I perched on it and looked out over the view Eliot had described as she sat warming her feet.

There was still a stretch of grass and pretty flower beds before me. But I could not see any hills beyond—only a dense growth of trees, like that which could be seen all around the neighbourhood. Then I remembered something I had learned from a local historian: that in the nineteenth century, there had been far fewer trees in Shottermill. In those days, the hills had been sparsely covered with grasses and heather. The trees had come later, and were due to changes in the local economy. Partly, their growth was tied to the decline of the broom industry, which had depended upon cutting down birch trees. But a more important change, the historian told me, had been the Education Act of 1880.

The Education Act, which ushered in mandatory elementary-school education for all children, was an inevitable consequence of the changes to the political landscape that had begun with the Reform Act of 1832—the transformative event that reverberates through *Middlemarch*. The Reform Act of 1832 led ultimately to the Reform Act of 1867, in which working-class men were given the vote for the first time. These new voters needed an education; as one disdainful parliamentary opponent of Reform put it to his colleagues, "I believe it will be absolutely necessary that you should prevail on our future masters to learn their letters."

But when Eliot saw Shottermill, the Education Act was still a decade in the future. When she knew the village many of its young boys were not in school, but were instead tending to the flocks of sheep that grazed its hills—sheep that trampled upon and ate up seedlings before they had a chance to turn into trees. Within not too many years, though, the village children were in school, required to learn writing and arithmetic instead of animal husbandry. Then the sheep left the hills, and the trees were free to grow unchecked.

As I looked out from the window towards the obscured hills, I felt a quiet thrill of excitement at the idea that the landscape itself had been transformed by the reading of books. The trees were there because ordinary children not much older than my late-Victorian grandfather—children close to the age of George Eliot's baby granddaughter, Blanche—had learned their letters. Some of them would have learned not just to read books but also to love them. Some of those children would have become writers themselves, and so would some among their descendants.

"Imagine me seated near a window, opening under a verandah," George Eliot had written. And I could imagine her there: I could conjure her more vividly than anywhere else I had pictured her in my travels. But through that window was a larger vista: a landscape changed by books, reshaped by reading, transfigured by the slow green growth.

Bibliographical Notes and Acknowledgements

Many books been written about George Eliot, and I am indebted
to the work of many biographers whose scholarship has revealed
the contours of her life, the processes of her work, and the devel-
opment of her thought. I first read Gordon S. Haight's *George
Eliot: A Biography* (Oxford University Press, 1968) as a teenager; it
remains indispensable. For readers wishing to learn about George
Eliot's life in greater detail, I recommend Rosemary Ashton's excellent *George Eliot: A Life* (Penguin Press, 1996) and Kathryn
Hughes's very readable *George Eliot: The Last Victorian* (Farrar
Straus and Giroux, 1998). Among critical biographies I particu-
larly admire Rosemarie Bodenheimer's *The Real Life of Mary Ann
Evans: George Eliot, Her Letters and Fiction* (Cornell, 1994), and
Barbara Hardy's *George Eliot: A Critic's Biography* (Continuum,
2006). As I was finishing this book, Nancy Henry's *The Life of
George Eliot* (Wiley-Blackwell, 2012) was published, offering a
fascinating critical reading of earlier biographies.

Before I began writing this book—but after I had published

an essay in the *New Yorker* about my love of George Eliot—I received out of the blue from K. K. Collins a kind note and a copy of his volume, *George Eliot: Interviews and Recollections* (Palgrave Macmillan, 2010). This fascinating collection of firsthand accounts of meeting George Eliot has been extremely useful, while its author, Ken Collins, has patiently answered many questions and pointed me to other sources. A number of scholars have graciously responded to my queries both for the *New Yorker* article and for this book, while others have been kind enough to engage in longer conversations with me. I am grateful to Rosemary Ashton, William Baker, Harold Bloom, Rosemarie Bodenheimer, Kathleen McCormack, Edward Mendelson, Jeff Nunokawa, Leah Price, and Ilya Wachs. I accosted James Arnett on the subway one day because I saw him reading Haight's biography; he subsequently invited me to sit in on the classes on *Middlemarch* he was teaching at Hunter College, and I am grateful for the insights of both James and his students. I am in perpetual debt to Roy Park and Helen Cooper, my own former tutors at University College, Oxford.

A note on naming: biographers have struggled with the question of what to call George Eliot, who went by many names in her life as well as adopting a literary pseudonym. She was, variously, Mary Ann Evans, Marian Evans, Marian Evans Lewes, and Mary Ann Cross, and I have switched between names as seems appropriate to the context. Many scholars do not refer to George Eliot by surname only, since, it is argued, there was not really a person called George Eliot. In the spirit of the naive reader I remain and aspire to represent, I think of George Eliot as a real person—just as I think of Mark Twain, Lewis Carroll, and George Orwell as real people—and therefore I do sometimes refer to her by surname only.

When quoting from the works of George Eliot I have used the following editions: *Scenes of Clerical Life* (Penguin Classics, 1998), *Adam Bede* (Penguin Classics, 2008), *The Mill on the Floss* (Penguin Classics, 2003), *Felix Holt, the Radical* (Penguin Classics, 1982), *Middlemarch* (Penguin Classics, 1994), and *Daniel Deronda* (Penguin Classics, 1995). Quotations from essays published anonymously in the *Westminster Review* and elsewhere are taken from *Essays of George Eliot*, edited by Thomas Pinney (Columbia University Press, 1963).

The most important sources I have used are George Eliot's own journals and letters, which her widower, John Walter Cross, drew on for the first biography, *George Eliot's Life, as Related in Her Letters and Journals* (Harper and Brothers, 1885). They have subsequently been edited in more scholarly fashion, and these are the editions I have used. All quotations from the journals come from *The Journals of George Eliot*, edited by Margaret Harris and Judith Johnston (Cambridge University Press, 2000). Quotations from George Eliot's letters come from Gordon S. Haight's nine-volume collection, *The George Eliot Letters* (vols. 1–7, Oxford University Press, 1954; vols. 8–9, Yale University Press, 1978). Haight included relevant letters of George Henry Lewes and John Blackwood, and several of Eliot and Lewes's other correspondents; when quoting them I have drawn from his edition. Lewes's letters have also been collected in *The Letters of George Henry Lewes*, edited by William Baker (English Literary Studies, 1995). Some of George Eliot's letters I read in manuscript at the Beinecke Rare Book and Manuscript Library at Yale University, where I also read

Thornton Lewes's letters, several of which are entirely or partially unpublished. I am grateful to staff there, particularly Timothy Young, curator of Modern Books and Manuscripts, who helped me decipher Thornie's handwriting.

Other institutions granted me generous access to their materials. I am extremely grateful to the British Library for making the manuscript of *Middlemarch* available to me; I would like to thank in particular Jamie Andrews, head of English and Drama; Helen Melody, curator, Modern Literary Manuscripts; and Rachel Foss, lead curator, Modern Literary Manuscripts. I am indebted to Isaac Gewirtz, curator of the Henry W. and Albert A. Berg Collection of English and American Literature, the New York Public Library, Astor, Lenox and Tilden Foundations, for permission to quote from George Eliot's notebook, and for showing me Charles Dickens's desk. At the Morgan Library & Museum, Declan Kiely, the Robert H. Taylor curator and department head, Literary and Historical Manuscripts, was extremely helpful. At the National Library of Scotland, I am grateful to Iain D. Brown, formerly the principal curator of the Manuscripts Division, and to his colleague Yvonne Shand, as well as to David McClay. At the Harry Ransom Center at the University of Texas in Austin, which holds George Eliot's proofs of *Middlemarch*, thanks go to Jenn Shapland for her assistance. Hannah Westall, archivist at Girton College, Cambridge, also receives my thanks, as does Elizabeth Adams, librarian of University College, Oxford.

At the National Portrait Gallery in London, I am indebted to Tim Moreton, Clementine Hampshire, Alexandra Ault, Kristina Macdonald, and Eleanor Macnair. Ali Wells, keeper of Collections (Social History and Natural History) at the Herbert Art

Gallery & Museum in Coventry, gave generously of her time, as did Catherine Nisbet and Janine Fox at the Nuneaton Museum and Art Gallery. At the Grolier Club, in New York, where I read the Sotheby's catalogue for the 1923 auction of Gertrude Lewes's estate, I am grateful for the assistance of Meghan Read Constantinou; thanks go to Sarah Funke Butler for pointing me there.

IN the Prelude, I cite Virginia's Woolf's article about George Eliot that appeared in the *Times Literary Supplement* (November 1919); it is reprinted in *A Century of George Eliot Criticism*, edited by Gordon S. Haight (University Paperbacks, 1966). Accounts of visits to the Priory, and of encounters with George Eliot, by Elizabeth M. Bruce, Charles Eliot Norton, William Hale White, and Sophia Lucy Clifford are taken from K. K. Collins's *George Eliot: Interviews and Recollections*. Fascinating images of the Priory, as well as other locations and individuals important to George Eliot's story, can be found in *George Eliot* by Marghanita Laski (Thames and Hudson, 1987). After my encounter with George Eliot's notebook I learned more of its history from *George Eliot's "Middlemarch" Notebooks: A Transcription,* edited by John Clark Pratt and Victor A. Neufeldt (University of California Press, 1979).

IN chapter 1, "Miss Brooke," I am indebted to the scholarship of Jerome Beaty, who in *"Middlemarch" from Notebook to Novel: A Study of George Eliot's Creative Method* (University of Illinois Press, 1960) described the process by which Eliot constructed *Middlemarch*. Mathilde Blind's *George Eliot* (Roberts Brothers, 1889) proved a fascinating source of firsthand accounts of George Eliot as a child; other recollections of George Eliot's school days, several of them anonymously published in contemporary periodicals, have been collected by Collins. As of this writing, George Eliot's desk is no longer on display at the Nuneaton Museum and Art Gallery; it was stolen in 2012. Nina Auerbach's suggestive comments about Dorothea are in an essay, "Dorothea's Lost Dog," which appears in *"Middlemarch" in the 21st Century,* edited by Karen Chase (Oxford University Press, 2006). George Eliot's notebook in which she wrote out her scheme for *Middlemarch*, known as *Quarry for "Middlemarch,"* is in the Houghton Library at Harvard.

IN chapter 2, "Old and Young," I relied upon Hermione Lee's *Virginia Woolf* (Vintage Books, 1999) for my characterization of Woolf's early years; the quotation from Vanessa Bell's memoir, *Notes on Virginia's Childhood*, is taken from Lee's book. Leslie Stephen's essay appeared in the *Cornhill Magazine* (February 1881) and is reprinted in Haight's *A Century of George Eliot Criticism*. My understanding of Coventry's nineteenth-century history is gleaned from Benjamin Poole's *The History of Coventry* (D. Lewin, 1852). I referred to *A Dictionary of British Place-Names* by A. D. Mills (Oxford University Press, 2011), and am grateful to Paul Cavill, of the University of Nottingham, for his further insight into English place-names. Emily Davies's letters are excerpted by Collins.

In chapter 3, I draw upon George Henry Lewes's diary, excerpted in Haight's *The George Eliot Letters*. In Rosemary Ashton's *G. H. Lewes: A Life* (Clarendon Press, 1991) I read about Lewes's first marriage; I also referred to David Williams's *Mr. George Eliot: A Biography of George Henry Lewes* (Franklin Watts, 1983). Nancy Henry's *The Life of George Eliot* (Wiley-Blackwell, 2012) provides a fascinating reexamination of the circumstances surrounding Lewes's separation from Agnes. Ruby V. Redinger's *George Eliot: The Emergent Self* (Alfred A. Knopf, 1975) offers interesting analysis of the family dynamics between the Evans children. In *The Real Life of Mary Ann Evans: George Eliot, Her Letters and Fiction* (Cornell, 1994), Rosemarie Bodenheimer devotes a chapter to George Eliot's stepsons; her insights have helped me develop my own. Thornie's portrait is reprinted in Arthur Paterson's *George Eliot's Family Life and Letters* (Houghton Mifflin, 1928). *Natal: A History and Description of the Colony* by Henry Brooks (L. Reeve, 1876) was illuminating. Marie Sanderson's letter to George Eliot is in Haight's edition. Collins cites Charles Lewes's defence of George Eliot in a letter to the *Times*, 27 December 1902.

In chapter 4, the anecdote about the archbishop of Dublin concealing *Middlemarch* in his hat is from a letter written by Lewes that appears in Haight's *The George Eliot Letters*. The *Spectator* review published 1 June 1872 is reprinted in *George Eliot and Her Readers: A Selection of Contemporary Reviews*, edited by Laurence Lerner and John Holmstrom (Bodley Head, 1966). Rosemary Ashton's *142 Strand: A Radical Address in Victorian London* (Jonathan

Cape, 2007) gave me insight into George Eliot's London milieu. George Eliot's review of Thomas Carlyle's *Life of Sterling* appears in Pinney's edition of her essays; one of her biographers, Frederick R. Karl, notes the consonance between Eliot's theory of biography and the practice of fiction in his *George Eliot: Voice of a Century* (Norton, 1995). Bessie Rayner Parkes's comment about George Eliot's angelic wings appears in Haight, and I am grateful to Girton College, Cambridge, for permission to reprint it. Letters from Alphonse D'Albert Durade's haggling over the price of his father's portrait of George Eliot are preserved in the archive at the National Portrait Gallery. Anne Fremantle's *George Eliot* (Duckworth, 1933) provides a perspective upon Eliot's reputation eighty years ago; Brenda Maddox's *George Eliot: Novelist, Lover, Wife* (HarperPress, 2009) does the same thing for our own time. Henry James's letter to his father is excerpted in Collins, as are the observations of Sara Jane Lippincott, who wrote under the pseudonym Grace Greenwood, of Ivan Turgenev, as reported by Sofia Kovalevskaya, and of Elizabeth Malleson. For a fascinating account of an attempt to identify George Eliot's painter suitor, see *Those of Us Who Loved Her: The Men in George Eliot's Life* by Kathleen Adams (George Eliot Fellowship, 1993). Bessie Rayner Parkes's essay, "Dorothea Casaubon and George Eliot," first appeared in the *Contemporary Review* in 1894. I draw upon Herbert Spencer's *Social Statics* (D. Appleton, 1865) and *An Autobiography* (D. Appleton, 1904). Spencer's letter to Youmans is excerpted by Haight. Barbara Hardy offers a particularly sensitive and sympathetic reading of Spencer's motives and actions in *George Eliot: A Critic's Biography*. Henry James's review of *Middlemarch* was published in the *Galaxy*, March 1873, and is reprinted in *The Art of Criticism: Henry James on the Theory and the Practice of Fiction*, edited by William Veeder and Susan M. Griffin (University of Chicago Press, 1986). I have drawn upon *Home Life with Herbert Spencer; By Two* (J. W. Arrowsmith, 1910).

In chapter 5, I cite J. Hillis Miller's essay from *George Eliot*, edited by Harold Bloom (Chelsea House Publishers, 1985). I have quoted from an essay "The Building of Oxford Covered Market," by Malcolm Graham, published in *Oxoniensia,* vol. 44, 1979. William Wordsworth's recollection is in Collins. For the life of Francis Pattison I have drawn upon Betty Askwith's biography, *Lady Dilke* (Chatto and Windus, 1969). Lady Dilke's published stories, *The Shrine of Death and Other Stories* (George Routledge and Sons, 1886), make for fascinating reading. Lord Dilke's memoir of his wife appears in *The Book of the Spiritual Life* by Lady Dilke (E. P. Dutton, 1905). For my understanding of Mark Pattison I read his *Memoirs* (Macmillan, 1885) and drew upon H. S. Jones's biography, *Intellect and Character in Victorian England: Mark Pattison and the Invention of the Don* (Cambridge University Press, 2007). Dilke's unpublished memoirs are cited by Askwith, among others. Haight's 1974 essay, "Poor Mr. Casaubon," appears in his volume *George Eliot's Originals and Contemporaries* (University of Michigan Press, 1992). Sparrow's lectures were published as *Mark Pattison and the Idea of a University* (Cambridge University Press, 1967). A. D. Nuttall's *Dead from the Waist Down: Scholars and Scholarship in Literature and the Popular Imagination* was published in 2003 by Yale University Press. V. S. Pritchett's essay on George Eliot appears in *A Man of Letters: Selected Essays* (Random House, 1985). Mary Augusta Ward's recollection appears in Collins.

In chapter 6, I cite *The Diary of Alice James*, edited by Leon Edel (Northeastern University Press, 1999). Elizabeth Hardwick's essay is in *A View of My Own: Essays on Literature and Society* (Ecco Press, 1982). "How I came to write Fiction" was not published in Eliot's lifetime; Cross excerpted it, and it appears in full in *The Journals of George Eliot*. Blanche Colton Williams's biography is *George Eliot* (Macmillan, 1936). Remarks by Eliza Lynn Linton and Margaret Fuller appear in Collins. I cite Joel Harvey Linsley's 1828 publication, *Lectures on the Relations and Duties of the Middle Aged*. Lord David Cecil's characterization of Ladislaw is quoted in Haight's *George Eliot's Originals and Contemporaries*; Leslie Stephen's appears in *George Eliot* (Macmillan, 1902), a volume in the ill-named English Men of Letters series. James's comments appear in his *Galaxy* review. David Trotter's essay appears in *"Middlemarch" in the 21st Century*. Several of Eliot's biographers have noted the parallels between Ladislaw and Lewes, including Ina Taylor in *A Woman of Contradictions: The Life of George Eliot* (William Morrow, 1989) and Lawrence and Elisabeth Hanson, who in their *Marian Evans & George Eliot* (Oxford University Press, 1952) call Ladislaw "that unfortunate blend of Shelley and Lewes." Annie Fields is quoted in Collins, as is the anonymous curtain-twitcher. Phyllis Rose's *Parallel Lives: Five Victorian Marriages* (Vintage Books, 1984) remains an exemplary work of sympathetic scholarship and has informed all my thinking about Victorian marriage and not-quite marriage. Robert Lowell's poem is reprinted in *Essays in Appreciation* by Christopher Ricks (Oxford University Press, 1996). George Eliot's translation of Feuerbach is quoted in *George Eliot: A Critical Study of Her Life, Writings, and Philosophy* by George Willis Cooke (Houghton Mifflin, 1895). Eliza Lynn Linton's *My Literary Life* was published by Hodder and Stoughton in 1899. John G. Lord's essay on Eliot appeared in his *Beacon Lights of History: Great Women* (Fords, Howard and Hulbert, 1886). Barbara Bodichon's letter is in Haight's *The George Eliot Letters*, as is Anne Thackeray Ritchie's. Research into George Eliot's foreign travels has been done by Kathleen McCormack in *George Eliot in Society: Travels Abroad and Sundays at the Priory* (Ohio State University Press, 2013).

In chapter 7, *"The Mill on the Floss": In Half the Time* (Phoenix, 2007) seems mercifully to be out of print. I referred to Michael Holroyd's *Lytton Strachey: The New Biography* (Farrar, Straus and Giroux, 1995). Benjamin Jowett's notes on Eliot appear in Collins. *The Letters of Lord Acton to Mary Gladstone* were published by Macmillan in 1905; his review of Cross's *Life of George Eliot* appeared in the *Nineteenth Century*, vol. 17, 1885. Disparaging summations of George Eliot appear in William Ernest Henley's *Views and Reviews: Essays in Appreciation* (Charles Scribner's Sons, 1890). George Saintsbury's observations appear in his *Corrected Impressions: Essays on Victorian Writers* (Dodd, Mead, 1895). Edmund Gosse's essay appears in his *Aspects and Impressions* (Cassell, 1922). Bessie Rayner Parkes's comments come from "Dorothea

Casaubon and George Eliot"; for a fascinating early critique of Eliot's underachieving heroines, see Abba Goold Woolson's *George Eliot and Her Heroines* (Harper and Brothers, 1886). Leah Price writes about the practice of excerpting George Eliot's wisdom in "George Eliot and the Production of Consumers," an excellent chapter in *The Anthology and the Rise of the Novel: From Richardson to George Eliot* (Cambridge University Press, 2000).

IN chapter 8, I am indebted to Stephen Gill's detailed analysis of George Eliot's Wordsworthian inheritance in *Wordsworth and the Victorians* (Clarendon Press, 2001). I referred to *The Buildings of Old Weymouth: Part Two* by Eric Ricketts (Weymouth Bookshop, 1976). Haight's essay on Mary Garth appears in *George Eliot's Originals and Contemporaries*. The translation of the epigraph from Victor Hugo is taken from the Norton Critical Edition of *Middlemarch*, edited by Bert G. Hornback (Norton, 2000).

IN the Finale, I refer to Stanley Fish's *How to Write a Sentence: And How to Read One* (Harper, 2011). Gillian Beer notes the biblical resonance of the view from Dorothea's window in *Darwin's Plots: Evolutionary Narrative in Darwin, George Eliot and Nineteenth-Century Fiction* (Ark, 1985). I gleaned the history of Shottermill from *Shottermill: Its Farms, Families and Mills, Part 2* by Greta A. Turner (John Owen Smith, 2005).

I am grateful to Daniel Zalewski, my editor at the *New Yorker*, and David Remnick, the magazine's editor, for encouraging me to write the essay about George Eliot that led to this book. I am grateful to Sameen Gauhar and Hannah Goldfield at the *New Yorker*, who were the fact-checkers on that essay, and to Elizabeth Pearson-Griffiths, who was the copy editor. Also at the *New Yorker* thanks go to Rhonda Sherman, Pam McCarthy, and Bruce Diones.

I have been extremely fortunate in my editors for this book, Vanessa Mobley at Crown and Bella Lacey at Granta Books, graceful and insightful readers both. Also at Crown I am grateful to my publisher, Molly Stern, as well as to Chris Brand, Miriam Chotiner-Gardner, Maureen Clark, Catherine Cullen, Luisa Francavilla, Elena Giavaldi, Min Lee, Mark McCauslin, Claire Potter, and Elizabeth Rendfleisch. Thanks go to Philip Gwyn Jones, my original publisher at Granta Books; also at Granta Books thanks to Laura Barber, Iain Chapple, Sara D'Arcy, Christine Lo, Anne Meadows, Colin Midson, Aidan O'Neill, and Sarah Wasley. I am grateful to Daphne Tagg and David Eldridge. Thanks to Michael Heyward, my publisher at Text Publishing, where I am also grateful to Jane Novak. Thanks go to Lynn Henry, the publishing director at Doubleday Canada, and Kristin Cochrane. My agent, Kathy Robbins, has been indispensable. I am grateful to her, as well as to Louise Quayle, Rachelle Bergstein, and Micah Hauser at the Robbins Office.

Rhoda Feng diligently tracked down contemporary reviews of *Middlemarch*, as well as more recent articles and scholarship.

I am very grateful for her assistance. Thanks also to Cathy Tempelsman and to Herman Edelman.

When several years ago I wrote to John Burton, the indefatigable chairman of the George Eliot Fellowship, asking for information about the organization's activities, he wrote back immediately not only to tell me about an upcoming study weekend devoted to *The Mill on the Floss* but also to invite me to be a speaker at it. The invitation was irresistible, as was the prospect of a charabanc tour of sites of George Eliot's childhood. Subsequently John made himself available to guide me around Coventry and opened many doors for me there and in Nuneaton. I am very grateful to him, and to other members of the Fellowship and local champions of George Eliot, including Bill Adams, Kathleen Adams, Lynda Burton, Michael Harris, Barbara McKay, John Rignall, and Vivienne Wood. Mike Wastell, the general manager of the Griff House hotel and restaurant, generously showed me around his family's home, once George Eliot's.

Jonathan Ouvry, a great-great-grandson of George Henry Lewes, and the president of the George Eliot Fellowship, welcomed me into his home and graciously answered my many questions; thanks go to him and to his wife, Marjorie Ouvry, for their kindness and generosity. David Ouvry, another Lewes descendant, and Daphne Clarke were equally welcoming when I visited them; I am grateful to them for their warmth, hospitality, and enthusiasm about this project. Margaret Langford generously showed me around Lincoln College, Oxford, where her husband, Paul Langford, was rector until 2012; thanks go to both of them. Alana Harris, Darby Fellow in History at Lincoln, was kind enough to allow me into her rooms, once the Pattisons'. In

Shottermill, Greta Turner conducted me around town and shared her encyclopaedic historical knowledge. I thank Melanie and Will Pitcairn, who welcomed me into their house, once the home of Anne Gilchrist; Melanie also generously sent me further documents and contacts. Mark and Lindsey Pepper, the current owners of Cherrimans, were equally welcoming; I am grateful to them for allowing me to look out of their window and to discover the end of my book.

Many friends have contributed to this book, in various ways. I am grateful to Christian Brammer, Richard Cohen, Nick Denton, Jonathan Derbyshire, Christine Schwartz Hartley, Jane Haugh, Paul Holdengräber, Emily Jackson, Henry Phillips, Annie Piper, Elisabeth Prochnik, Carne Ross, Karmen Ross, Shari Spiegel, Katherine Barrett Swett, Benjamin Swett, and Barbara Wansbrough. My brother, Matthew Mead, and my sister-in-law, Julia Mead, have been supportive throughout.

This book is dedicated to my mother, Barbara Mead, and to my late father, Brian Mead, who died while I was halfway through writing it. My debt to them is on every page. I am grateful to my stepsons, Yona, Tzvi, and Zach, for everything they have taught me about young men, and for so much else. My son, Rafael, brightens my world; I hope he will read *Middlemarch* one day. The last word goes to my husband, George Prochnik, my own George. Without his kindness, encouragement, and inspiration, not a word of this book could have been written.

Keep in touch with
Granta Books:

Visit grantabooks.com to discover more.

GRANTA